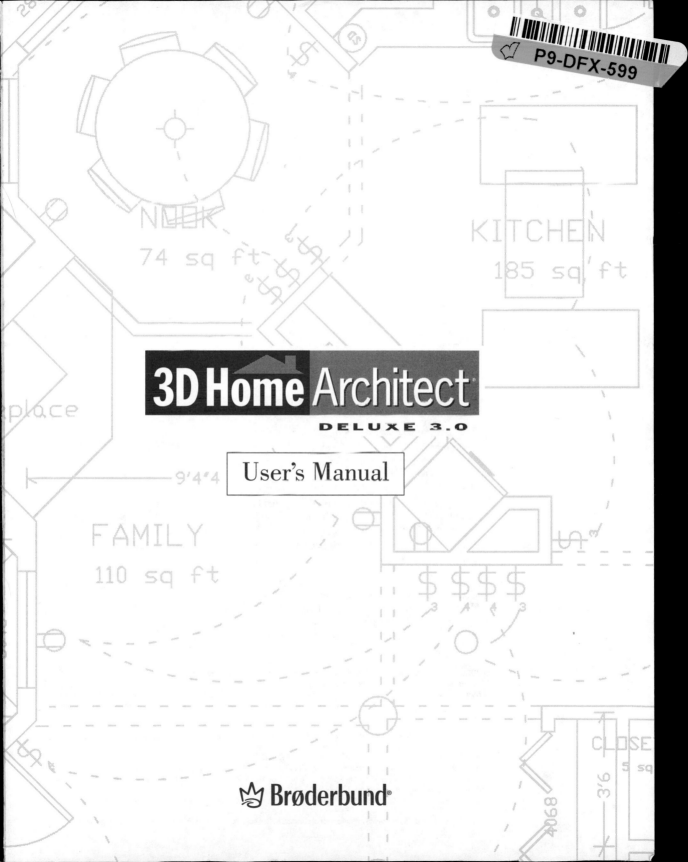

P9-DFX-599

3D Home Architect

DELUXE 3.0

User's Manual

👑 Brøderbund

Mattel Interactive: 500 Redwood Blvd., Novato, CA 94947, Tel:319-378-7319, Web Site: www.mattelinteractive.com

IMAGETECTS™
Many of the textures supplied are from the ImageCELs® libraries. For a free color catalog or questions, please contact IMAGETECTS, M-F 9am-5pm Pacific time, at 408-252-5487. 24-hour fax number is 408-252-7409. IMAGETECTS, P.O. Box 4, Saratoga, CA 95071.
Email: info@imagecels.com or imagetects@aol.com; WWW: http://www.imagecels.com

In the interest of product improvement, information and specifications represented here are subject to change without notice.

Table of Contents

Congratulations on your purchase of **3D Home Architect® Deluxe 3.0,** the complete software solution for easy home design. With **3D Home Architect Deluxe**, you can quickly and easily produce accurate and complete floor plans for a remodel, an addition, or even an entire home. The program will handle multiple floors, check your design for obvious errors, determine building materials you will need, and even let you see and work with your design in three dimensions. The program will automatically take care of lining up walls, measuring and adding dimensions, and doing most of the other tedious work necessary to create building plans. Your job will be to use the tools the program gives you to design a remodel, addition, or entire home that works for you.

At the end of the manual you will find answers to common questions, a user's guide to **3D Home Architect Deluxe Tips**, and an index for fast referencing.

The *"Introduction"* covers hardware and software requirements, installation, and program features you'll be using to create your plans.

The *"Tutorial"* takes you through the creation of a basic plan. You will learn to edit a plan in different views. Finally, you will see how to use special features like automatic dimensions, electrical outlet placement, and PlanCheck™ and how to create a Materials list for estimating cost. The roof tutorial shows you how to create two industry standard roofs for your plan. The tutorial walks you through the creation of these roofs, and then helps you view them using three-dimensional view tools.

"Basic Techniques" shows you how to manipulate objects in **3D Home Architect Deluxe** and includes a more thorough tutorial showing you how to create such things as staircases, custom windows, cabinetry, decks, and multiple stories.

"Advanced Roofing Techniques" teaches you how to build eight different roof structures. With this knowledge, you can combine any of these styles to create your own custom roofs. This chapter also introduces two tools that help in the roof creation process, and includes

an introduction to placing dormers in your roof.

The *"Reference"* provides an item-by-item explanation of each command the program offers, organized by the toolbar and menus. This is the definitive source of information on the program.

The *"Introduction to Residential Design"* gives a brief overview of some of the aspects of residential building design relevant to the home architect.

Other Materials

The QuickStart Guide lays out the most important commands and drawing tools for easy reference, and the program itself features an extensive, context-sensitive Help system. A separate booklet illustrates some of the sample plans that are available on the program disc.

A Word about Windows

3D Home Architect Deluxe is a Microsoft Windows application and it follows the interface standards established by Windows. This manual assumes you are familiar with Windows and basic Windows techniques, such as using the mouse and menus. If you are new to computers, or unfamiliar with Windows, learning the basics with the Microsoft Windows documentation will allow you to focus on *3D Home Architect Deluxe*.

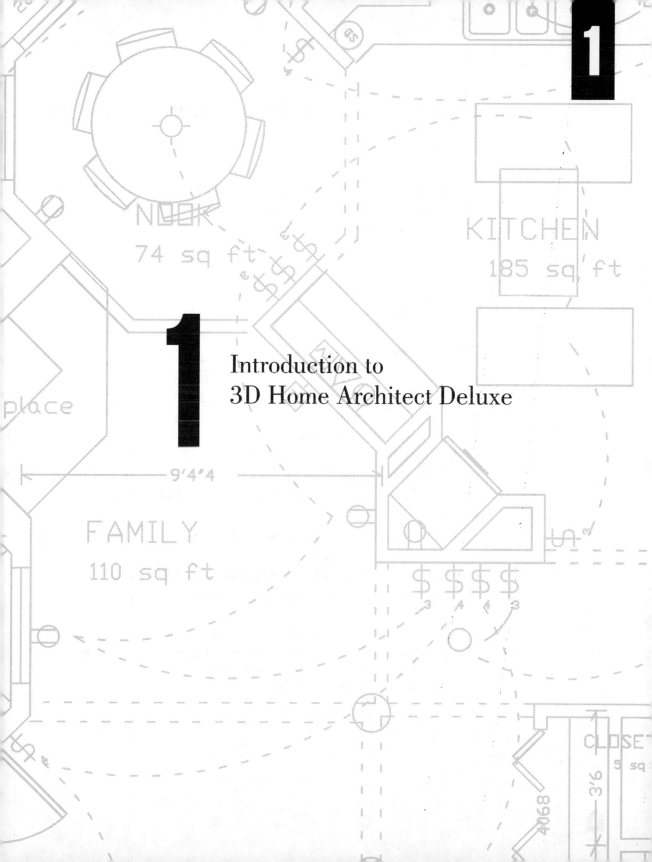

1

Introduction to
3D Home Architect Deluxe

Chapter 1

Introduction to 3D Home Architect Deluxe

Materials

Your *3D Home Architect Deluxe* package should include the following materials:
- One CD-ROM
- User's Manual
- QuickStart Guide
- One Sample Plan Booklet
- Registration Card

System Requirements

WINDOWS® CD-ROM*
- Windows 95 or Windows 98
- 100MHz Pentium® or faster
- Minimum 16MB hard disk space
- 2X CD-ROM drive or faster
- 800x600 display, 256 colors; High and True Color supported
- Windows-compatible mouse
- Printer support: Works with most popular printers (monochrome and color) supported by Windows.
- Optional: Modem and Internet Service Provider account** for TotalHomeNetwork access; Windows compatible sound device for Tutorial audio

*System configuration: May require minor adjustments to the configuration of your operating system and/or updates to the hardware component drivers.

**User is responsible for all Internet access fees and phone charges.

Installing 3D Home Architect Deluxe

Windows 95 or Windows 98
To Install

- Begin at the Windows desktop.
- Insert the CD-ROM into your CD-ROM drive.
- The **3D Home Architect Deluxe** startup window will appear.
- Click the **Install** button and follow the on-screen instructions to install the program.

If the **3D Home Architect Deluxe** startup window does not appear automatically on screen, you can install the program manually.
- Click the **Start** button on the taskbar and choose **Run**.
- Type **D:\SETUP.EXE** in the line labeled **Open**. (If your CD-ROM drive uses a letter other than **D**, substitute that letter for **D**.)
- Click the **OK** button and follow the on-screen instructions to install *3D Home Architect Deluxe*.

To Run

After successfully installing the program, click the **Run** button at the **3D Home Architect Deluxe** startup window to start the program. The startup window will usually appear each time the CD-ROM is inserted into the CD-ROM drive.

If the **3D Home Architect Deluxe** startup window does not appear automatically on screen:
- Begin at the Windows desktop.
- Click the **Start** button, point to **Programs, Broderbund Home Products**, and then to **3D Home Architect Deluxe 3.0**.
- Click the **3D Home Architect Deluxe 3.0** menu item to start the program.

To Remove

If you need to remove *3D Home Architect Deluxe*, begin at the

Windows desktop. Click the **Start** button, point to **Programs,
Broderbund Home Products**, and then to **3D Home Architect
Deluxe 3.0**. Click the **Uninstall** menu item to uninstall the program.

What 3D Home Architect Deluxe Can Do

3D Home Architect Deluxe is a simple yet powerful program for
creating complete, professional-looking residential floor plans. By
combining the point-and-click commands of Microsoft Windows with
"intelligent" objects, the program lets you, the amateur "home
architect," design a remodel, an addition, or even an entire home. You
can view and edit it in three dimensions, and print out plans for use by
professional architects and builders. You can record and show walkthroughs (animated 3D representations) of your house. You can add
exterior landscaping objects such as trees, shrubs, and flowers. You can
search for plans in a database that match your criteria. Accurate
dimensions and other details are created automatically, as are itemized
lists of materials which help you estimate materials costs. You can print
your plan to any scale either as a floor plan, a 3D view, or interior
elevation. The program can even check your plans for compliance with
certain building standards and rules of thumb. Most importantly, *3D
Home Architect Deluxe* will greatly simplify the task of accurately
drawing your plans, letting you visualize them and experiment with
possible alternatives, and then convey your ideas to others involved in
the project. Using *3D Home Architect Deluxe*, you can experiment
and sketch out how you want your home to look, without agonizing over
every line and measurement, while you remain confident that your plan
can then be used to build the home you imagined.

What 3D Home Architect Deluxe Will Not Do

3D Home Architect Deluxe does a good job of creating plans,
interior elevations, exterior elevations, cross sections, and details of
foundation, wall, floor, and ceiling/roof construction. Construction
details, which show the fine points of how walls, floors, and ceilings are
built, are usually determined by local building codes and practices, so
you must consult with a licensed contractor to see what works and what

is required. This program is intended to help you with designs that use standard construction techniques. For designs that require more specialized construction, like multiple-story homes on steep sites, you should definitely consult professional architects and builders.

Finally, **3D Home Architect Deluxe** will only help you design your home; it will not design your home for you. You will decide room size, where rooms will go, what will be in them, and how light, air, and people will move about, between, and within them. This means studying different designs, trying them out, and thinking about how you and your family will really live in and use the home you design. While the program cannot do this work for you, this is where you will really appreciate it, because by simplifying the process of drawing precise, detailed plans, **3D Home Architect Deluxe** frees you to experiment and play around with different design ideas. By taking care of the drawing and helping you to fully visualize the end result before building, the program lets you concentrate on the design and avoid costly mistakes.

Windows and Views in 3D Home Architect Deluxe

3D Home Architect Deluxe uses the familiar Windows graphic interface featuring multiple program windows, drop-down menus, dialog boxes, scroll bars, sliders, and buttons. A brief summary of Windows basics will be given later in this introduction. Besides ease of use, **3D Home Architect Deluxe** employs Windows capabilities to provide you with multiple independent windows, or views, of your work. You can open multiple windows on your plan, each with a different view and use, and even multiple versions of each view. This means that while you are designing a home or addition, you can see a variety of views at once and go quickly from one to another to work in the appropriate view, all views automatically reflecting every change you make.

Views in **3D Home Architect Deluxe** are just different ways of looking at your design: each shows a different aspect of your design, each has a different use, and each a different window. Most views are opened from **Plan** view, which is like a blueprint. This is the view displayed when you first open a file. **Wall Elevation** view shows part of your design directly from the side. **Plan Camera** view shows a three-dimensional perspective of the interior of your design. **Overview** shows your entire plan in three dimensions, from any angle you specify, with ceilings stripped away. **Full Camera** view includes ceilings in the three-dimensional rendering. **Cross Section** view shows a three-dimensional cross-section view of your design, including roofs. **Overview** shows your floor plan in three dimensions and includes multiple stories, but does not show the roof. (**Full Overview** is similar to **Overview**, but it includes the roof.) **Applied Materials** view, a new view in *3D Home Architect Deluxe 3.0*, allows you to see your house with materials such as brick and clapboard applied to it. **Materials** displays a worksheet listing the building materials your design will need, and can calculate total costs based on unit costs you enter. You can move and change objects in all the windows except **Materials**, but can only add objects and change walls in the **Plan** window. All views except **Materials** will automatically reflect changes in other windows.

Plan view is the heart of the program, where you will do most of your work. In it, you see a two-dimensional blueprint view of your design. Here you can add, edit, and see all the elements of your plan, from walls and doors to furniture, dimensions, and labels. It is only from **Plan** view that you can open the other views. This view, with its detailed information, is the most important for actually building your design. You can have a number of plans for your home design, one for each floor, and each with its own associated views. With the exception of special "reference" floors, to keep things simple only one floor can be worked on at a time.

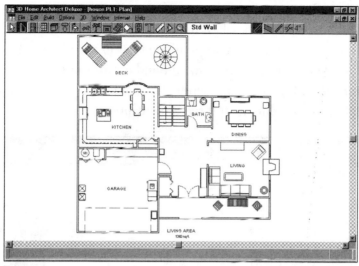

Plan View

Wall Elevation view is two-dimensional, but of the vertical plane so it shows width and height. Along with **Plan** view, it provides information crucial for actual construction of your design. Although you cannot add objects or change walls in this view (or in any view other than **Plan** view), you can change objects like doors, windows, cabinets, and furniture. You will find this view ideal for lining up objects precisely, because you can see them straight on and view their height relative to one another.

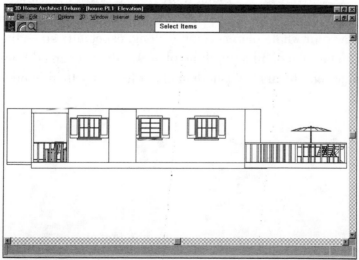

Wall Elevation View

Plan Camera view is a three-dimensional view of your plan, showing you how it will look when finished, complete with fixtures and furniture. Besides providing a more realistic view of your home, **Plan Camera** view also makes it easier to edit and arrange objects like cabinets and furniture. It gives you a better sense of how everything fits together and lets you edit objects in three dimensions.

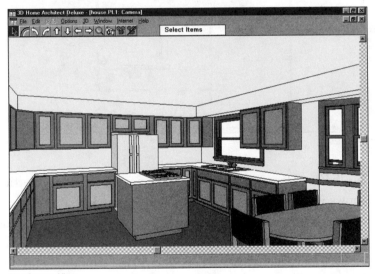

Plan Camera View

Overview is also a three-dimensional view, but instead of showing a perspective within a room, it provides a bird's-eye view of the entire plan, with ceilings stripped away. This makes it ideal for determining how your whole plan is coming along, especially since the view angle can be rotated all around the plan. While you can edit objects in this view too, the angles usually make it less easy than in other views.

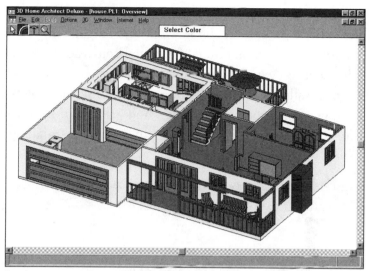

Overview

Full Camera view is another three-dimensional view of your plan showing you how it will look when finished, complete with fixtures, furniture, and cathedral ceilings. **Full Camera** view also shows a perspective view of an entire multistory model.

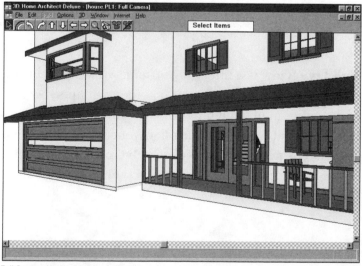

Full Camera View

Cross Section view is a three-dimensional view including roofs, but of the vertical plane so it shows width and height. Along with **Plan** view, it provides information crucial for actual construction of your design. Although you cannot add objects or change walls in this view (you can change walls only in **Plan** view), you can change objects like doors, windows, cabinets, and furniture. You will find this view ideal for lining things up precisely, because you can see them straight on and view their height relative to one another.

Cross Section View

Full Overview is a three-dimensional view also, but instead of showing a perspective within a room, it provides a nonperspective bird's-eye view of the entire plan, including multiple-level designs with roofs. This makes it ideal for determining how your whole plan is coming along, especially since the view angle can be rotated all around the plan. While you can edit objects in **Full Overview**, the angles usually make it less easy to do so than in other views.

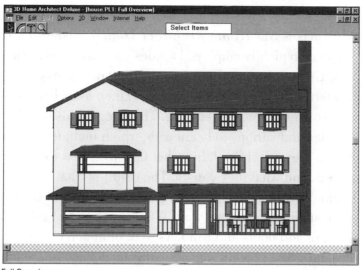

Full Overview

Materials is not a view of your plan, but a window containing a worksheet listing the materials your plan will need, with a column for you to enter unit costs. Once you have created the list and entered the cost factors, the worksheet will calculate building costs. Besides being handy for buying materials once your design is finished, the **Materials** window is also useful for determining what you can afford while you are still designing. It is the only window that does not automatically update to reflect changes made in other views.

	ID	Flr	Size	Item	Count	Un	Quantity	Price	Tot. Cost	Code	Comment
1											
2	GN1	1		heated wall area	1060	sqft	1				
3	GN2	1		heated glass are	257	sqft	1				
4	GN3	1		heated door area	79	sqft	1				
5	GN6	2		heated wall area	1140	sqft	1				
6	GN7	2		heated glass are	256	sqft	1				
7				Subtotal:							
8											
9	FO1	0	8x24"h	concrete grade b	11.41	cuyd	1				
10	FO2	0	2x6"	treated mud sill	231	ft	1				
11	FO3	0	1/2x6"	foam sill seal	231	ft	1				
12	FO4	0		foundation bolts	50		1				
13	FO5	0	no. 4	steel rebar	996	ft	1				
14	FO6	0	12"diam x 120	drilled pier hole	45		1				
15	FO7	0	no. 4	steel rebar (piers	1200	ft	1				
16	FO8	0		concrete for piers	13.08	cuyd	1				
17	FO9	0	90x55x12"	slab for fireplace	1.27	cuyd	1				
18	FO10	0	4x8"	foundation girder	71	ft	1				
19	FO11	1	4"x732 sq ft	concrete slab	9.04	cuyd	1				
20	FO12	1	732 sq ft	steel mesh for sl	732	sqft	1				
21				Subtotal:							
22											
23	M1	1		masonry fireplac	1		1				

Materials Window

Objects in 3D Home Architect Deluxe

What makes **3D Home Architect Deluxe** easier to use than the CAD programs typically employed for design is its object-oriented approach. Most CAD and general-purpose drawing programs create simple geometric objects like lines and arcs, then associate these to each other to create more complex entities. This program uses objects that are more complex and various to begin with, which include information not only on how they are shaped, but what they *are*, how they relate to other objects, and what they can do. The result is what we call SmartParts™ Technology. Instead of carefully drawing lines and calling them a wall, you just click and drag a wall. When you connect this wall to other walls, or add doors and windows to it, or attach cabinets, the program recognizes the objects you are using and what you are doing and responds accordingly. Much of your drawing is then done automatically; you do not have to worry so much about positioning and sizing things exactly. The program will even warn you when you are breaking the "rules." You spend less time drawing and more time designing.

The object-oriented nature of **3D Home Architect Deluxe** also enables the program to have its PlanCheck feature. This feature will check your plan and indicate if you have violated any standard building principles. For example, PlanCheck will notify you if haven't made a garage door wide enough, if you have not placed any smoke detectors, or if you haven't placed enough electrical outlets.

Getting Around

3D Home Architect Deluxe follows Microsoft Windows conventions for manipulating files and issuing commands. When you start the program, two windows display, one for the application and one for a plan. The application window includes title and menu bars, toolbar, minimize and maximize/restore buttons, and vertical and horizontal scroll bars. The **Plan** view window has its own title bar and window controls.

You can move around within each window by dragging or clicking the scroll bars, and you can resize each window by clicking and dragging the borders and corners. Click and drag the title bar to move the window itself. To switch to other programs and windows or close the active window, click the program icon to open the program menu and then click the appropriate command. To reduce the active window to an icon, select **Minimize** from the program menu or click the **Minimize** button.

Minimize button

Maximize button

To have the window fill the screen or be restored to its original size, click the **Maximize** button. (You will probably always want the **Plan** view window maximized to give you the most working space.) Remember, the program will display multiple, independent windows, so you can have several views of a single plan open at once (say **Plan**, **Wall Elevation**, and **Camera** views), plus several versions of each view (say, **Camera** views from two angles), and even several different plans (for comparing your designs). Each view will have its own window, and each window can be separately moved, resized, opened and closed, and even printed. To make a window active, just click it, or press **Ctrl+Tab** to cycle through the open windows. To change your view within a window, zooming in and out, use the **Window** menu commands, or the **Zoom** mode tools. A maximum of ten windows can be open at any given time.

All the menus and commands in the program can be used by clicking the toolbar or menu. Many can also be used from the keyboard by pressing **Alt** and the first underlined letter of the menu to open it, then typing the first letter of the command, or by using the hot-key shortcuts listed in the menus.

Modes and Menu Commands

Modes set the program to create objects or carry out commands, like drawing walls, placing windows, and changing views. Once you have selected a mode, you then select a tool within that mode and then execute a command by clicking the tool. For instance, to build a wall, first you select **Wall** from the **Build** menu (or the toolbar, a shortcut that will be discussed later), then select the type of wall (for example, **Std Wall**), then click and drag to actually create a standard wall in your plan. Menu commands come in four basic types. Executing commands carry out tasks immediately when selected. Toggling commands are toggled on or off, and when on are preceded by a check mark in the menus. Dialog box commands, followed by an ellipsis (...), bring up dialog boxes. Finally, drop-down menu commands, followed by an arrow, bring up submenus.

Dialog boxes are used to enter information by typing in text boxes, choosing from option lists, or selecting check boxes or option buttons (any number of check boxes in a dialog box can be enabled at once, while only one option button can be enabled at a time). Dialog boxes also include buttons to indicate you are finished and want the program to accept new settings, to get help, to escape, and to jump to other menus and dialog boxes.

Some commands set modes, like the **Wall Mode** button or the **Cabinet Mode** button. Others let you select particular tools, which determine what will happen when you next click in your drawing. Still others, executing commands like the **Overview** tool, will carry out a task immediately upon selection.

Toolbar

The toolbar, the strip of buttons under the main menu, provides a shortcut to the most commonly used commands. You can do almost all of your work using only the toolbar. Each button represents one command. For example, the **Wall** command on the **Build** menu is represented by the **Wall** button. The toolbar conveniently places the mode buttons on the left side and the tool buttons on the right side. When you press a mode button on the left side, all the tool buttons that are available in that mode are displayed. The first tool button is depressed by default, since it is the most commonly used. For example, when you click the **Wall Mode** button, the **Standard Wall** tool is automatically selected and you can begin to draw walls.

In addition to both mode and tool buttons being depressed when selected, the status box in the middle of the toolbar displays the name of the active tool. Also, when the pointer passes over a button, a brief message appears in the status bar at the bottom of the screen that provides information about the button. The toolbar changes as you make different windows active, reflecting what you can do in each window,

Most of the buttons on the toolbar are mode buttons which yield a set of tool buttons that are appropriate to that mode. The exceptions are the **Fixture**, **Furniture**, **Stairs**, **Outdoor Objects**, and **Outdoor Images** tools (when you click these tools, a dialog box appears) and the **Fireplace**, **Text**, and **Stairs** tools (after you click these tools, you must click in the **Plan** window to add a fireplace, text, or stairs).

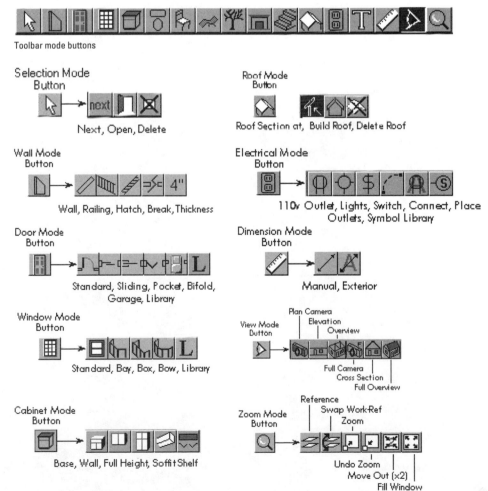

Toolbar mode buttons

Selection Mode Button
Next, Open, Delete

Wall Mode Button
Wall, Railing, Hatch, Break, Thickness

Door Mode Button
Standard, Sliding, Pocket, Bifold, Garage, Library

Window Mode Button
Standard, Bay, Box, Bow, Library

Cabinet Mode Button
Base, Wall, Full Height, Soffit Shelf

Roof Mode Button
Roof Section at, Build Roof, Delete Roof

Electrical Mode Button
110v Outlet, Lights, Switch, Connect, Place Outlets, Symbol Library

Dimension Mode Button
Manual, Exterior

View Mode Button
Plan Camera
Elevation
Overview
Full Camera
Cross Section
Full Overview

Zoom Mode Button
Reference
Swap Work-Ref
Zoom
Undo Zoom
Move Out (x2)
Fill Window

Menus

For the most part, you will probably rely on the toolbar for most of your work. However, there are commands and options available in the menus for which there are no toolbar equivalents. All commands in *3D Home Architect Deluxe* are accessible from drop-down menus listed in the menu bar. To display a menu, just click its title, or press the **Alt** key and the first letter of the menu. Each menu item then displays a list of commands appropriate to it, some of which bring up dialog boxes and submenus with their own commands. For a complete discussion of the menus, check the menu descriptions in the "Reference" section, chapter 5.

NOOK
74 sq ft

KITCHEN
185 sq ft

2 Tutorial

place

9'4"4

FAMILY
110 sq ft

CLOSE
5 sq

3'6

4068

Chapter 2

Tutorial

You will find **3D Home Architect Deluxe** simple to use, especially considering what it does. This tutorial will help you get started; it walks you through the design of a simple two-room cabin. You'll learn how to change the length of walls, put in doors, windows, fixtures, furniture, and landscaping, and design a roof. You'll also learn how to switch between the various 3D views, check your plan, and then generate a materials list for the design.

Building a Simple Plan

Drawing Walls

You should start the tutorial with a blank slate. If you do not have the program already running, click the Windows **Start** button, and then point to **Programs**. Point to **Broderbund Home Products**, then point to **3D Home Architect Deluxe 3.0**, and then click the **3D Home Architect Deluxe 3.0** menu item to start the program. If the program is running, on the **File** menu, click **Close All**, and then on the **File** menu, click **New**. In either case, a **Plan** view window should be open, ready for you to start drawing. (Using the **Close All** command instead of **Close** removes all plans from memory.)

When you start a new plan, **Wall** mode is the default mode, and the **Standard Wall** tool is the default tool.

Wall Mode button

Standard Wall tool

This means you can start drawing walls immediately. Move the pointer to the top left of the screen, and then click and drag out a wall to the right. As you drag, you will notice that the status box in the toolbar indicates how long the wall is. Make this wall approximately 20 feet in length. (Don't worry about being exact.)

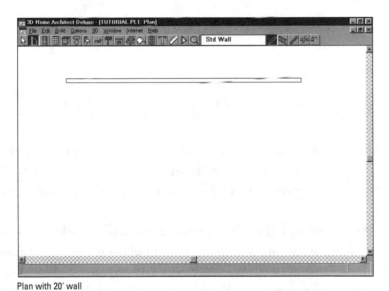

Plan with 20' wall

You can draw angled walls, but the angle is restricted to increments of 15 degrees. This ensures that parallel walls will be parallel, which is especially important if you intend to export your plans to CAD programs, since lines that are not parallel will be very obvious. Also, your builders will thank you, because they like walls to be oriented along simple angles, which are easier to build.

Now that you have drawn the top wall, use the same technique to drag out a wall on the right side. You do not need to begin this wall exactly where the other wall ends—just get it close, and the new wall will

automatically snap to the existing wall. When the second wall is
finished, draw two more walls to make a box.

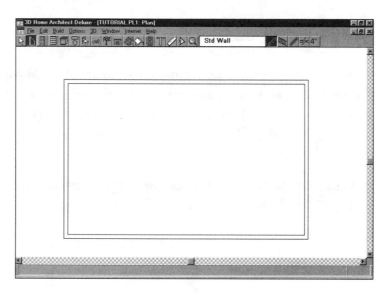

If you make a mistake, just draw over a wall again, or click the wall with
the pointer, then press the **Delete** key. If you get into trouble and would
like to start over, select **Close** from the **File** menu and then **New**.

If you want to adjust the spacing of the walls, click a wall. You will see a
dimension line stretching out to the opposite wall, and three handles:
one in the middle of the selected wall, and one at either end. Try the
following: to move a wall, click the wall, and then drag its center handle.
To resize a wall, click the wall, and then drag one of its end handles.
When you move a wall, the lengths of all connected walls are adjusted
automatically, keeping them connected. This makes it very easy to
sketch out a rough design, which you can adjust for precise dimensions
later.

Dimension Mode
button

While on the subject of dimensions, our plan will need some, so click
the **Dimension Mode** button on the toolbar.

Notice that two additional tools are now available on the right side of the
toolbar. The first tool is for creating manual dimension lines. The second

Exterior Dimensions tool

tool, the **Exterior Dimensions** tool, creates exterior dimension lines automatically. Click that tool and see what happens.

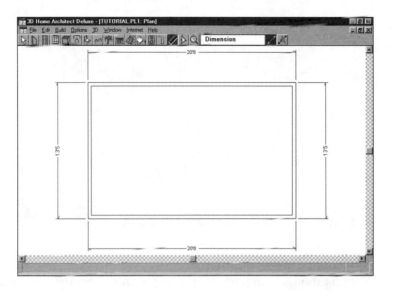

Zoom Mode button

Undo Zoom tool

Fill Window tool

If you want a closer view, click the **Zoom Mode** button. Drag a box around the area you want to see in detail; the area will then fill the screen. To return to the original view, click the **Undo Zoom** tool.

Should your plan ever grow larger than the screen, the **Fill Window** tool will resize the plan so it fits within the screen perfectly. In fact, you may need to use it now if the exterior dimension lines are not all visible on screen.

Finally, divide the room into two rooms by drawing another wall within the enclosure, using the **Standard Wall** tool as you did earlier. The plan should look something like this:

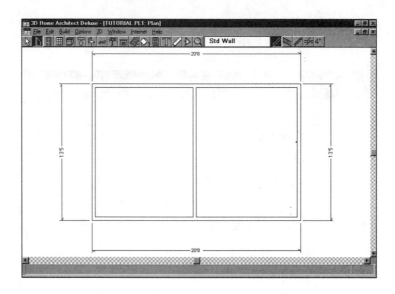

Naming Rooms

Naming rooms is important in this program because rooms have special qualities that are not available until they are named. Click the **Selection Mode** button, and then double-click the room on the left. The **Room Specification** dialog box appears.

Click the box next to **Room Name**, and then in the list that appears click **Kitchen**.

Now click **OK** to leave the dialog box and return to the **Plan** view. Notice that the room is now labeled KITCHEN.

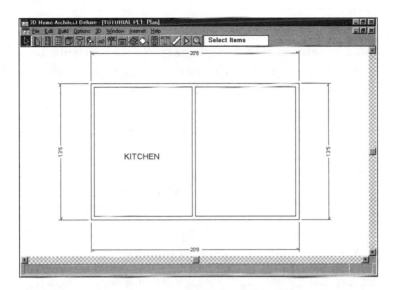

Let's label the other room as the Bedroom. Double-click the room on the right, select **Bedroom** in the **Room Name** list, and then click **OK**. The plan should now look like this, with both rooms labeled:

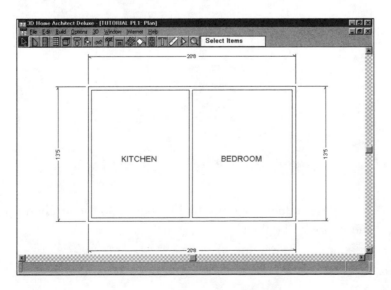

Door Mode button

Standard Door(way) tool

Placing Doors and Windows

Now we'll add some doors and windows to our cabin. Click the **Door Mode** button.

Notice there are now a number of tools on the right side of the toolbar; these represent different types of door commands. By default, the active tool is the **Standard Door(way)** tool.

Let's put a standard door in our cabin. Move the pointer to the bottom wall at the midpoint of the bedroom and click. A doorway is placed in the wall. Notice that there is no door visible in the doorway. That is because you need to first show which way you want the door to open. To do this, click the doorway. Three handles will appear, just as they do when you click a wall. Next, click an end handle, and then drag in the direction that you want the door to open.

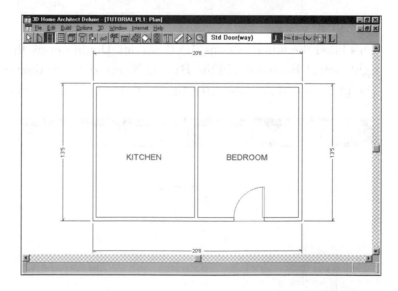

Now place a doorway from the bedroom into the kitchen. The plan should look like this:

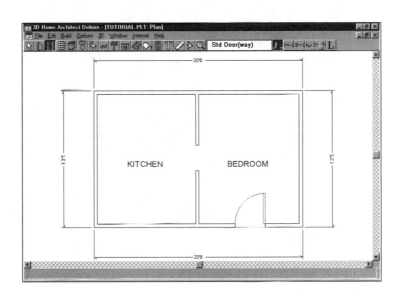

Window Mode button

To place a window, click the **Window Mode** button to get into **Window** mode.

Standard Window tool

As with **Door** mode, you will now see a number of tools on the right side of the toolbar which are specific to **Window** mode. By default, the **Standard Window** tool is active.

You can see by the other tools that you can easily place other types of windows, such as bay windows. (You can also click the **Windows Library** button, which gives you an even wider assortment.) Let's place a standard window: click the top wall at the midpoint of the bedroom.

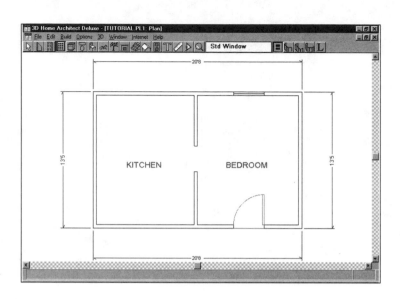

Placing Cabinets

Cabinet Mode button

Base Cabinet tool

Now let's place some cabinets. Click the **Cabinet Mode** button.

As with the other tools we have used, the tools specific to cabinets now appear on the right-hand side of the toolbar. These tools place different types of cabinets: base cabinet, wall cabinet, full-height cabinet, and shelving. By default, the **Base Cabinet** tool is active.

Place some cabinets against the left wall in the kitchen. If you put a cabinet in the wrong place, click it again to make it active and move it, or delete it and start over. Don't worry about correctly orienting the cabinets; when placed near a wall, a cabinet is automatically placed against the wall with its front facing out. Also, when cabinets are placed next to each other, they attach to one another to form an extended cabinet. (Cabinetry in a modern kitchen is made up of modular units linked together.)

The arrow on the cabinet tells you which way the cabinet is facing. To rotate a cabinet, click the **Selection Mode** button, and then click the cabinet. Click the **red arrow** at the rear of the cabinet, and then drag in a circular motion. Use the side and center handles to move and resize the cabinet. The default movement for a cabinet is up/down/left/right. To have unrestricted movement, click the cabinet, press **Ctrl**, and then drag the cabinet.

Your plan should now look like this:

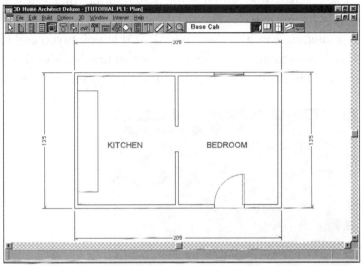

Plan with cabinets placed in kitchen

Placing Fixtures

Fixtures Mode button

Several objects are meant to be placed in cabinets, such as sinks and some appliances. Let's try adding a sink to one of our cabinets. To do this, click the **Fixtures Mode** button.

The **Fixture Library** dialog box appears.

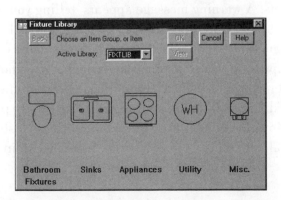

When you open the Fixture Library, it displays five categories of fixtures; each time you click a graphic, you narrow your choice within that category. Click the item labeled **Sinks** and you will be brought to the next level in the Fixture Library. (You can return to a previous level by clicking the **Back** button.) Now click **Kitchen Sinks**; then **24"** **Single Kit. Sink**, which is the actual object that you will place. (You can tell when you've reached the actual object because when you click it, a rectangle appears around it.) At this point, you can either click the **OK** button to place the sink or you can preview the sink in color and three dimensions. Let's preview the sink by clicking the **View** button.

Fixture Library dialog box with preview of 24" kitchen sink

When you are finished viewing, you can either return to the Fixture Library by clicking the **Back** button or you can place the object by clicking the **OK** button. Let's place the sink by clicking the **OK** button. Notice the pointer is shaped like a toilet. This means you are in a mode for placing fixtures in the plan. Click in the middle of the Kitchen, away from the cabinets. A warning message appears, telling you that you must place that particular fixture in a cabinet. The program will not let you place the sink anywhere but in a cabinet. There are many other warnings that appear if you try to do something that does not make sense, like placing a window in an interior wall. Some of these warnings can be bypassed; others, like the sink warning, let you try placing the object again. Move the pointer over the cabinet that is closest to the center of the wall and click. A sink has now been placed in the cabinet.

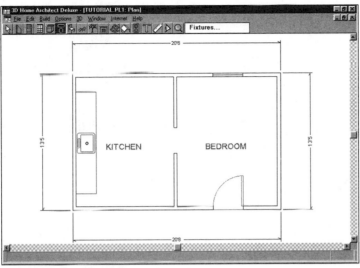

Plan with 24" sink placed in cabinet

Let's place a dishwasher. Click the **Fixtures Mode** button. (Even though the **Fixtures Mode** button is already selected, you must click the button each time you want to place a different fixture.) A dishwasher is an appliance, so click the **Appliances** category, and then **Other**. Click **Kitchen**, and then click the **Dishwasher**. If you want to preview the dishwasher, click the **View** button. Click the **OK** button to go to the plan and place the dishwasher into a cabinet. Make sure you don't click the same cabinet where you placed the sink; if you do, the dishwasher will replace the sink.

Note that any fixture that would typically be placed in a cabinet requires that you place the fixture in a cabinet that is large enough to accommodate it. This means that you must create the cabinet, adjust its size if necessary, and then place the fixture in it.

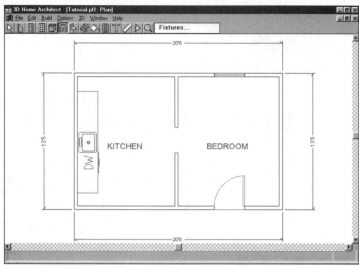

Plan with dishwasher placed in cabinet next to sink

Window Mode button

Now that we have a sink in our kitchen, let's add a window above it. To do this, click the **Window Mode** button as we did earlier.

Again, by default the **Standard Window** tool is active. Click the wall above the cabinets and sink. A window appears above the sink.

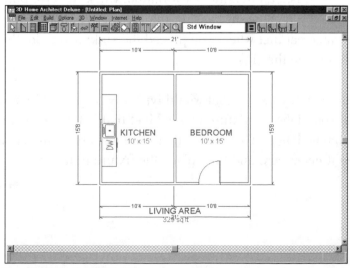

Plan with window placed above sink

Working in Three Dimensions

View Mode button

Camera tool

Let's see what our cabin looks like in three dimensions. To do this, click the **View Mode** button.

By default, the **Camera** tool is selected.

(Notice that the pointer now looks like a camera.) Let's make a view from the doorway, looking into the kitchen. Click just inside the doorway, then drag toward the kitchen a short distance (about an inch on the screen). Then release the mouse button.

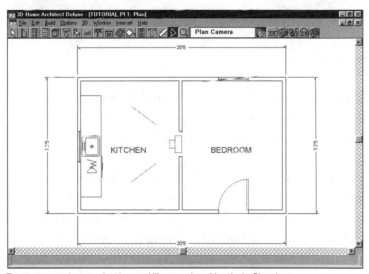

The camera can be moved and rotated like any other object in the Plan view.

A new window appears which shows a three-dimensional view of the kitchen (**Camera** window.)

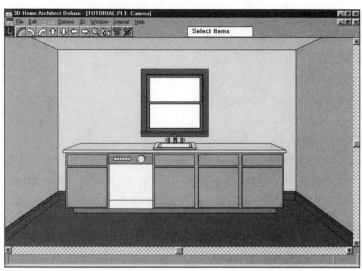

Resulting Plan view

If you click the **Window** menu, and then click **Untitled: Plan** to bring the **Plan** window to the front, you'll see that a red camera appears on the plan where you clicked, pointing into the kitchen.

To change the view in the **Camera** window, make the **Camera** window active, and then click one or more of the arrow tools in the toolbar. Each time you click a tool, the scene in the **Camera** window is redrawn. To make several clicks without having to wait for a redraw each time, hold down the **Shift** key while clicking the tools. To make a particular window active, click the name of the window on the **Window** menu, or press **Ctrl+Tab** to cycle through all open windows. If you want to view all open windows on-screen at the same time, click the **Tile** command on the **Window** menu.

Editing in 3D Views

You can edit and arrange objects in the **Camera** window (and in other windows, too). Any changes you make in a **3D** window are automatically reflected in the **Plan** window, and vice versa. Make sure the **Camera** window is active, and then click the window above the sink. Move the pointer over the center handle in the middle of the kitchen window; the pointer changes to a cross. Click and drag the handle to reposition the window. The new position of the window is shown automatically in the **Plan** window. If you want to resize the window, click and drag one of the handles located on each side of the window.

Besides moving and resizing, you can also change the details of objects in the different views. Let's change the window above the sink. Click the **Selection Mode** button, and then double-click the window. The **Window Specification** dialog box appears, allowing you to change the type and look of the window.

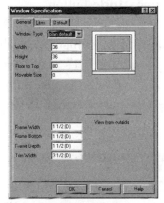

Window Specification dialog box

All the object specification dialog boxes work in pretty much the same way. So, what you learn here about the **Window Specification** dialog box will be applicable to the dialog boxes for walls, doors, cabinets, and other objects, even whole rooms.

There are several option boxes that enable you to change the look of the window. Experiment by selecting different types from the **Window Type** list box. To see the results of your changes, look at the window graphic in the dialog box. When you're done experimenting, click **OK** to return to the **Camera** window and check to see how the window in your plan looks.

Adjust Color tool

3D Home Architect Deluxe also lets you experiment with color in the different views. Click the **Adjust Color** tool on the toolbar.

Click a wall in the **Camera** window. The **Adjust Color** dialog box appears, allowing you to pick different colors for the wall. Create a new color by moving one or more of the sliders in the dialog box, and then click **OK**. Note that by default all walls have the same color; a single default color is assigned to every object of the same type to maintain consistency in your plans.

Placing Furniture

Placing furniture is similar to placing fixtures. Make the **Plan** window active, and then click the **Furniture Mode** button.

The **Furniture Library** dialog box appears. Just like with fixtures, furniture items are arranged in a hierarchy. Let's place a queen-size bed in the bedroom. Click **Bedroom**, then **Large Beds**, then **Traditional**, then **Queen Bed**, and finally the **OK** button. Click in the bedroom to place the bed.

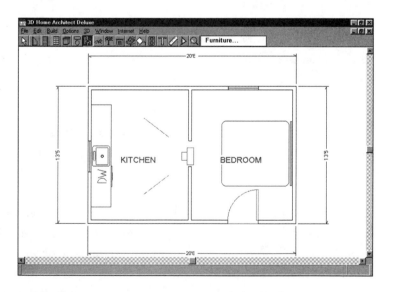

Note that once you have placed a certain object, you can place as many of that type as you want by simply clicking again and again in the plan. To change the type of object that you are placing, click again on the depressed **Furniture Mode** button. This reopens the **Furniture Library** dialog box, and you can repeat the steps for choosing a furniture object. To delete a furniture object, click the **Selection Mode** button, click the object, and then press the **Delete** key. Here's an example of what your plan might look like with more furniture:

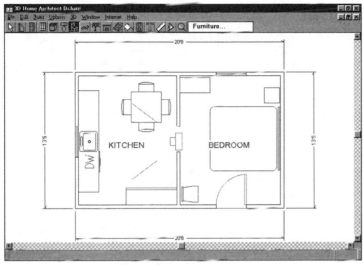

Plan view with additional furniture objects

Oops! No bathroom?

Actually, we did that intentionally. Many of you are going to be using **3D Home Architect Deluxe** to design a remodel or an addition for your existing home. In those cases, the best thing to do is to recreate your existing floor plan in **3D Home Architect Deluxe**, and then modify it from there. Adding a bathroom to our existing cabin is a typical example.

Zoom Mode button

Walls are the essential building blocks of this program, so you can think about walls as a first step in any project. Switch to the **Plan** window by clicking **Plan** on the **Windows** menu. Let's add a bathroom off of the bedroom. First, click the **Zoom Mode** button:

Move Out (x2) tool

Now "zoom out" by clicking the **Move Out (x2)** tool.

This gives us more room to work with. Now let's add the walls (use the **Wall** mode tools as you did earlier) so the plan looks like this:

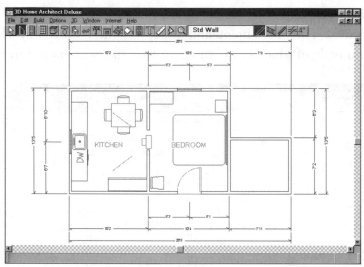

Plan view with bathroom walls added

Remember that it's very easy to move walls around once they are placed. When you move a wall, the walls connected to either end get longer or shorter so that the connection is maintained. If you place cabinets against a wall and then move the wall, the cabinets move with the wall. This means you don't have to be precise when you first add walls, because it is easy to adjust them to the dimensions you want later.

Now that we have added the walls, let's name the room. Click the **Selection Mode** button, and then double-click inside the room to open the **Room Specification** dialog box. Click the **Room Name** list box, click **Bath**, and then click **OK** to return to the plan. Now, to place a doorway between the bedroom and the bathroom, select the **Door Mode** button as you did earlier and then click the wall between the bedroom and bathroom. To make the doorway into a door, click the doorway once. Click the top handle of the door, then drag into the bathroom. As you can see, the door has been created:

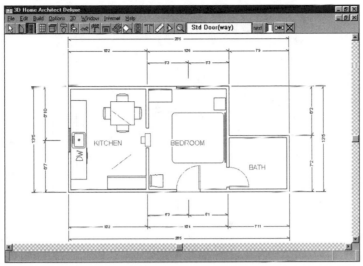

Door opening into bathroom from bedroom

Now let's place some bathroom fixtures; we'll add a toilet first. Click the **Fixture** tool. When the dialog box appears, click **Bathroom Fixtures** and then click **Toilets**. Click your preferred toilet (you can preview it if you like), then click **OK**. In the bathroom, click the location where you want to place the toilet.

Now let's place a sink. Click the depressed **Fixtures Mode** button; in the dialog box, click **Sinks** and then **Bathroom Sinks**. Click the **Oval** bathroom sink, and then click **View** to preview. The **Oval** bathroom sink is set in a cabinet, so this sink requires that we first create a cabinet to place the sink in. We don't want to do that right now, so let's preview another sink. Click the **Back** button to exit the preview. Next, click the **Oval Free Standing** sink, and then click the **View** button. Notice that this fixture does not require a cabinet. Click **OK** to accept this sink, and then place the sink by clicking the location you want in the bathroom. Your plan should look something like this:

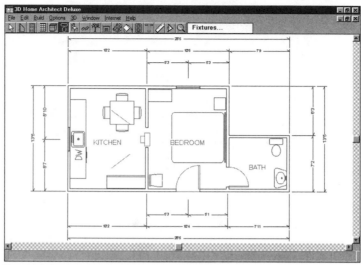

Plan with bathroom fixtures placed

Finally, let's put a shower into the bathroom. Click the depressed **Fixtures Mode** button, then **Bathroom Fixtures**, then **Showers**, then **Rectangular Showers**. Click the **33x42" Shower,** and then click **View** to preview the shower. Click **OK** to accept the shower, and then place the shower by clicking the bathroom in the location you want. Here's how the bathroom should look:

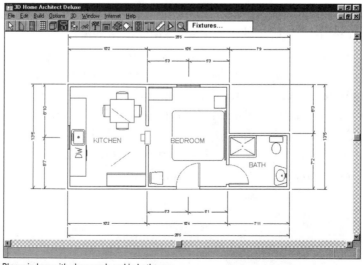

Plan window with shower placed in bathroom

View Mode button

Overview tool

View Angle Tool

Great! We're done with our bathroom. Since we have made substantial changes to our plan, it is best to reset all 3D views. On the **3D** menu, click **Remove 3D** to close all open 3D views. Now let's get a bird's-eye overview of the entire plan. To do this, click the **View Mode** button and then click the **Overview** tool from the right-hand tools.

Your plan appears in the **Overview** window. To change the view angle, click the **View Angle** tool. You can now experiment with the sliders and options in the **View Angle** dialog box, or you can exit the dialog box by clicking **Cancel**.

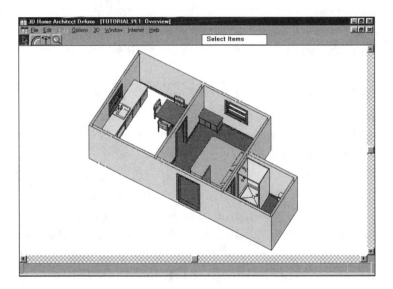

When you're finished experimenting with the **Overview** window, you can close it by selecting **Close** on the **File** menu.

Applying a Material to Your Cabin

Let's add to the realistic look of your cabin by applying a material to an outside wall and then viewing the wall.

Click the **Selection Mode** button, and then click your plan about 1/2 inch outside the left-hand wall. The **Assign Colors** dialog box should appear; if the **Wall Specification** dialog box appears instead, click **Cancel**, and then try clicking your plan a little further from the wall.

In the **Assign Colors** dialog box, click **Material**, and then click **Choose Material**. This opens the **Select Image** dialog box; click a category, then click a subcategory, and then click the material you want to apply. Click **OK** two times to exit the dialog boxes and apply the material.

Even though the material has been applied, you can't see it in the **Plan** window. To view the material, click the **View Mode** button, and then click the upper-left corner of your screen and drag toward the left-hand wall. This opens a **Camera** view; next, on the toolbar, click the **Applied Materials** tool (which looks like a camera). An **Applied Materials View** window opens, displaying the material you chose. When you are done viewing this window, click its **Exit** button to close it.

Adding Landscaping

Just as you can add a material to a wall for a more realistic look, you can add a ground covering to the ground surrounding your cabin. The first step is to build the lot your cabin resides on. On the **Build** menu, click **Build/Move Lot**; this places a 50'x100' lot. To see the boundaries of the lot, click the **Zoom Mode** button, and then click the **Zoom Out** tool. Click the **Zoom In** tool when you are finished to reset the view. Let's also turn off the dimension lines for now; on the **Options** menu, click **Show Items**. Click the check box next to **Automatic Dimensions** to clear it. Click **OK** to exit the dialog box.

On the **Options** menu, click **Show Items** and then make sure **Beam/Soffit** is selected. This ensures that your ground covering will be visible. Click **OK** to exit the dialog box. On the **Build** menu, click ground covering, and then click in the upper-left corner of the **Plan** window. This places a 3'x3' ground covering. To make it larger, click the ground covering, then click the red handle located on its right side, and then drag to the right edge of the window. Click the ground covering again, and drag the lower red handle to the north wall of the cabin. The ground covering should now cover a large portion of your backyard.

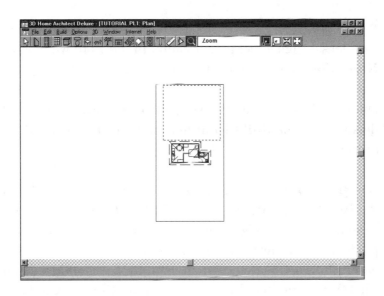

Now let's apply a material. Double-click the ground covering to open the **Ground Cover Size** dialog box. Click **Color & Material**, click **Material**, and then click **Choose Material**. Click **grnd_cvr**, click **lawn**, and then click **light**. Here is where you choose the actual material; double-click **lawnlt06**. (You can also single-click your choice, and then click **OK**.) Click **OK** twice to apply the material.

Once again, we need to create an **Applied Materials** view to see the ground covering. Click the **View Mode** button, and then click the upper-left corner of the **Plan** window and drag toward the upper-right corner. This opens a **Camera** view. Next, on the toolbar, click the **Applied Materials** button (which looks like a camera). An **Applied Materials View** window opens, displaying the ground covering with the material you chose. When you are done viewing this window, click its **Exit** button to close it.

Lets turn the Dimension marks back on: on the **Options** menu, click **Show Items**. Click the check box next to **Automatic Dimensions** to select it. Click **OK** to exit the dialog box.

Roof Mode button

Building the Roof

Now let's design a roof for our cabin. In the **Plan** window, click the **Roof Mode** button on the toolbar.

Roof Mode
Button

Roof Section at, Build Roof, Delete Roof

On the right side of the toolbar, the **Roof Section at** tool (this is the default tool), the **Build Roof** tool, and the **Delete Roof** tool are displayed.

By default, *3D Home Architect Deluxe* will build a hip roof. Click the **Build Roof** tool, and the **Build Roof** dialog box appears. The Automatic Roof Designer in the program takes the information on roof pitch, overhang, and rafter thickness and translates that into, in this case, a hip roof. For our first attempt, let's accept the defaults and see what Automatic Roof Designer will build. Click **OK** to build the roof. Your plan should look something like this:

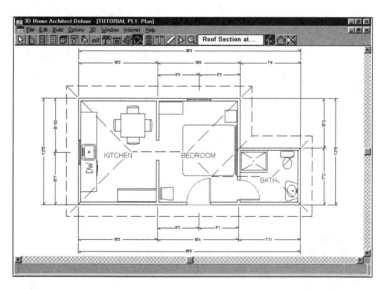

View Mode button

Full Overview tool

Now let's take a look at the cabin in a three-dimensional view using the **Full Overview** tool. To do this, click the **View Mode** button, then select the **Full Overview** tool from the right-hand tools.

Direction Tool

Your plan appears in the **Full Overview** window. To change the view angle, click the **Direction** tool.

Experiment with the **View Angle** dialog box, or click **Cancel** to exit the dialog box. Your view should look like this:

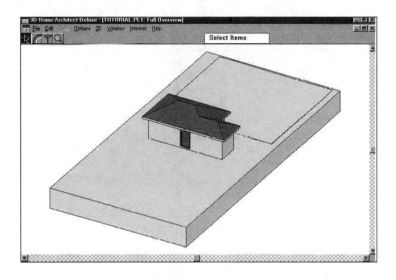

View Mode button

Full Camera tool

When you're done experimenting with the **Full Overview** window, close the window by selecting **Close** on the **File** menu. Let's take one more look at the cabin with the **Full Camera** tool. To do this, click the **View Mode** button. Then click the **Full Camera** tool from the right-hand tools.

Notice that the pointer now looks like a camera; this tool works like the standard **Camera** tool. Let's make our view toward the front door, looking at the front of the cabin. Click about five inches outside the doorway and drag toward the door a short distance (about an inch on the screen). Your plan appears in a **Full Camera** window that looks something like this:

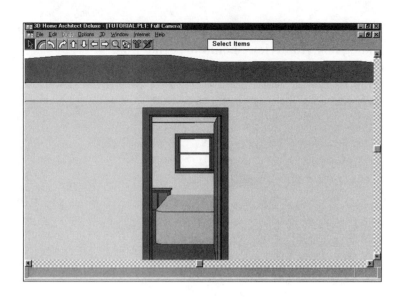

You can move around the view by using the tools available in the menu bar. When you're done experimenting, close the view by selecting **Close** on the **File** menu.

Roof Mode button

Roof Section at tool

Now let's change this hip roof to a gable roof. In order for Automatic Roof Designer to build a gable roof, we must tell it where we want the gables to be. The **Roof Section at** tool will help you do this. Click the **Roof Mode** button; the **Roof Section at** tool on the right side of the toolbar is selected by default.

Let's make the gables on the east- and west-facing walls of our cabin. First, click the west-facing wall. The **Roof Section at Wall** dialog box appears with the default settings for this wall.

Click **Full Gable wall**. That's all we will change for now, so click **OK** and you will be taken back to the plan. Now do the same thing for both the east-facing walls. We have now instructed Automatic Roof Designer to place gables in each of these walls. Let's build the roof and see what it looks like. Click the **Roof Mode** button and select the **Build Roof** tool. We don't want to change any of the settings in this dialog box, so click **OK** to build the roof.

View Mode button

Now let's view the cabin with its gable roof. Click the **View Mode** button, then select the **Full Camera** tool, and then click in the upper-right corner and drag toward the middle of the window.

Full Camera tool

Your plan appears in the **Full Camera** window. It should look like this:

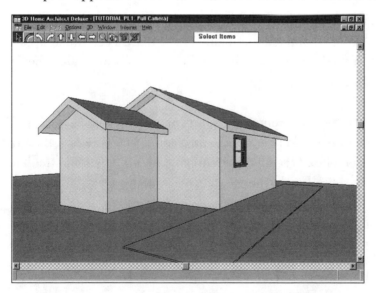

When you're done experimenting with the **Full Overview** window, close the window by selecting **Close** on the **File** menu.

This completes the basic roofing techniques part of this tutorial. For more detailed information on creating roofs, including instructions for creating other roof styles, placing gables over doors and windows, and placing dormers in your roof, see chapter 4, "Advanced Roofing Techniques."

Electrical Symbols

Electrical Mode button

Place Outlets tool

Electrical symbols are an important part of a building plan. They indicate where switches, outlets, and lighting are to be located. They also indicate how switches are wired. ***3D Home Architect Deluxe*** can do all of these things quickly and easily. We'll try using just one of the tools which are available, in order to place some electrical outlets. In the **Plan** window, click the **Electrical Mode** button, and then click the **Place Outlets** tool.

Click each of the three rooms in the plan. 110V electrical outlets are placed in each room at standard intervals, and light fixtures are placed over the sinks.

Outdoor Images

Outdoor Images button

We've completed the inside of the plan. Let's finish up our landscaping on the outside of the house. Zoom out 2X and click the **Outdoor Images** button.

The **Select Image** dialog box opens. As you can see, you can add flowers, rockery, shrubs, and trees. Click **flowers**, then **margdisy**, and then click **OK**. In the **Plan** window, click outside the house next to the north wall eight times. Your plan should look like this:

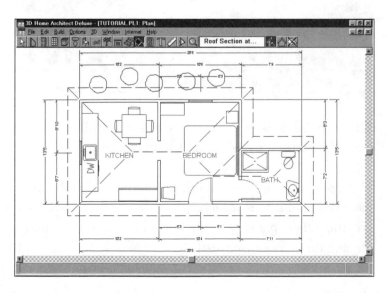

Next, click the depressed **Outdoor Images** button, then click **large tree**, **lg trees**, and **sweetgum**. Click **OK**, and then click above the flowers twice to place two trees.

Let's view the plan with outdoor images in 3D. Click the **View Mode** button, and then click the **Full Overview** button. This defaults to a front view. Let's change it to see the landscaping additions we have made. Click the **Direction** tool, and then in the **View Angle** dialog box, click **Elevation** and **Back**. Click **OK** to exit the dialog box. Click the **Zoom Mode** button, and then click the **Zoom to Fit** tool. Your plan should look something like this:

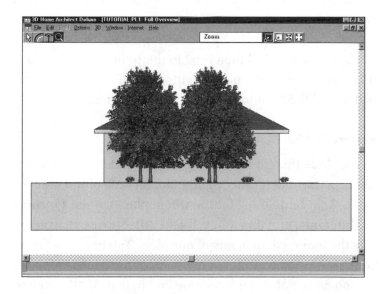

To close the **Full Overview** window, click the **Exit** button in the upper-right corner of the window.

PlanCheck

PlanCheck checks your plan for blatant design errors. It will not verify that the plan is up to code, because codes vary greatly depending on local ordinances. PlanCheck will alert you to any rules of thumb that you may have violated, and it will also give you some design tips.

Let's check our plan now. Make sure the **Plan** window is active, and then on the **Options** menu, click **PlanCheck**. The **PlanCheck** dialog box will appear. Read any message that is displayed, and then click **Next** to move on to the next message. When you're finished, click the **Done** button. You can now make corrections to the plan. For example, PlanCheck has noted that the light above the kitchen sink (placed there automatically by the **Place Outlets** tool), is not wired to a switch. To wire it, make sure the **Electrical Mode** button is selected, and then click the **Switch** tool.

Switch tool

Connect tool

To place a switch, click the inner surface of a kitchen wall in the location you want. To connect the switch to a light, click the **Connect** tool.

Click the switch, and then drag to the light you want to attach it to. When you release the mouse button, a curved line appears between the switch and the light to indicate the connection.

Materials List

To conclude this tutorial, let's generate a Materials list for our cabin. We can generate one for the whole plan, an area of the plan, or a single room. We'll build a list for the whole plan. On the **Options** menu, point to **Materials**, and then click **Build All Floors**. A window opens which lists the major components of our plan. You can enter material costs in the **Price** column. To learn more about the **Materials** window, see the section on the **Materials** window in chapter 5, "Reference."

When you are done, select **Close All** on the **File** menu. A dialog box appears asking if you wish to save the plan before closing. You can save it if you like, or click **No**.

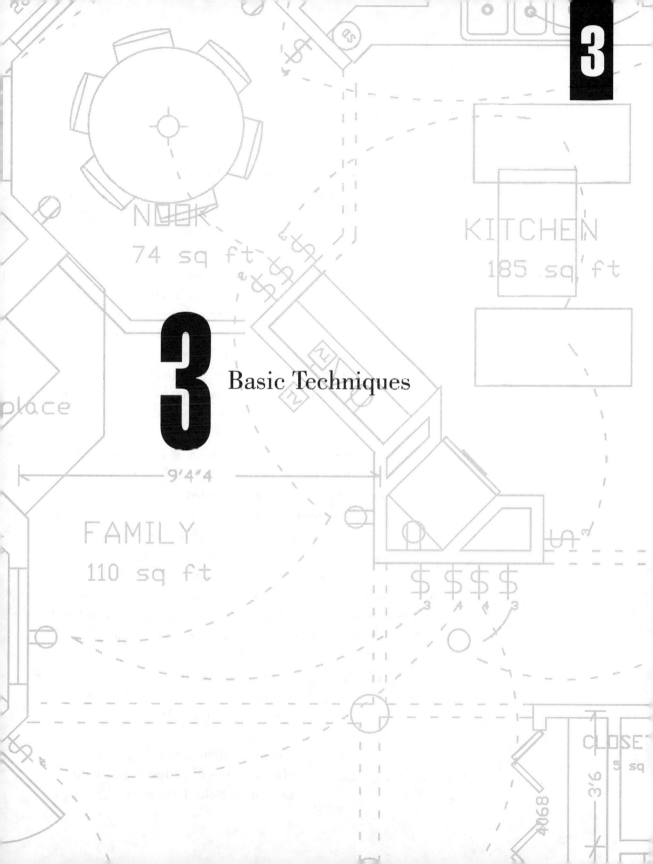

3

Basic Techniques

Basic Techniques

Drawing a Plan

Drawing plans in *3D Home Architect Deluxe* is really pretty simple—all the different items you might want in a plan are grouped into categories, and all members of a given category act in much the same way.

Moving, rotating, resizing, and deleting operate almost identically for every kind of object. Once an object has been placed in your plan, clicking it with the pointer will enable you to change it in different ways. The first thing you will notice is that walls, text, and outdoor images display three squares, called handles, one at each end and one in the middle. Moving the pointer over the middle handle changes it to double-sided arrows; by dragging the pointer you can move the object. Dragging one of the end handles in or out lets you resize the object.

Other objects, like cabinets and furniture, have at least two handles: a triangle on one end and a square in the middle. When dragged over the square, the pointer changes to a double-headed arrow and you can move the object. Pointing at the triangle changes the pointer to a circling arrow; dragging this lets you rotate the object. Note that objects displaying a square and triangle can only be moved orthogonally, that is, vertically and horizontally; to move them freely, press and hold **Ctrl**, and then drag. Cabinets will display four squares, a triangle, and an arrow. The center square and the triangle move and rotate. The other three handles resize, and the arrow indicates which way the cabinet is facing.

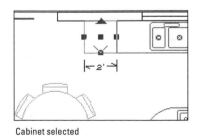

Cabinet selected

To delete any selected item, use the **Delete** command on the **Edit** menu, the **Delete** key, or the **Delete** tool.

To edit an item, first select it. To do this, click the **Select Mode** button on the toolbar, or **Select Items** on the **Edit** menu. This switches the program to **Select** mode. When you select an object, as many as four right-hand tools will appear in the toolbar, depending on the type of object selected: the **Next, Open, Copy,** and **Delete** tools. The last two are easy enough; click the appropriate tool to copy or delete the object. If copying, the pointer will change to a Copy pointer, which you click to place the copy (as with the **Paste** command on the **Edit** menu).

Next tool

The **Next** tool lets you select items that are stacked, like staircases, or incorporated into other objects, like standard windows within bay and bow window structures. The **Open** tool corresponds to the **Open Item** menu command on the **Edit** menu, or to double-clicking an object. These commands open a dialog box where you can change the specifications of the object selected.

Open tool

Copy tool

Delete tool

In addition to the **Open** tool or command, you can also open an object by double-clicking it while in **Selection** mode, or with the tool that created the object. You can open just about every item in your plan, and in almost every view. Even rooms can be opened, which is important because the **Room Specification** dialog box is where you can do things like naming a room. (To select a room, click inside it anywhere except on an object; the room will then be outlined.)

Walls are created by either using the **Wall** mode tools in the toolbar or by selecting the **Wall** command on the **Build** menu, then just clicking and dragging out walls. To draw a wall at an angle, move the pointer in a circle as you drag—the wall will snap to 15-degree increments. Drawing one wall close to another will cause the walls to snap together. To extend a wall, either select it and drag an end handle, or simply drag a new wall near the end so it is in line with the old. To shorten a wall, perform these steps in reverse. While you are dragging a wall, its length displays in the status box in the toolbar. Here is the first rule for drawing walls: Draw straight through a doorway, window, or other opening. Put the opening in later. The picture below does not show two horizontal walls of different lengths. There is only one horizontal wall that has a doorway near its end. You must draw it as one wall and then place a doorway in it. If you try drawing it as two walls, the program will not let you put in a door or draw a very short wall. If it did, it would be hard to line everything up.

Doors, like windows, are openings in walls that you create by selecting the appropriate command or tool, then clicking the area of the wall where you want the opening. While holding the mouse button down, you can move the door back and forth along the wall; dimension lines will display showing the door's position in the wall. Once you have placed the door, you can change it by moving and resizing or "opening" it to change its specifications. To determine the direction that the door will open, highlight the door and then click either end and drag north or south in the direction you want the door to open.

Windows are created like doors, only using **Window** mode and commands. Just select the kind of window you want and where you want it, and click. Besides changing the width of a window, you can also adjust its height from top to bottom by dragging the middle handle in or out. As you drag, four-digit numbers are displayed in the middle of the window. The last two digits show the window height in feet and inches; the first two digits show width.

Cabinets can be placed anywhere in a plan where there is room by selecting a cabinet tool and clicking. If you click near a wall, the cabinet is automatically attached to that wall. Cabinets are considered "modules" that fit together, so when you create several in a row they seem to join into one. As modules, they are also a standard size (which you can set and change, of course). But note that the size of the cabinet, which way it faces, and even its type can change automatically depending on where you put it. For example, if you place a cabinet in a corner, it automatically becomes a corner cabinet.

Fixtures, furniture, and outdoor objects are grouped by type and then item group into a hierarchical dialog box. To select and place fixtures, first click the **Fixtures Library** button, which opens a dialog box, then work through the dialog box from item group to item group until you find the item you want (items, as opposed to groups, will be outlined when selected). You can preview a fixture item by clicking the **View** button; when done with the preview, click **Back** to return to the selection dialog box. When you have the piece you want, click **OK** and then click in your plan where you want to locate the fixture item. Follow through this process for each fixture, piece of furniture, and outdoor object you place in your plan. Some fixtures, like sinks, are placed in cabinets. Others, like refrigerators, are free-standing. Fixtures placed in cabinets are edited with the cabinets, while free-standing fixtures, furniture, and outdoor objects are edited individually.

Outdoor Images
button

Outdoor images are also grouped by type and item group in a hierarchical dialog box. To select and place an outdoor image, click the **Outdoor Images** button on the toolbar—this opens the **Select Image** dialog box. Click the name of the group of outdoor images you want to place in your plan (for example, shrubs), and then click the graphic that shows the outdoor image you want. For more information about the object you chose, view the text window which appears in the lower-left corner of the dialog box. When you are finished with the **Select Image** dialog box, click **OK**. In your plan, click the location where you want to place the outdoor image.

Roofs are best created after all other design aspects have been completed, but before electrical items are placed in the plan. By using the appropriate roofing tools, you can add gables above doors and windows and place dormers in the attic of your plan. *3D Home Architect Deluxe* uses Automatic Roof Designer to generate roof structures. The default roof will be a hip roof, but you can always modify this, as you will learn later on in this manual.

Electrical Mode
button

Electrical outlets (both 110V and 220V), switches, and light fixtures can be selected and placed pretty much like cabinets. Select the type of

Symbol Library
tool

Connect tool

Place Outlet tool

Text tool

Dimension Mode
button

Exterior
Dimensions tool

object and click where you want it. Clicking near a wall places items in it. Clicking away from a wall places light fixtures in the ceiling. Switches can only be placed on walls. Besides these standard electrical symbols, others can be obtained and placed through the **Symbol Library** dialog box, which is used like the fixture and furniture libraries. The **Symbol Library** tool becomes available on the right side of the toolbar when **Electrical** mode is selected. To move any electrical symbol, click and drag it. To show which light fixtures and outlets are controlled by which switches, click the **Connect** tool, then starting with the first switch and ending with any additional switches, drag a line to each item on the circuit. To disconnect items, just click them. The **Place Outlets** tool places all the outlets in a room automatically when you select the tool and click the room.

Text is created by using the **Text** tool or by selecting the **Text** command on the **Build** menu and clicking the location in your plan where the text is to be placed. A dialog box appears where you type the actual text. Here you can choose to have a moveable arrow placed with the text. Once created, text boxes can be moved and resized like other objects by clicking their handles. Note that text is drawn as an object, so it scales up or down as you zoom in or out of the plan. Text is sized in plan inches, as in CAD programs, not in points, as in word processors.

Dimensions are created in two ways. Manual, interior dimension lines are "built" like walls, by dragging a dimension line out perpendicularly between two walls with the **Manual Dimension** tool. Exterior dimension lines are created automatically by using the **Exterior Dimensions** tool; you can also point to **Dimension Lines** on the **Build** menu, and then click **Exterior Dimen**. Once created, dimension lines can be moved, but not resized; their ends will move automatically if the associated walls move. Note that the exterior dimensions do not always update completely when you change your plan, so it is best to reissue the command if changes have occurred, as the exterior dimension lines are completely redone every time you select the command. You can set the attributes of the dimension lines in the **Dimensions Setup** dialog box. On the **Options** menu, click **Dimension Setup**.

View Mode
button

Plan Camera tool

Wall Elevation
tool

Plan Overview
tool

Full Camera tool

Cross Section
tool

Full Overview
tool

Views and Windows

In addition to working with your plan as a "blueprint," *3D Home Architect Deluxe* also offers seven other views on your design. These are the **Plan Camera** window, the **Wall Elevation** window, the **Plan Overview** window, the **Full Camera** window, the **Cross Section** window, the **Full Overview** window and the **Materials** window, which is available on the **Options** menu. The first six windows are accessed by the tools under the **View Mode** button, or through the commands in the **3D** menu. All open a separate window, and all are used by selecting the command while a plan is open. To select a camera view or an interior elevation view, select the command, then drag a line of sight toward your area of interest. For an overview, the **Full Overview** window showing the whole plan will be displayed immediately after the command is issued. The **Materials** window shows a different view of your plan, namely, a list of the materials needed to construct it. You can also use the **Materials** window to generate a cost of materials based on unit costs that you enter. The **Applied Materials** window shows you the same views as the **Plan Camera** and **Full Camera** windows, but with the selected building materials applied. For example, in this view you can see the bricks in a brick wall. The view in the **Applied Materials** window can be saved as a bitmap graphic image. You can change the way this window is displayed by clicking **Set Up Applied Materials Windows** on the **3D** menu, and then choosing options in the dialog box that appears.

Setting Up Applied Materials View

On the **3D** menu, click **Applied Materials View Setup**. In the dialog box that appears, under **Color Model**, click **Color** if it is not already selected. (This will give you the highest quality view, but may cause an improper display on some older computers. If this happens, return to this option and choose **Ramp**.) Under **Shade**, choose **Flat** if you want the shading in your view to be faceted (broken up). Choose **Gouraud** if you want shading to be smooth. Select **Show Images** if you want to include bitmap images (for example, plants and statuary) in your view. Select **No Default Lights** if you do not want to include lights by default. Select **Ambient Light** if you want to illuminate all surfaces in your view. Use the scroll bar on the right to specify the amount of **Ambient Light** you want. To change the background of your view, click **Backdrop**, then choose an image and a color. Click **OK** when you are done.

Multiple Floors

3D Home Architect Deluxe can handle up to four separate floors in a plan, an attic, plus a foundation, which is a special case. Floors are worked on one at a time. However, you can superimpose one floor, called a reference floor, on your working floor to keep things lined up, and you can easily swap working and reference floors back and forth. The relevant commands are listed on the **Window** menu. To keep the different floors of the design distinct, yet together, the program uses the same file name for each, simply changing the extension to indicate different floors. A foundation plan is termed "FILE.PL0," a first floor plan, "FILE.PL1," and a second floor plan "FILE.PL2," and so on.

Thinking about Drawing a Plan

When you start drawing your plan, don't think in terms of drawing lines. Think in terms of building things. Here is a good sequence to follow:

1. Draw walls.
2. Name rooms.
3. Put in doorways and windows.
4. Place cabinet modules in kitchen and bathrooms.
5. Place fixtures and appliances.
6. Place furniture.
7. Build roof.
8. Place electrical outlets, light fixtures, and switches.
9. Create a lot.
10. Place landscaping and outdoor objects.

Of course, you will want to use the 3D views extensively as you are following these general steps, both to check on your design and to make changes, especially to doors and windows.

Creating a Complete Plan

Having completed the first tutorial, you should have a pretty good idea of just how capable, and even fun, **3D Home Architect Deluxe** is. You might now be ready to go on to drawing your own designs. But in case you want to know more of the program's special features and tricks, we have included this second tutorial. It is longer than the first, and more involved, but worthwhile in taking you all the way through the process of designing a house, learning along the way special techniques many designs will require. The finished plan, called "TUTORIAL.pl1," is located in the **My Plans** directory. To look at the plan in 3D, use the **Plan Camera** tool. Use the **Show Floors** command to switch to the plan for the foundation and second floor.

Thinking about Drawing Walls

When designing a new home with **3D Home Architect Deluxe**, the very first thing is to think about how you will live in your new home, and what designs will reflect that. After this conceptual stage, you'll begin drawing up your ideas to see what they look like.

There are three things to remember to take full advantage of **3D Home Architect Deluxe**. First, the rooms within your home are defined by walls, and walls alone. If a space is not completely surrounded by walls, it is not a separate space. Second, openings in walls are best made by placing actual opening objects, like windows and doors, in the walls, not by leaving out a section of wall. Third, the program will measure and align walls for you, and will even move and resize walls to make them connect. You can relax, sketch out the general shape first, and fine-tune later.

Creating the Exterior of a House

First we'll draw exterior walls that will completely enclose our plan. This will make it absolutely clear what is inside and outside. To draw these exterior walls, select **Wall** mode, either on the **Build** menu or the toolbar. Next, before we start drawing, we'll set the wall thickness. We could do this later, but it is best to get a proper start (it will also make it

Wall Mode button

easier to align walls of different types and thicknesses, as we will see). The default thickness for standard walls is four inches, as they are considered interior walls (this basically amounts to two-by-four studs with a half-inch of sheetrock and plaster on each side). Exterior walls are usually thicker, so click the wall **Thickness** button, at the right end of the toolbar, until it reads **6"**.

Now that we have set the proper wall thickness, use the techniques that you learned in the first tutorial to start dragging out the exterior walls. As in the accompanying illustration, make two "rooms"; one will be a garage, which is usually (but not always) separated from the rest of the house by exterior walls, since the garage is usually at outside temperature.

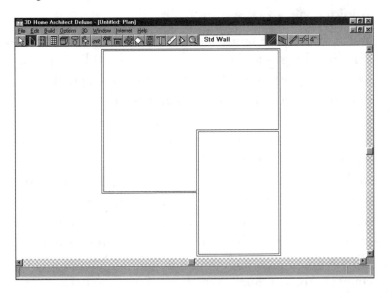

Dimension Mode button

Exterior Dimensions tool

Once you have drawn the walls, make sure they are the right length. As an aid, let's have exterior dimension lines automatically placed on our plan. Click the **Dimension Mode** button, then the **Exterior Dimensions** tool (note that you may need to use the **Fill Window** tool to make everything fit on screen). Dimension lines will be drawn all around the plan, locating all the walls automatically. (Of course, because the plan is already completely enclosed, you could check each wall's length just by clicking a wall and then clicking its center handle. This would display a temporary dimension line showing the distance from one perpendicular wall to the next. We used exterior dimensions here just so you can see everything at once.) Now that you can see how long all the walls in your plan are, make any necessary adjustments so that the dimensions match those in the illustration below. For example, the wall across the top should be exactly 40 feet long. If not, select it and drag the center handles of an attaching wall until it is.

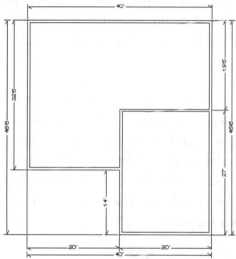

To adjust the length of the top wall, move either of the vertical walls that attach to its end points.

Fill Window tool

Move Out (x2) tool

If you cannot see the whole wall on screen, go to **Zoom** mode and select either the **Fill Window** tool or **Move Out (x2)** tool to increase the visible portion of the plan. As you move walls around, you may notice that not all the exterior dimension lines update; to make sure they are accurate, just select the command again, and the program will redraw all of them.

Note: For the purpose of clarity, many of the plan illustrations in this tutorial do not show the exterior dimension lines. The exterior dimension lines are turned off by clearing the **Automatic Dimensions** check box in the **Show Items** dialog box.

Selecting Material for Exterior Walls

You can specify a texture and material for an exterior wall. To do this, click the **Selection Mode** button, and then click your plan about 1/2 inch outside the wall you want to decorate. The **Assign Colors** dialog box should appear; if the **Wall Specification** dialog box appears instead, click **Cancel**, and then try clicking your plan a little further from the wall. In the **Assign Colors** dialog box, click **Material**, and then click **Choose Material**. This opens the **Select Image** dialog box; click a category, then click a subcategory, and then click the material you want to apply. Click **OK** two times to exit the dialog boxes and apply the material.

Even though the material has been applied, you can't see it in the Plan window. To view the material, click the **View Mode** button, and then click inside the window and drag toward the wall. This opens a Camera view; next, on the toolbar, click the **Applied Materials** tool (which looks like a camera). An **Applied Materials View** window opens, displaying the material you chose. When you are done viewing this window, click its **Exit** button to close it.

Selecting Colors for Exterior Walls

You can apply a color to the exterior walls of a floor. To do this, click the **Selection Mode** button, and then click your plan about 1/2 inch outside the wall you want to color. The **Assign Colors** dialog box should appear; if the **Wall Specification** dialog box appears instead, click **Cancel**, and then try clicking your plan a little further from the wall. In the **Assign Colors** dialog box, click the color you want, and then click **OK**.

To view the colored wall, click the **View Mode** button, and then click inside the window and drag toward the wall. This opens a Camera view, which displays the wall with the color you chose. When you are done viewing this window, click its **Exit** button to close it.

Drawing Interior Walls

As exterior walls define the basic shape of our house, interior walls define individual rooms. Then we can assign special properties to each room and its contents. Create these walls just like exterior walls, but first change the wall thickness to four inches by clicking the **Thickness** button until it reads **4"**. We will want our walls to line up like those in the next picture, so move and resize each interior wall until they all measure up. That is more than a pun, because now that we have all the exterior walls up, every time we select and move a wall, either the exterior dimension line will show what is going on, or a temporary dimension line will appear, showing how far away the wall is from the neighboring perpendicular walls. The idea is to place your walls quickly by dragging them out roughly first and then adjusting for position and length later.

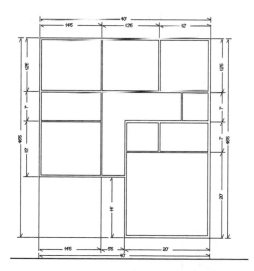

Once you have drawn one interior wall, like the horizontal wall below the top exterior wall of the plan, you will notice that you cannot draw another wall completely across it. Instead, you must draw one crossing the wall on one side, and the second on the other. This is not difficult, however, because the program will snap the wall ends together, keeping them lined up.

Note that although we have drawn real, standard walls to create our rooms, that does not mean we cannot have an "open" plan. Remember, we are putting in all these walls just to define space. There are two ways

Wall Specification dialog box

to wall off rooms while keeping your rooms and plan open. The most obvious is to use invisible walls. These are not really built, they just help the program identify rooms. To use these, either select the command from the **Wall** submenu in the **Build** menu and create new walls or open the **Wall Specification** dialog box for an existing wall by double-clicking it. Then check the **No Locate** and **Invisible** options. Try this out on the first horizontal interior wall from the top on the left. If you draw that long horizontal wall first, it will be one wall all the way across the house. To create a section, either erase the relevant portion and then draw a short section in its place, or use the **Break Wall** command, by selecting the tool and clicking once where the walls cross.

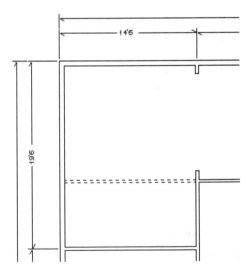

Dotted lines represent a Room Definition wall, used to help define an area which is not really enclosed.

The other method is to use a real wall, but place a wide doorway in it. We are going to do this to the first vertical interior wall on the left, in the section nearest the top exterior wall. Change to **Door** mode by clicking the **Door Mode** tool, then select the **Standard Door** tool (it should already be selected, as it is the default tool for that mode), and place it in the wall. Next, drag the end handles to make the door wide enough, say 10 feet, but do not drag open a door.

Naming Rooms

Selection Mode button

Open tool

Now that we have our rooms defined with walls of different kinds, we are going to give them names. To do this, first select each room, by first choosing the **Selection Mode** button. Next, click anywhere inside the top-left room. A red line should appear, following the walls that outline the space. Now we can use the **Open** tool to display the **Room Specification** dialog box. You can also display the **Room Specification** dialog box by double-clicking the room.

To name the selected room, click the box next to **Room Name**, and then in the list that appears, click **Kitchen**. While in this dialog box, take a look at some of the other changes we can make to rooms. Notice the **Color & Material** button; you can change the floor material or color by clicking this button and then using the same series of steps you used earlier to change the wall material and color. When you are finished with this dialog box, click the **OK** button. Notice that text showing the room name ("KITCHEN") and the room's dimensions have now appeared in the room. Double-click and name all the rooms in the plan so that it looks like the following:

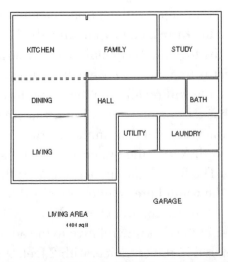

Room-name labels are text objects that can be repositioned with the pointer, as has been done here for the Hall.
To hide room dimensions, on the Options menu, click Show Items, and then under Room Labels, clear the Size option.

Selecting Textures and Materials for Interior Walls

You can specify textures and materials for interior walls. To do this:

1. Click the **Selection Mode** button, then double-click the room you want to work on. The **Room Specification** dialog box displays.

2. Click **Color & Material** then click **Material** and choose a material or texture to apply.

When you apply a texture and material to an interior wall, it affects all the walls in that room.

Selecting Colors for Interior Walls

You can apply a color to the interior walls of a room. To do this:

1. Click the **Selection Mode** button, then double-click the room you want to work on. The **Room Specification** dialog box displays.

2. Click **Color & Material**, and then click the color you want.

3. Click **OK** twice to close the dialog boxes and apply the color.

When you apply a color to an interior wall, it affects all the walls in that room.

Placing Doors

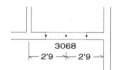

First create the doorway...

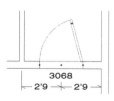

...then create the door by "swinging out" one of the end handles.

Now we can determine how people will get from room to room in our plan. To place doors, go to **Door** mode by clicking the **Door Mode** button. On the right of the toolbar, the default tool, **Standard Door**, should be selected. That is fine, because we will start by creating the front door to our house. You will recall from the first tutorial that the **Standard Door** tool has a two-step nature. First, you create a doorway, and then, if you wish, you can put a door in the doorway. Add a new doorway to the bottom wall. Notice the dimensions that display while you place this doorway. The four-digit number indicates the width and height of the doorway; the width here is automatically 3 feet and the height is 6'8", which is standard for an exterior doorway. The other figures locate the center of the doorway relative to the adjacent walls. Make the doorway centered in the entrance, with 2 feet, 9 inches to either side.

Now we'll put a door in the doorway. Click the doorway to make it active, then click and hold on either the left or right handle and drag in the direction that the door opens. Exterior doors open in. Traffic patterns affect how most doors open, and to which side, but be sure to check for any regulations or standards.

Pocket Doors tool

Widening a single pocket door automatically creates a double pocket.

Now that you have placed a standard door, try some special items. First, a double-pocket door in the wall between the dining and living rooms. Select the **Pocket Doors** tool, then place the door so it is centered in the wall. Remember to check the locate dimensions. You will have a door when done, but instead of a double-door, it is a single door. To make it a double, click the door (you can select it with the **Pocket Doors** tool), click a side handle, and then drag the doorway out to six feet. When you release, a double-door will display. (Note that pocket doors cannot be pulled open, but with single doors you can determine the side the door opens from by dragging that side out from the wall.)

Next, let's add a door to the doorway between the kitchen and family room. Instead of using a tool, we will use the **Door Specification** dialog box. To do so, double-click in the doorway. Our doorway width should be set to 10 feet (120 inches) already, but if it is not, set the

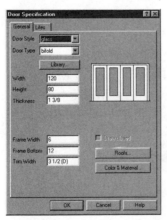

Door Specification dialog box

width in the **Width** edit box. We'll change the door type and style by picking **bifold** from the **Door Type** list box. This will place folding doors in our doorway, which is wide enough to need double folds. Next, select **glass** from the **Door Style** list box. Take a look at the preview to see what we will get, then click **OK**. Let's also change the style of our pocket door in the dining room to glass. This will allow us to use doors for privacy and quiet, while keeping the kitchen and adjacent rooms full of light.

Garage Doors tool

Now add the remaining interior doorways and doors. With the **Standard Door** tool, first place the doorway, and then create the door (if there is one) to look like the plan below. Click the **Garage Doors** tool, and place a pair of these in the garage.

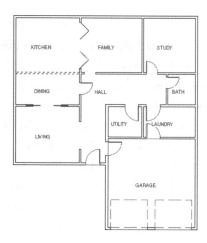

Library tool

Other door types that you can add are available in the Doorways Library. To access this library, click the **Door Mode** button, and then click the **Library** tool.

Window Mode button

Standard Window tool

Placing Windows

Doors are openings for allowing the movement of people; windows for the movement of air and light. Windows are placed almost exactly like doors, so you should have a pretty good idea of what to do. First, enter **Window** mode by clicking the **Window Mode** button, then select the **Standard Window** tool. Now, place standard windows as shown in the illustration.

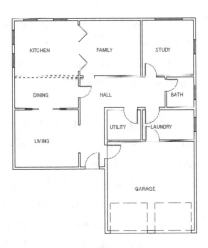

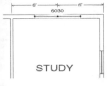

Dragging the center handle of a window changes its vertical dimensions.

Notice that standard windows default to three feet wide and three feet high (shown by the four-digit number above the window). Let's make the window in our study wider; select it, then click and drag an end handle until the window is six feet wide. Next, we'll change the height of our laundry and bathroom windows, which are usually shorter. Select the bathroom window and drag the center handle perpendicular to the wall. You will see the last two digits of the displayed dimension changing, indicating the varying height, top to bottom. Change the height to one foot. Note that it is probably best to change window heights in the **Camera** or **Elevation** views where it is easier to see changes in the vertical dimension. (Zooming in on the window will make it easier to see the dimensions.)

Of course, we do not want these two windows as low on the wall as others either, for the sake of privacy and security, and we should make some other changes too. To change this, we will need to open the **Window Specification** dialog box. Start with the bathroom window: double-click to open the dialog box. The preview will show a three-foot wide, one-foot high double-hung, wood-frame window. We want something different,

Window Specification dialog box

so in the **Window Type** list box, select **left sliding**. Next, set the **Trim Width** to **0**, and finally, set the **Floor to Top** dimension to **86"**. (The **Floor to Top** list box moves the entire window up, while changing the height affects the size of the window.) Click **OK**.

Selection Mode button

Copy tool

Delete tool

To make identical changes to our laundry room window, we could open a dialog box and repeat these steps. Instead, we'll use the **Copy** tool in **Selection** mode. First, change to **Selection** mode (either by clicking **Select Items** on the **Edit** menu or clicking the **Selection Mode** button), then select the existing laundry room window, and click the **Delete** tool to remove it. Next, click the bathroom window we just changed, and then the **Copy** tool, on the right side of the toolbar. The pointer will change to the **Copy** tool, which you position where the old window was, and click. A copy of the bathroom window now displays in the laundry room.

Bay Window tool

Now we are ready to place some special windows. To make our living and dining rooms more inviting, we'll add a bay window to the one, and a bow window to the other. In **Window** mode, select the **Bay Window** tool. Click the dining room exterior wall to place it, then drag the end and center handles to resize the window until it is one foot deep and six feet wide at the wall.

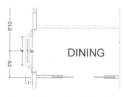

Bay window placed in wall

Selecting a 7-section bow window

Finally, let's add a bow window on the bottom wall of the living room. We could do this the same way we placed the bay window, but the **Bow Window** tool in the toolbar makes only a five-section bow, and we want something bigger. Instead, on the **Window** submenu in the **Build** menu, select the **Bow, 7 Sect** command. Now click the wall to place it. Notice all those dimensions? They are all needed to properly dimension the bow. Because of these complex dimensions, the component windows cannot be changed individually, as doing so would throw things off. To change them, click the bow window, click the **Next** tool, and then click the **Open** button. This opens the **Window Specification** dialog box, which in this case applies to all the windows in the bay window. You can move and resize the whole bow, and should do so to make it match this depiction.

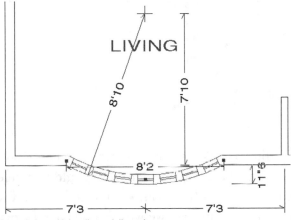

Bow window with handles and dimensions

Placing Cabinets

Now that we have all the walls, doors, and windows for this floor, we should have a pretty good idea of the basic design, and can start furnishing the rooms. To see how this is done, we will add some kitchen cabinetry. Before we do, we should clean up our display a bit, as it may have gotten messy with all our previous work. First, click the **Dimension Mode** button, then the **Exterior Dimensions** tool. This will redraw all the automatic, exterior dimension lines, so that they accurately reflect our current design. At this point, adjust the dimensions of your plan if you like.

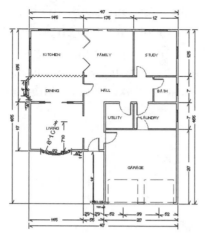

Plan with exterior dimensions

Now that our dimensions are accurate, we can choose not to show them, as some of you may have already done. We could just delete all the lines, using either the **Delete Items** command on the **Edit** menu, or by deleting each line, but instead we will just change the display so that no dimension lines, other than temporary, show up. To do so, go to the **Options** menu and select the **Show Items** command. This will display the **Show Items** dialog box controlling the display of different objects. Take a look at what it can do, then remove the check from the **Automatic Dimensions** check box and click **OK**. As in the illustration below, the lines will be hidden, but still accessible. To make them visible again, just reopen the dialog box and check the box.

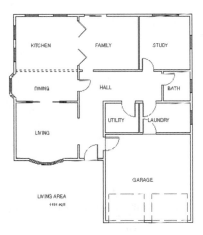

Plan with Automatic Dimensions turned off in
Show Items dialog box in the Options menu

Cabinet Mode button

Having cleaned up the display, let's put our cabinets in. First, use the **Zoom** tool to focus in on the kitchen. Then, click the **Cabinet Mode** button in the toolbar, then the **Base Cabinet** tool from the right-hand tools (it will be the default tool).

The top-left corner could be awkward once we place other cabinets, so we should fill that corner first. Often in a corner like this, a specially configured corner cabinet would be placed automatically by the program were we to click right in the corner. Instead, click along the north wall, under the window. This places a base cabinet. Select the cabinet, and take a close look. Notice the triangle and arrow? The triangle is a rotation handle; by dragging this, you can rotate the cabinet. The arrow indicates which way the cabinet faces. This one should be facing away from the wall, because if you place a cabinet close enough to a wall the program will know which way it should go, and will even attach it to the wall, so moving the wall will also move the cabinets.

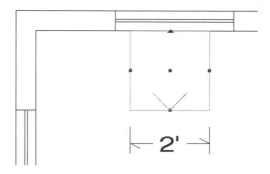

All we want to do is push our cabinet into the corner, so that we have a standard cabinet there instead of a corner cabinet. To move it, just select the cabinet and drag. If the windows and walls are properly sized, the standard, two-foot wide cabinet should just fit. Next, place another cabinet alongside it, under the window. Make sure the second cabinet is in line with the first by moving it sideways and against the wall. When properly placed, the line dividing the two modules will disappear. We want this cabinet to match the width of the window, so drag its side handles until it reads three feet. Now, your two cabinets should look like the following illustration.

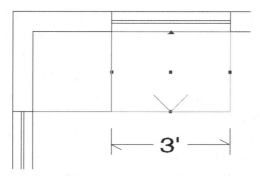

First cabinet has been moved into left corner, second cabinet widened to 3'.

Note: An important point about cabinets is that **3D Home Architect Deluxe** will "stretch" a countertop across a corner, if the cabinets on either side facing in are close enough together, which means we could have left this corner empty. This "blind" cabinet will offer a little extra storage, however.

Even though our two cabinets now look like one, they are still separate, which you can see by clicking the cabinet under the window. Now place similar cabinets under the other three windows: copy this cabinet, then paste and align a copy under each of the other three windows. Notice how the cabinets place differently according to what is next to them. Finally, let's finish the counter by placing two base cabinets in the two gaps on the left wall. The result should look like the next picture. If the dividing lines still display, make sure all the cabinets are facing the right way, then "push" the one on the bottom against the rest. They should fit snugly now.

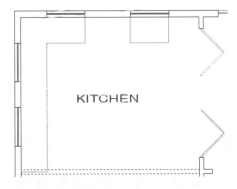

To finish off the cabinets along the walls, we will place a full-height cabinet along the top on the right, just as we placed the base cabinets. Use the **Full Height Cabinet** tool to place this cabinet and fit it snug to the base cabinet on the left. The module line will not disappear because these are different kinds of cabinets. Next, choose the **Wall Cabinet** tool and click once in the top-left corner to place a corner cabinet. (You must click very close to the corner; otherwise, the cabinet will be a regular, not corner, cabinet.)

Full Height Cabinet tool

Wall Cabinet tool

The wall cabinets are shown with a dashed line. Now place two regular wall cabinets, one between the windows on the left side, and the other on the wall section dividing the kitchen and dining room. The results should look like the following illustration.

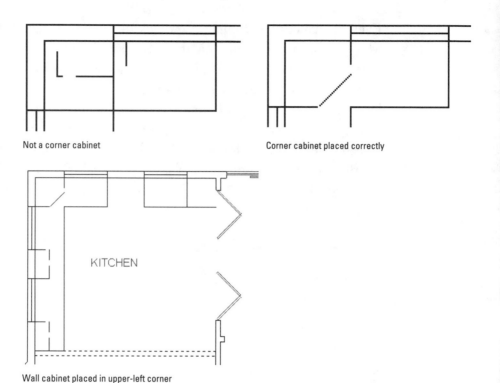

Not a corner cabinet

Corner cabinet placed correctly

KITCHEN

Wall cabinet placed in upper-left corner

Cabinet Mode button

Soffit tool

Now let's create cabinet soffits between the wall cabinets and the ceiling of our plan. To do this we need to use the **Soffit** tool. Select the **Cabinet Mode** button, and choose the **Soffit** tool from the right-hand tools. Click this tool as if you are placing a wall cabinet, and it will place a soffit in that area. Notice that the soffit extends about an inch past the wall cabinet already present. Continue to place soffits above each set of wall cabinets, until the area above each wall cabinet contains a soffit.

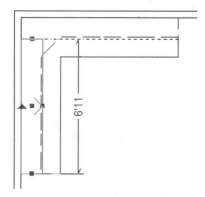

Next, we are going to use base cabinets to create an island in the middle of the kitchen. To do this, place the base cabinets as we've been doing, but this time out in the middle of the room. There being nothing to attach to, the first cabinet will just "float." Select it, and drag the rotation handle so it faces to the right. Next, place another cabinet below it, and another below that. All three should line up facing to the right, with the last two snapping into place. Next, add a fourth cabinet, just to the left of the bottom one. The program should snap the back of this one to the back of the other, creating the reverse L you see below. (Exact location in the room is not crucial, but allow a comfortable distance, say three feet, between the island and other counters. You can use the **Show Items** dialog box to turn off the Kitchen label, as has been done here.)

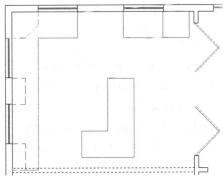

Kitchen with L-shaped cabinet island

And finally, for the finishing touch to our kitchen cabinetry, we'll add a second island, this one suspended above the first. How is this done? Simple, just create two banks of three wall cabinets, one facing left, and one right, and center it all above the base island. Wall cabinets not attached to walls float 54" above the floor. Add soffits above the wall cabinet island to attach it to the ceiling.

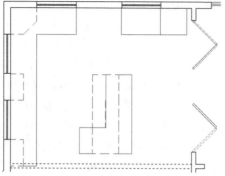

Wall cabinets placed away from walls become ceiling cabinets.

Placing Fixtures

Now that we have this wonderful cabinet setup, we need to add fixtures and appliances to make the kitchen useful. Using the Fixture Library in **3D Home Architect Deluxe**, this is as easy as seeing what you want and dropping it in the plan. First we'll place a sink in our kitchen cabinet beneath the first window on the left. Select the **Fixtures** tool, which opens the **Fixture Library** dialog box showing the first level in the library. Next, choose the **Sinks** item group, then **Kitchen Sinks**, and finally the **32" Double Kit. Sink**. Click the **OK** button, then point with the **Fixtures** tool in the cabinet. Click once, and there should be a sink. The counter should now look like this:

Fixtures tool

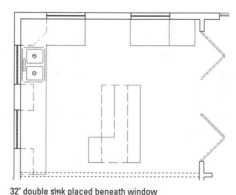

32" double sink placed beneath window

Keep in mind that the cabinet that is to hold the fixture must be big enough, so you need to exercise some forethought. While placing and aligning cabinets all at once makes sense, it also pays to make sure your cabinets will hold your fixtures, because if you really want a particular fixture, and its cabinet is too small, you may have to redo all the cabinets to make things fit.

Now that we have the sink in, go ahead and add a trash compactor and dishwasher, as shown below.

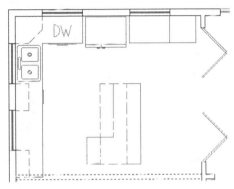

Trash compactor placed to the left of sink

Having placed built-in fixtures, now we are going to add some movable ones. The big gap in the top wall is for a 36-inch side-by-side refrigerator, while the nook in the center island is for a 36-inch professional gas range. Place these like the other fixtures, but just out on the floor. The center and rotation handles can be used to move and rotate them. The kitchen should now look like this:

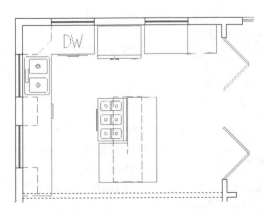

Looking at a Room

As with everything else, you can see what your cabinets and fixtures look like by double-clicking each one to open a dialog box that will let you preview or make changes. Double-click one of the wall cabinets above the island. Check boxes, such as for dimension and style, control

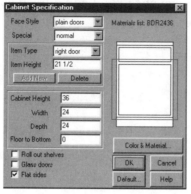

Cabinet Specification dialog box for base cabinet

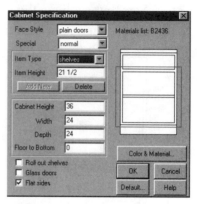

Cabinet Specification dialog box with shelves instead of right door

individual pieces of an object, determining, for instance, size or whether a cabinet has doors or drawers. To see how this works, click in the middle of the wall cabinet preview. An area will be outlined in red, and **Item Type** should read **right door**. Click the **Delete** button in the dialog box to create a blank space, then select **shelves** in the **Item Type** list. Now the preview will show three shelves where there was a door. Click **OK**, and the changes will be accepted. Go ahead and experiment with other options in other cabinets, like adding cutting boards, or drawers, or changing doors to glass.

You can use the same technique to change fixtures, too, or to resize. (To have fixtures, free-standing ones anyway, display and resize like cabinets, select the **Fixture/Furniture resize enable** option in the **Plan Setup** dialog box in the **Options** menu.)

Plan Setup dialog box

View Mode button

Wall Elevation tool

Another way to see and edit your work is to try out the different views. Click the **View Mode** button on the toolbar, and then the **Wall Elevation** tool. In the kitchen, click near the top wall, say in front of the refrigerator, and drag a line of sight.

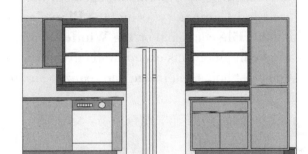

Elevation view of a kitchen wall

As you can see, there is still plenty of work to do. For instance, we could add some wall cabinets above the refrigerator and clean up the window trim, since the defaults do not seem to work that well here. While we are in the **Elevation** view, we cannot add anything, but we can move objects and open dialog boxes for them. To try this, double-click one of the windows, experiment with changing the trim, and see how it looks. Remember, the changes made here will be automatically reflected in **Plan** view and all other views.

Plan Camera tool

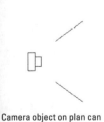

Camera object on plan can be moved and rotated like any other object.

For another view (you can close the **Elevation** window first), click the **Plan Camera** tool, then place the camera in the plan and drag a line of sight. If you do not like the view, try adjusting the camera by moving

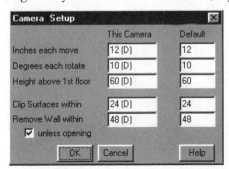

Camera Setup dialog box

and rotating it, either as an object in **Plan** view or using the special camera movement tools in the **Camera** window. Another method is to double-click the camera itself in the **Plan** view, opening the **Camera Setup** dialog box in which you can set the increments of movement and rotation, camera height, even what will be clipped (deleted) from the field of view.

The two views below show the kitchen from the left side of the dining room, with the first view being from a camera four feet off the floor, and the second from six feet. As an experiment, open several views—for example, our two **Plan Camera** views and the **Plan** view—and tile them by clicking the **Tile** command on the **Windows** menu. Remember, you can select and edit all objects except walls in these views, so see what combination most helps you image and realize your design.

Camera at 48" height

Camera at 72" height

Furniture tool

Placing Furniture

Having seen how to place fixtures, you should already have a pretty good idea of how to handle furniture. For practice, try placing a few simple pieces in the dining room. First, choose the **Furniture** tool. Then, with the same techniques used for fixtures, place a dining room table, a china cabinet, and perhaps some side chairs.

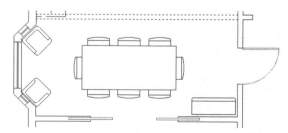

Pressing the Ctrl key when moving an object lets you place it inside a bay window.

Selecting Colors and Materials for Furniture

You can apply colors and materials to furniture.

To apply a color, click the **Selection Mode** button, and then double-click the furniture you want to work on. Click **Color & Material**, and then in the **Assign Colors** dialog box, click the color you want. Click **OK** twice to close the dialog boxes and apply the color.

To apply a material, click the **Select Mode** button, and then double-click the furniture you want to work on. Click **Color & Material**, then **Material**, and then **Choose Material**. In the **Select Image** dialog box, click the category of material you want, then click a subcategory, and then click the actual material you want. Click **OK** to choose that material. (You can also double-click the material to choose it.) Click **OK** two more times to exit the dialog boxes and apply the material to the furniture.

You must create a 3D view to see any color or material you apply. Click the **View Mode** button, and then click and drag to create a Camera view that includes the furniture. (Adjust the view after creating, if necessary.) This shows you the color you applied; to see the material, on the **3D** menu, click **Setup Applied Materials View**. In the **Applied Materials View Setup** dialog box, under **Color Model**, click **Color** if it is not already selected, and then click **OK**. On the **3D** menu, click **Applied Materials View**. When you are done viewing this window, click its **Exit** button to close it.

Placing Fireplaces

Next in our design scheme, we will place a fireplace in the living room. This is pretty simple, and of course builds on what you have already seen, but there are some wrinkles. The first is that fireplaces come in two types: prefabricated metal and built-in masonry. The metal fireplaces are listed in the Fixture Library in the **Utility** category. They are handled like free-standing fixtures (with one exception: you usually build walls to encase them).

Masonry fireplaces can be placed either in walls, in which case they act like doors and windows, or out in the room, where they act like cabinets. Either way, the first step to building a masonry fireplace is to select the **Fireplace** command on the **Build** menu or click the **Fireplace** tool on the toolbar, then click where you want it. Try this out by selecting the command or tool, then clicking the middle of the left wall in the living room, to continue with our current example. The plan should look something like this:

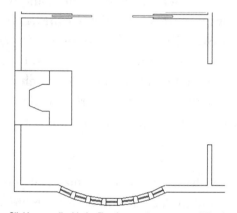

Clicking a wall with the Fireplace tool creates a wall fireplace.

We could leave this fireplace as is, once it is centered in the wall, but we do not want it projecting into the room. To fix this, click the fireplace, and then while pressing the **Ctrl** key, drag the fireplace back through the wall so that the edge of the firebox lines up with the inner edge of the wall. It should look like the fireplace below.

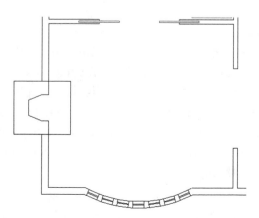

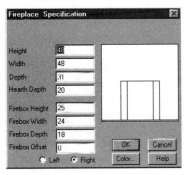

Fireplace Specification dialog box

Next, let's change the depth of the hearth. Double-click the fireplace, toward the back. The resulting **Fireplace Specification** dialog box is pretty straightforward; all we need do is enter **10** for the **Hearth Depth** option, and click **OK**.

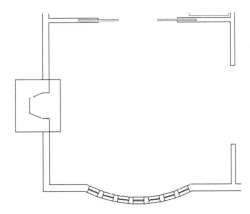

Building Decks and Porches

Wall Mode button

Railings tool

Remember that sliding door we placed in the family room? We'll build a deck off that wall of the family room. *3D Home Architect Deluxe* makes adding a deck easy. To create a deck, all we need do is drag out walls, as if we were creating a room. The trick is to drag out walls that are railings. To do that, click the **Wall Mode** button, then select the **Railings** tool. Then drag out the railings to form the deck. (Another way to do this is to just draw regular walls, then change them to railings using the **Wall Specification** dialog box for each wall.) We want our deck to be wide, from the left wall of the house up to the right side of the family room. Draw the walls so they look like the following.

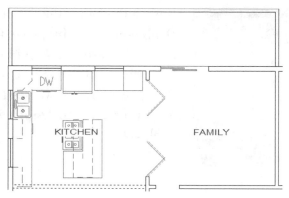

Railings dragged out to create a deck

The first thing after drawing out the deck railings is to declare this "room" a deck. That will let the program know this area has the properties of a deck. To do that, click the **Selection Mode** button and then double-click within the deck to access the **Room Specification** dialog box. Then, select **Deck** as the **Room Name** and click **OK**.

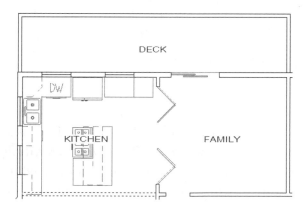

To see how it looks, place a camera outside the house looking toward the deck.

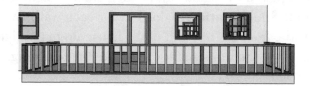

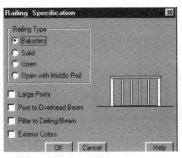

Railing Specification dialog box

Notice that the railings are constructed of plain uprights (these are called "balusters"). This is the default. To set other styles, double-click the railing to get a specification dialog box. But with two views up, where do we select the railing? It really does not matter. If we select the railing in **Plan** view, the **Wall Specification** dialog box will appear; clicking the **Define** button will cause the **Railing Specification** dialog box to display. Opening the railing in a 3D view will take us straight to this. Our railing is fine already, but experiment to see how the different styles will look, if you wish. When done, close the **Camera** window.

To see the **Railing Specification** dialog box in action, we will create a porch just outside the front door running from the garage to the left edge of the house. A porch differs from a deck in that a porch will usually have a roof. As with the deck we created, you want to name the new room a porch as soon as possible. Go ahead and draw the two rails so they match the drawing below, then double-click the room with the **Selection Mode** button and select **Porch** from **Room Name**.

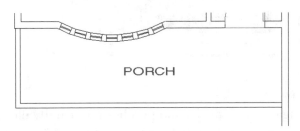

PORCH

To set the railings, all we have to do is open a specification dialog box for each railing by double-clicking it, and selecting the **Balusters** and **Post to Overhead Beam** options. Click **OK** and we are all set. (To save time, we could have set the style in the dialog box before drawing the rails, instead of having to open a dialog box for both.)

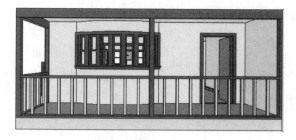

To check the effect, place another camera, this time in front of the house, looking back toward the porch. Notice anything funny? There's no way to get off the porch! To fix this, we need to place a doorway in the railing. Go to **Plan** view (you can select **Plan** view from the bottom of the **Window** menu or you can press **Ctrl+Tab** to cycle through the open windows to **Plan** view as a shortcut). A standard doorway is fine, just make it a little wider and keep it in line with the front door. When done, go back to **Camera** view (again, either through the **Window** menu or with **Ctrl+Tab**).

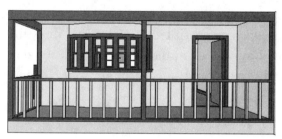

Posts are automatically added to frame doorways.

Creating Stairs

Besides being covered, decks and porches are usually elevated, which means we will need some staircases for our two outside rooms. Before we do that however, we will place one in the hallway, leading up to the second floor. Stairs are quite complicated pieces of construction, because the length, height, and number of steps must be balanced so the staircase climbs the right amount within the horizontal distance allowed. If this sounds like a job for SmartParts Technology, you are exactly right. *3D Home Architect Deluxe* will handle all the calculations necessary to construct a stair section; all we have to do is click the **Stairs Mode**

Stairs Mode button

button, and click and drag in our plan where we want the stairs, in the direction they are to rise. The program will create a staircase with all the risers, treads, and stringers. All we have to do is make the staircase long enough to contain enough steps to reach the next floor. We can even make a landing—the platform between two staircase sections—by dragging out one staircase, then dragging another with its bottom near the top of the first, and then clicking the gap between them.

With three factors—step number, height, and width—determining the height of the staircase (and its length), you can bet there is a detailed specification dialog box for stairs. While you do not need to use this dialog box to create a staircase, it can be handy.

To see what it is all about, click the **Stairs Mode** button, then drag in the hall to create a short staircase with seven or so steps. Notice that the staircase will be labeled Up in the direction of the drag. Now, double-click it to display the dialog box. Most of the settings just show the calculations going on to figure out how to make the staircase work. If so inclined, you can enter numbers yourself to set the length of the section, and the width and number of treads. Note that these figures are interdependent, so adjusting one will cause the other two to change. That is what makes the **Make Reach** button so nice. When this button is clicked, the program will figure out everything necessary to make your stairs reach the next floor, and will adjust the staircase length and tread dimensions automatically.

A stair section

Because we drew our staircase too short, the message at the top of the dialog box should read **Staircase does NOT reach next floor**. To fix this, click the **Make Reach** button. Notice the numbers changing, then click **OK**. Look at the **Plan** view and see how the staircase has been lengthened.

Staircase Specification dialog box

The staircase will probably not be in the right place. To move it, select it and drag it by the center handle, just like a cabinet. (Dragging the side handles will change the width of the stairs, while dragging the end handles will change the length, and so the number of steps.) Move the staircase against the wall outside the family room, with the foot near the family room entrance, as shown below.

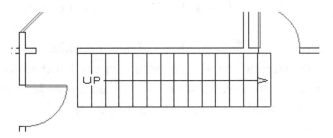

Now, open an **Elevation** window by clicking with the **Wall Elevation** tool and dragging next to the staircase, then use the **Tile** command in the **Window** menu to see the **Plan** and **Elevation** views side by side. You can see we have some problems. First, our staircase has a wall coming down from it, covering the door to the study. Second, the staircase as drawn is too close to the door on the left.

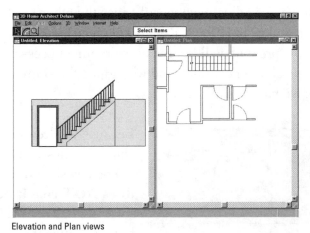

Elevation and Plan views

The wall is easy to fix. Double-click the staircase, in either view, to open the **Staircase Specification** dialog box. Then click the **Style** button. As with railings, this will display a dialog box for controlling the appearance of the selected staircase. Now, check the **Open**

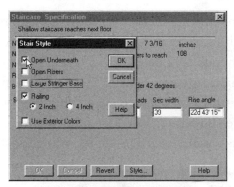

Staircase Specification dialog box

Underneath option, and clear the **Large Stringer Base** option, then click **OK** both in the **Stair Style** and **Staircase Specification** dialog boxes. Look in the **Elevation** view to see how the staircase has changed.

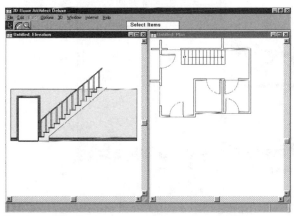

Elevation and Plan views

As you can see, we still have a problem: we can reach our door now, but the staircase foot still is too close to the door. To correct this, we can move the staircase to the right, shorten it, which will mean removing some steps and making the rest higher, or we could move the door. Moving the staircase would be easy, but then it would stick out into the main hallway. Moving the study door would be easiest, since there is room at that wall. (Note that you can select both staircase and doorway in the **Elevation** view, but only move the doorway.) This is probably the best course, and you should experiment with both, but for the fun of it, we are going to change the stairs.

So double-click the staircase (try it in **Elevation** view) to open a dialog box, then change the **Tread width** setting to 8 inches. Press the **Tab** key, and you should see the numbers in **Length** change from 140 inches to 112, with tread width staying at 8 inches, and number of treads at 14. Since the number of treads, and the height of each, is not changing, the staircase will be as high, only now a little steeper. To confirm this, check the **Plan** and **Elevation** views, then go ahead and drag the staircase back into position (the shortening was done at the bottom, shifting the case over). The results should look like the following illustration.

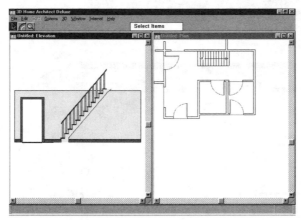

Elevation and Plan views

If you have ever climbed up a medieval staircase, or a Mayan pyramid, you can appreciate modern building regulations covering staircase configurations. *3D Home Architect Deluxe* will usually keep you out of trouble, but when adjusting step width and height as we did above, take care to follow the rules.

That last example of building staircases made it seem much harder than it really is, for the sake of showing you some special details. With a little forethought, you will almost always be able to place staircases just by dragging them out, and at most using the **Make Reach** command. To see how easy building stairs can be, we are now going to add two more staircases, one each for the deck and porch.

First, we will add a staircase off the porch. Close the **Elevation** view, then zoom in on the front porch. Now, with the **Stairs** tool selected, press the **Shift** key, then drag the stairs out from the opening in the porch down to about the front of the garage. Next, resize and position the stairs (notice they say DN for down) so they look like those in the following picture.

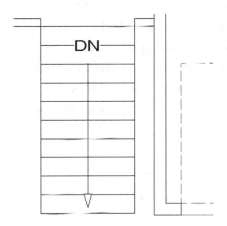

Now, double-click the stairs to open the dialog box. The stairs will probably not reach the next floor but that is fine, since we are assuming a half floor only for the foundation. Click the **Style** button, and make sure the **Railings** option is selected. Click **OK** twice to exit the dialog boxes, then place the camera to view our new porch staircase.

Now for the back deck. What we will do here is create three shallow stair sections coming off the right side of the deck, with two landings dividing them. The first step is to create a stair section off the deck, just as we did with the porch, by dragging with the **Stairs** tool while pressing the **Shift** key. Next, reposition the stair section so it is snug against the deck, centered and away from the back wall. Next, drag out another section going down (again holding down the **Shift** key as you drag), in the same direction as the first section. Make sure to leave an area between the sections for the landing that will go between them. Notice that this section will automatically have the same width as the last. Finally, drag out another down section, but this time at a right angle to the first two sections, and again leaving space for a landing. The results should look like those below.

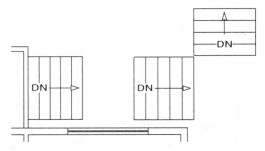

To create landings, all we have to do is click the gaps between staircases with the **Stairs** tool. The program will do the rest.

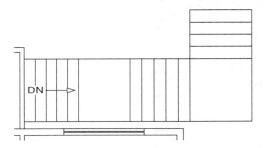

Now we have a complete, three-section, two-landing staircase. To fine-tune the whole thing at once, double-click a piece, such as the first section. Notice that the **Staircase Specification** dialog box includes the number of sections and landings, and the tread setup for each. What we want is to go to the **Stair Style** dialog box (click the **Style** button) and make sure everything except **Large Stringer Base** is selected. Exit the dialog boxes, then create a **Camera** view of the back steps.

Notice that the options that we set in the **Stair Style** dialog box make these stairs look like exterior stairs commonly seen on decks. You will also see a railing on the right side of the deck, blocking access to the stairs. As you did with the porch, simply switch back to the **Plan** view (try pressing **Ctrl+Tab** to effect the switch) and put a doorway in the deck railing where the stairs connect to the deck. Then, switch back to the **Camera** view (by pressing **Ctrl+Tab** again) so that you can inspect your work.

The technique given above for creating multiple-section staircases works well for both Up staircases and Down staircases. The tricks to remember are:

- Have a clear picture in your mind for the layout of the stairs.
- Drag out the stair sections first, leaving room for landings.
- Click between the sections to create the landings.
- Use the **Make Reach** button if you need to.
- Setting style attributes for one stair section applies to the entire staircase.

Stairs are one of the most complicated objects in a house, because there is such a large variety of possibilities. ***3D Home Architect Deluxe*** can create many types of staircases. It is really very simple, as long as you keep in mind the above steps.

Adding Additional Floors

So where are all these stairs going? Well, in the case of the deck and porch, just down to ground level, past the foundation. The hall stairs will lead up to the second floor. Although you can have only one floor in each plan file in *3D Home Architect Deluxe*, you can create separate files for each floor. Doing this by hand could be a real hassle, but the program makes it fairly simple using two techniques. The first is displaying one floor plan on top of the one on which you are working; this makes it easy to keep items lined up. The second is automatically generating the basics of a new floor plan from the outlines of an existing one. To see how this works we will now create floor plan files for a foundation, and the second floor.

We will start with the foundation. From the **Plan** window, go to the

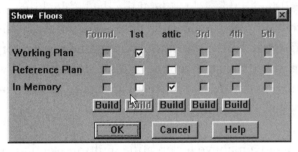

Window menu and select the **Show Floors** command. This will open the dialog box shown here.

You may be prompted to save your plan first, which you should do. Select **Save As** in the **File** menu and a dialog box will appear in which you can name your plan. Name the plan MYPLAN unless you prefer a different name. Once the plan is saved, again select **Show Floors** from the **Window** menu and proceed.

This may look complicated at first, but it is really simple. All the check boxes are just showing the different floor plan files for a given design, and the status of each. For example, right now we have designed only one floor, the first, which is checked Working Plan (meaning we can work on it). If we had other floors (the program allows four plus a foundation), they too would be available, but not necessarily checked. There can be only one working plan and one reference plan at a time, with the reference plan being the one we can display on top of the working plan. (Placing plans "in memory" makes it possible to rename all the plans of a given design at once using **Save As,** or to export all to a **DXF** file using **DXF All**.) Remember that to keep all the plans of a design together, the program gives the same file name to each, but adds an extension indicating the floor, so filename.PL1 is the first floor, filename.PL2 is the second, and so on. Notice the buttons labeled **Build** at the bottom of each column. Existing files will have dimmed **Build** buttons; clicking the button for a nonexisting file will bring up the **New Working Plan** dialog box, in which you can build a new plan by tracing the exterior walls of the current working plan, or open a blank file, or simply change the existing plan's name so that it becomes the plan for a different floor.

We will use this dialog box later to make the second floor, but for now we want to make the foundation, so click the **Build** button under the **Foundation** column. This will open the same dialog box, but selecting the **Derive** option will then make the foundation the working plan in the **Show Floors** dialog box.

New Working Plan dialog box

Show Floors dialog box with Foundation active

Foundation Setup dialog box

Clicking **OK** now causes the **Foundation Setup** dialog box to appear, with option boxes for specifying the foundation.

We can set the thickness and height of the foundation walls, and decide whether footings or piers should be used, with edit boxes for the dimensions of each. Change the wall height from **24** to **48** inches, then click **Done**. A foundation plan will display in the window, with solid lines showing the wall and dashed lines the footings (the wide bottoms of foundation walls). Notice the file name in the title bar—the extension for a foundation file is always PLO.

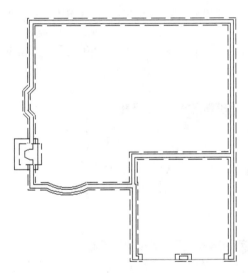

Next, we will create the second floor, using pretty much the same technique. The first step is to get the first floor plan back. We could do this by just opening it, but instead let's use the **Show Floors** dialog box. Open this up, and you will see that the foundation plan is now checked as **Working Plan**. To change this, just check the **Working Plan** box in the **1st** column. The first floor will now be a Working Plan, and the foundation will switch to the Reference Plan.

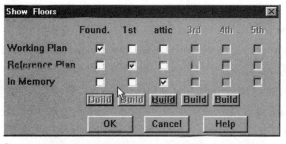

Show Floors dialog box with Foundation checked as the Working Plan

Show Floors dialog box with second floor as the Working Plan

Next, click the **Build** button in the **attic** column Note that with the three options in the **New Working Plan** dialog box, we can create a second floor by either tracing the first floor, or by bringing up a blank file to start from scratch, or by switching the first floor plan so it becomes the second. Normally you will want to use the **Derive** option, because it is easiest, so check it and then click **OK**. Now the **Show Floors** dialog box will appear with the second floor active, and when we click **OK** here we will get the second floor plan below.

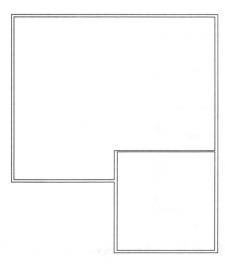

As you can see, all we get is a simple tracing of the exterior walls, but these will be helpful in creating our upstairs. Note that we can edit these walls freely, just like any other plan. Before we make any changes, however, we want to display the first floor as a reference plan so we can keep our interior walls lined up also. To do this, just go back to the **Show Floors** dialog box, and check the **Reference Plan** box for the first floor. After clicking **OK**, select **Reference Toggle** from the **Window** menu. The first floor plan will now display in red on the second floor's view. You cannot change anything on the first floor, but you can turn the display on and off and can change which plan is working and which is referenced by using **Show Floors**, **Reference Toggle**, and **Swap Work-Ref** commands in the **Window** menu. (These will also be available from the toolbar when the **Zoom Mode** button is selected.)

Now that we have a basic second floor plan up and the first floor plan displayed as a guide, we can experiment with creating a new plan. We will not go all the way through the process, but try dragging out some walls so that they look like the illustration below. (Note that here the reference plan is toggled off, to make the plan clearer.)

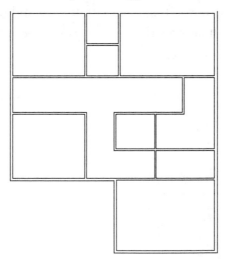

It is not necessary for the walls and rooms on the second floor to match the first, but doing so can make construction easier. This is especially true for lining up bathrooms because it will save on plumbing construction (and make future repairs easier). What we will eventually have here is a master bedroom occupying the top-right corner, with two walk-in closets to the left, and a large master bathroom above the bathroom and laundry room of the first floor. Other bedrooms can be arranged around the rest of the plan as desired. Of course, we could remove some space from the plan by deleting or moving exterior walls, or make part of the interior a deck or balcony by changing the wall definitions. For example, in this arrangement the top-left room could be a bedroom, or perhaps a balcony.

A finished second floor plan would include doors, windows, room names, furniture, and fixtures. We will not go through all that since you have already seen how to go about doing those things, but there is one special technique we will look at. Looking at our second floor plan, you may notice something missing: there are no stairs connecting down to the first floor.

Since our first floor plan shows a staircase, all we need to do is show that same staircase on the second floor. We can do this in one of two ways. One, used frequently in plans, is to show an area marking the stairwell and label it Open Below, usually with some notes about the stairs coming "up." The second is to show a staircase labeled Down, identical to the one labeled Up, from the first floor.

To see how these approaches work, first make sure the first floor is visible as a reference plan. Next, zoom in on the staircase with the **Zoom** tool, then wall the staircase off using **Railings** and a **Room Definition** wall at the right end. (The walls can be either standard walls or railings. Many contemporary homes are designed so that there is a room on either side of the stairs. That is not the case here, so we are going to add railings for the sake of safety. For the finishing touch, double-click the newly created "room," and then in the **Room Specification** dialog box, select **Open Below** from the **Room Name** list box. Click **OK** and the second floor plan should look like this. (Again, the first floor is toggled off for clarity.)

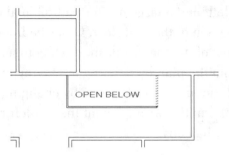

This, and perhaps a label, is all that is really needed, but we can show a staircase. Defining the Open Below room may seem like an unneeded step, but it allows us to see the stairs coming up through the floor in a **Full Camera** or **Overview** view. The result, in **Plan** and **Full Camera** views, should look like the following:

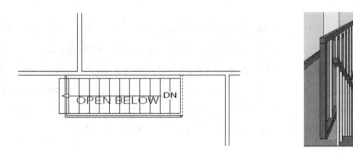

Fine-Tuning Rooms

Using the room name Open Below basically instructs the program to remove the floor. Other room names also have special properties. For instance, calling a room a bathroom will cause special electric outlets to be used, and rooms named Closet need not have windows, while a room called Court will have a concrete floor and no ceiling. Now that we have seen how to create all the major structural components of a plan, plus most of the physical fixtures, we are going to see how to use this **Room Name** list box and the **Room Specification** dialog box to add special features to our rooms and plan.

Note that the **Room Name** list box has several names, and many of these have special features. Let's try experimenting with what we can do with rooms. Double-click the living room in **Plan** view to open the **Room Specification** dialog box. Let's change all of the flooring material on this floor to wood. Click **Floor Defaults,** and then click **Color & Material.** In the **Assign Colors** dialog box, click the box to the left of **Floor** to place the pointer there. (This tells the program that these next few selections should apply to the floor.) Click **Material**, and then click **Choose Material**. In the **Select Image** dialog box, click **wood**, then **flooring**, and then **light**. This displays your actual material choices; click the one you want. Click **OK** to choose that material. (You can also double-click the material to choose it.) Click **OK** three more times to exit the dialog boxes and apply the material to the floor.

You must create an **Applied Materials** view to see any material you apply. Click the **View Mode** button, and then click and drag to create a **Camera** view that includes the floor. (Adjust the view after creating, if necessary.) On the **3D** menu, click **Setup Applied Materials View**. In the **Applied Materials View Setup** dialog box, under **Color Model**, click **Color** if it is not already selected, and then click **OK**. On the **3D** menu, click **Applied Materials View**. When you are done viewing this window, click its **Exit** button to close it.

While back in the **Room Specification** dialog box, check out the options at the bottom. These control the display and dimensions of three types of wall moulding. Base moulding runs along the bottom of walls, and is common in most houses (they make finishing walls and floors easier); crown moulding is less common. It is the moulding that runs along the top of walls. Sometimes this is called a picture rail because specially shaped hooks can be attached, allowing you to hang objects without pounding nails. The **Chair Rail** runs along the middle of the wall. The program defaults to base moulding, but not crown or chair rail. We want a picture rail in our living room, however, so set **Crown mould.** to a width of **4** inches. Since this is our living room, we can get fancy, so let's also add a chair rail of the same thickness by setting **Chair Rail** also to **4**. Click **OK**, then place a camera in the room so we can see what we have done.

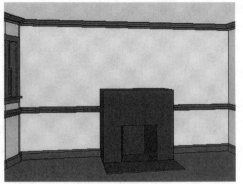

Living room with base, chair rail, and crown mouldings

Plan View Colors dialog box

Adding Colors

Another thing we can do with rooms is color their contents differently from the rest of the plan. This allows us some ability for interior design work, to make the elevations and three-dimensional views more realistic and interesting. Bear in mind that two color schemes are used in *3D Home Architect Deluxe*. The first can be viewed in the **Plan View Colors** dialog box, which you open by clicking **Plan View Color** on the **Options** menu. This is used to distinguish different types of objects in **Plan** view, so that it is easy to tell walls from windows, for instance. These colors do not have anything to do with how the objects will look when built. The second color scheme does try to show how things will look when built, and that is what is affected by room definitions.

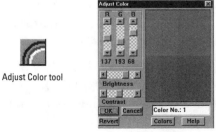

Adjust Color dialog box

Adjust Color tool

The second scheme is what we see in the **3D** view windows, and it is what we change when we use the **Adjust Color** tool available in the toolbar for those windows. Since we already have a **Camera** window opened on our living room, click the **Adjust Color** tool, and click a wall in the view. The **Adjust Color** dialog box will appear, showing the current color for that object, and a number of controls for changing that color. Before checking these out, consider that, as with plan colors, all the colors here are assigned not just to individual objects, but to whole classes of objects. That means if you select a wall and change its color, all the walls in the plan will have that new color.

All the kinds of objects in your plan already have default colors assigned to them. The controls in the **Adjust Color** dialog box let you change those default colors. Because you will be seeing these colors on a video monitor, they are created using the same RGB color model as used for televisions. This just means all the colors you see are really a blend of three primary colors—red, green, and blue—where 100 percent of each color makes white, zero black, and in between gray. Having more red than green or blue makes the color redder. The three sliders on the left of the dialog box control and show this color mix. (The numbers at the bottom of each slider, 0 to 255, show the 256 possible shades of each.) To change a color, simply move the sliders, or click a palette color. Moving the Brightness slider adds more light, and the Contrast slider changes the degree of shading used in the three-dimensional views.

All the objects that display in three dimensions can have their color manipulated, so try it out and see what you get. You should also try the **Use Exterior Colors** option in the **Stair Style** dialog box and the **Exterior Colors** option in the **Railing Specification** dialog box. These change the color scheme used for these objects to make it easier to tell exterior pieces from interior ones.

Getting Wired

Having gotten the walls up, placed windows and doors, added fixtures and furniture, and learned how to fine-tune your plan with various settings, it is about time to add the electrical system. We could do this at any time, but it is generally a good idea to wait until after other decisions have been made, because the location of electrical items does not affect other objects.

Electrical items in **3D Home Architect Deluxe** are a special kind of object in that the program treats them like symbols, more like labels than "real" objects, like walls or cabinets. For this reason they do not show up in the three-dimensional or elevation views.

The items we can place are fairly simple: 110- and 220-volt outlets, lights, switches, and special items like telephone jacks. We can even create circuits. Most of this is easy, and much can be done from the toolbar. The program will automatically change outlets to the proper type for a given room, so that water-proof and safety-grounded outlets are used for outdoor rooms and bathrooms, and will locate switches and lights in the walls, floors, or ceilings, depending on whether you place the item in a wall or out in the room. There is even one command that will place all the outlets in a room for you, using standard criteria.

Electrical Mode tools

Place Outlets tool

To see all this, we are going to wire our kitchen. The first step will be placing outlets, which we can do automatically. Click the **Electrical Mode** button, and then click the **Place Outlets** tool. Click the room we want wired, in this case the kitchen, and then take a look at the results.

All the outlets needed for the room have been placed, with their type and location determined by the program. Notice that a light has even been added above the kitchen sink. Outlets behind counters will be at counter level, unless an appliance is present in the cabinet, in which case the outlet will be directly behind. Those in open walls will be above the floor. Although we cannot open specification dialog boxes for the electrical symbols, we can move them about and delete them by selecting them with the pointer. (Note that outlets behind cabinets cannot be selected without first removing the cabinet.) Notice that we also have outlets in the dining room now. This is because, for the sake of placing outlets, invisible walls are ignored (because they will not block a cord).

Switches tool

Lights tool

We need more than outlets here, so now we will use the **Switches** and **Lights** tools from the toolbar to place some of these. Select a tool, then click and drag to position each item, until your plan looks like the one below.

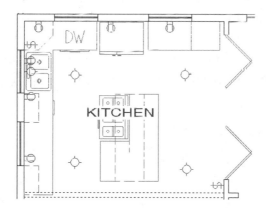

See the two switches? We are going to use these to create a two-way circuit in the kitchen, so that the lights can be turned on and off from either the switch above the sink, or that near the dining room. To do so, select the **Connect** tool, then click and drag from item to item to connect them, starting with one switch and ending with the other. The results should resemble those below. We left the outlets off the switch circuit, but you can add them if you like. To disconnect an item from the circuit, just click it with the **Connect** tool.

Connect tool

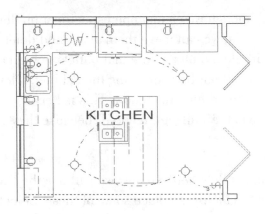

Finally, we are going to add a couple of special symbols to our kitchen, to represent a smoke detector and telephone jack. Unlike outlets, switches, and lights, these are added by using a Symbol Library, just like that used for fixtures and furniture. To try it, select the **Symbol Library** tool, then go through the dialog boxes to select and place the smoke detector and telephone jacks, so your plan looks like the following.

Symbol Library tool

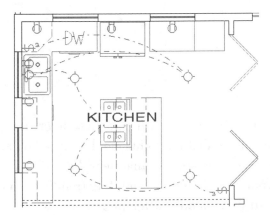

Making a List and Checking It Twice

This design is far from finished: we still need to add furniture, fixtures, wiring, and special features for each room in our two-story plan. But it is far enough along to give you an idea of how everything works, so now we are going to see if the plan really does work, and whether it will work for our budget.

To test whether our plan meets basic building standards and practices, and common sense, *3D Home Architect Deluxe* includes the **PlanCheck** command in the **Options** menu. When this command is selected, the program will go through every room and analyze its contents, determining whether it is big enough, has enough windows and doors, electrical circuits, and so on. It does this by comparing what it thinks should be in a room of a given type with what is really there. Room names are important so the program can tell what it is looking at.

After analyzing the plan, the program will open a **PlanCheck** dialog box, which will display problems and tips regarding the plan, with the total number of issues noted, along with the number of the current one. The objects or areas in question will be outlined in red in the plan. Click the **Next**, **Hold**, and **Done** buttons to see the next question, place PlanCheck on hold and fix a problem, or finish. When returning to PlanCheck after putting it on Hold, you will be taken to the next item on the list. This is because PlanCheck assumes you have corrected the previous problem, and wish to see the next. If you use Hold while running PlanCheck, it is important to restart PlanCheck one last time to make sure all of the areas of concern have actually been fixed.

PlanCheck is best used near the end of designing, because otherwise it will question things that have not been done yet, like adding windows, fixtures, and telephone jacks. Sometimes it will even question things that are, in fact, correct. On the other hand, PlanCheck will also automatically correct some things that have been changed in your plan. For example, doors given thresholds because they were in exterior walls will have them removed if they are now in interior walls, and walls moved up to cabinets (instead of the other way around) will be attached.

Once you have your plan checked, you can then use the **Materials** command to check on whether you can afford it. Selecting this command from the **Options** menu brings up a submenu that allows you to create a list for the whole plan, a room you click, or an area you select by dragging.

The result is a **Materials** window, showing all the required items, in the units of measure and amounts, with a column in which you can add local cost factors. Clicking the total column will calculate the cost of that item. The window will not update automatically, so you must run it whenever changes are made. For sophisticated cost estimates, perhaps including labor costs, you can export this worksheet data to a more powerful worksheet program using the **Export TXT** command on the **File** menu.

A Finished Job

"Checking it twice" is actually meant seriously in the preceding section, because that is what you will have to do. The Materials list and PlanCheck are both just tools to provide rough estimates of your progress. Before you can actually build anything, you will need much firmer cost estimates, and much more thorough plan checking, certainly by building officials and preferably by professionals who can help you avoid problems and extra costs. Just because you can draw something in *3D Home Architect Deluxe* does not mean you can build it, and even if you could build it that does not mean it would be safe or legal. So save yourself a lot of trouble and do your homework before you start your plan, and have it checked thoroughly before you finish.

And remember, if you have to make changes, relax, because that is what the program is all about—letting you try different things quickly and easily; sketch out a plan, detail it like we have done here, then print out different versions. (Note that you can use a variety of commands, like **Show Items**, **Dimension Setup**, and **Print**, to change how your plan looks.) Take these around to people, get suggestions, look at other plans, and make changes if you want to. There is a practically infinite number of variations you could come up with, so go ahead and experiment.

3D Walkthrough

You can record and play back a walkthrough of your plan. A walkthrough is a 3D representation of what your finished house would look like if you walked around or through it.

Recording a Walkthrough

To record a walkthrough, switch to a 3D view of your house using the **Plan Camera** or **Full Camera** options. Start from the position where you would like your walkthrough to begin (for example, out on the patio). Click the **Record Walkthrough** tool on the toolbar, or on the **3D** menu, click **Record Walkthrough**.

Record Walkthrough tool

In the **Write Movie File** dialog box, enter a file name for your walkthrough (for example, MYPLACE.WLK). Using the navigation tools on the toolbar or the arrow keys on your keyboard, move the camera is if you were walking through your plan. Each time you move the view, the program records the new view as a frame in your "movie." When you are finished, click the **Stop Recording** tool or click **Stop Recording** on the **3D** menu.

Stop Recording tool

Showing a Walkthrough

Once you have recorded a walkthrough, you can play it. To do this, click the **3D** menu, then click **Show Walkthrough**. In the **Open Movie File** dialog box, select the file for the walkthrough you want to view. (All walkthrough files' names end with .WLK.) Click **Open**. The application begins to play the walkthrough. To reverse the walkthrough, click it with the right mouse button. To pause the walkthrough, click it with the left mouse button. To resume playing the walkthrough, click it again with the left mouse button.

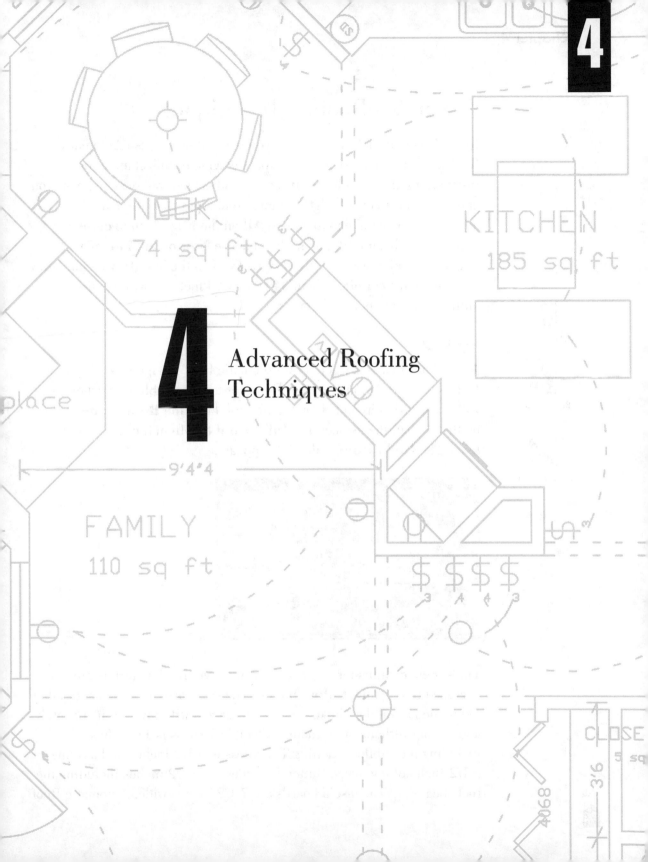

4

Advanced Roofing Techniques

Chapter 4

Advanced Roofing Techniques

In the basic tutorial in chapter 2, you learned how to use Automatic Roof Designer to construct basic roof designs. In this chapter, detailed instructions are given for creating more advanced roof designs. Now you can learn how to create eight common roof types that are more advanced. To begin, choose **Close All** on the **File** menu to close any plans you've been working on, then choose **New** on the **File** menu to begin a new plan. Choose **Move Out (x2)** on the **Window** menu. Draw a rectangular floor plan, about 34 feet by 24 feet. We will use this outline to design our roof shapes.

Roof Mode button

Build Roof tool

Delete Roof tool

Hip Roof

The default roof constructed by Automatic Roof Designer is a hip roof. Unless you tell Automatic Roof Designer to put a gable somewhere, you will get a basic hip roof. To get a hip roof, click the **Roof Mode** button on the toolbar, then select the **Build Roof** tool from the right-hand tools. The **Build Roof** dialog box appears.

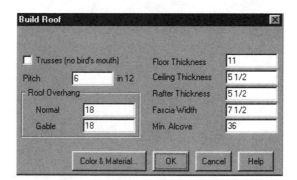

The system defaults for roofs are shown above. Roof materials are accessed through the **Colors** button. The steps are the same as for other items such as outdoor images. Your initial roof will have a 6 in 12 pitch and a roof overhang of 18 inches. Floor Thickness is 11 inches including the subfloor. Ceiling Thickness is 5 1/2 inches and assumes 5 1/2-inch ceiling joists. Rafter Thickness is 5 1/2 inches including the roof sheathing. The fascia boards are 7 1/2 inches wide. Automatic Roof

Designer takes the information on roof pitch, overhang, and rafter thickness and translates that into, in this case, a hip roof. If the **Trusses** check box is left clear, the rafters will have a bird's mouth cut in them as they come over the top plate of the wall. If the **Trusses** check box is selected, the rafters will sit on top of the wall top plate and will not have a bird's mouth cut. Click **OK**. For each roof shape generated, we will show pictures of the floor plan after the roof has been designed, as well as a Full Overview.

 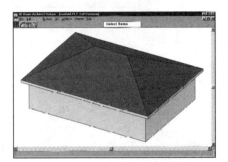

Basic hip roof

Feel free to experiment with altering the pitch and/or overhang as you build these basic roof shapes. Also, view the model and its roof with all of the full structure camera views that are available. Generating a cross section of each basic roof shape should be particularly instructive. Place some windows and doors in the model if you wish. When you have finished experimenting with alternate views and pitches and overhangs, reset the parameters before proceeding to the next basic roof shape.

Gable Roof

Roof Section at tool

To create a basic gable roof, you tell Automatic Roof Designer to put gables on the walls you have selected. Let's place gables on the long walls of the model. Click the **Roof Mode** button, and then click one of the long walls. The **Roof Section at Wall** dialog box appears.

Clicking the Roof Section at tool on a wall leads to the Roof Section at Wall dialog box.

Click the check box next to **Full Gable wall**. (This will cause a gable to appear above the wall.) Repeat these steps for the other long wall. Next, click the **Build Roof** tool, and then click **OK** in the **Build Roof** dialog box. To view the roof in 3D, click the **View Mode** button, then click the **Full Overview** button.

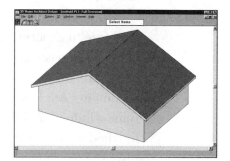

Gable roof with gables over the longer two walls

Shed Roof

Now let's turn this gable roof into a shed roof. A shed roof has just one sloping roof section. Walls at two sides of the roof section have gables over them. Of the other two walls, one is under the high end of the pitch of the roof section and the other is under the low end.

Before we can build the shed roof, we must decide which of the four walls will have gables above them and which will be the high wall under the shed. Let's have the upper horizontal wall be the high wall under the shed while the two vertical walls have gables over them. That means we have to access all four walls in the model by entering **Roof** mode and clicking each wall in turn with the **Roof Section at** tool to access the **Roof Section at Wall** dialog box for each wall.

Make the following changes:
- For the vertical wall on the left, check the **Full Gable wall** box.
- For the vertical wall on the right, check the **Full Gable wall** box.
- For the lower horizontal wall, clear the **Full Gable wall** box since we want a normal roof section over this wall to begin at the top plate.
- For the upper horizontal wall, clear the **Full Gable wall** box, and check the box for **High Shed/Gable wall**.

Now let's have Automatic Roof Designer build a shed roof. Click the **Build Roof** tool to access the **Build Roof** dialog box. Since we have already told *3D Home Architect Deluxe* exactly what we want to occur at each of the four walls, all we have to do is click **OK**. Click **OK** to build the shed roof.

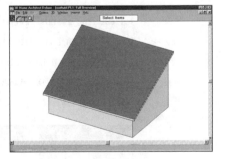

Basic shed roof

Note that since there is only one roof section, there is only one baseline. The baseline is the lower horizontal wall.

Saltbox Roof

Let's convert our shed roof into a saltbox. A saltbox is a type of gable roof with the ridge off-center because there is a different pitch on each of the two roof sections. The smaller roof section has a steeper pitch. What we will do here is assign different pitches to each of the two roof sections. This is done through the **Roof Section at Wall** dialog box for the wall that supports each of the two roof sections. Click the **Roof Mode** button in the toolbar, and use the **Roof Section at** tool to modify our shed roof in the following way:

- Leave the two vertical walls as they are. They already have gable information stored in them from before, when we built the shed roof.
- When you access the **Roof Section at Wall** dialog box for the upper horizontal wall, clear the box that says **High Shed/Gable wall**. Change the pitch for the roof section above this wall to 12 in 12. The roof section above this wall will be steep and will be the smaller of the two roof sections.
- At the lower horizontal wall, change the pitch to 3 in 12.

Roof sections will be built over the lower and upper horizontal walls, with gables over the two vertical walls. The different pitches declared for each of the two horizontal wall roof sections will assure a saltbox roof.

Click the **Build Roof** tool to access the **Build Roof** dialog box. Leave the pitch set in this dialog box at 6 in 12. It will have no effect when we build the roof because any pitch that has been set in a **Roof Section at Wall** dialog box overrides the roof default pitch. Click **OK** to build the saltbox roof.

Basic saltbox roof

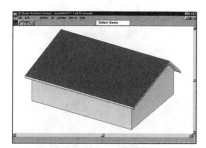

Gambrel Roof

Now let's turn the saltbox roof into a gambrel roof. A gambrel roof has two pitches on each side of the ridge. The first (lower) pitch on either side is steeper than the pitch near the ridge. Here is how to convert the saltbox to a gambrel. Let us make the lower pitch 12 in 12 and the upper pitch 6 in 12. Have the upper pitch begin 60 inches (5 feet) above the top plate.

Make the following changes to the roof sections over each wall using the **Roof Section at** tool for each wall.

- Make no changes to the two vertical walls. They remain gable ends.
- For the upper horizontal wall, keep the first **Pitch** as 12 in 12. **2nd Pitch** is already listed as 6 in 12 because that is the default pitch for the whole roof, as determined in the **Build Roof** dialog box. Type **156** in the **Starts at** box. The second pitch will begin 60 inches (5 feet) above the top plate, since the top plate is at 96 inches and 96 plus 60 =156.
- Change the roof section at the lower horizontal wall's specifications to read the same as those for the upper horizontal wall (first pitch is 12 in 12; 2nd pitch is 6 in 12 and starts at 156 inches).

Here is what the **Roof Section at Wall** dialog box should look like for both the upper and lower horizontal walls.

Now click the **Build Roof** tool to access the **Build Roof** dialog box.

Altering the pitch here will not affect the roof, since we have overridden the pitch designations for the entire roof by the information we have supplied for each of the walls. Click **OK** to build a gambrel roof.

Gambrel roof

Feel free to experiment with alternate pitches and overhangs. Also, try varying the height at which the second pitch comes in so that you can see the effect it has on your roof design.

Gull Wing Roof

A gull wing roof is the reverse of a gambrel. A gull wing has two pitches on either side of the ridge, as does a gambrel, but a gull wing has the first pitch shallower than the second pitch, usually much shallower. These types of roofs are seen in resort areas on cottages and on residences in eastern Canada as well as in certain parts of Europe. Let's convert our gambrel roof to a gull wing. Let the upper pitch be 12 in 12 and the lower pitch be 3 in 12. Let the pitch change at 114 inches (18 inches above the top plate).

Make the following changes to the roof sections over each wall using the **Roof Section at** tool for each wall.

- Do not change anything for either of the two vertical walls. They remain as gable ends.
- For both the upper and lower horizontal walls, make the first (lower) **Pitch** 3 in 12. Make the **2nd Pitch** 12 in 12 and make it start at 114 inches.

This should show the gull wing effect nicely. Here is the way the **Roof Section at Wall** dialog box should look for both the upper and lower horizontal walls.

Click the **Build Roof** tool to access the **Build Roof** dialog box. Click **OK** to build the gull wing roof.

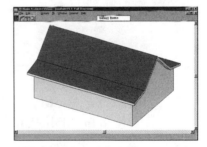

Gull wing roof

Half Hip Roof

A half hip roof has two gable ends. At the top of each gable is a hip that extends to the ridge. Let's convert the gull wing roof to a half hip. We will retain the system default of 6 in 12 pitch for the two major roof sections. Let the two hips have a 3 in 12 pitch so that they gently slope back to the ridge. Let the hip begin at 144 inches (4 feet above the top plate).

Make the following changes to the roof sections over each wall using the **Roof Section at** tool for each wall.

- For the two horizontal walls, make the first **Pitch** 6 in 12 and click the check box next to **2nd Pitch** to clear it.
- For the two vertical walls, leave the **Full Gable wall** box selected for both. Select the **2nd Pitch** box. Make the **2nd Pitch** 3 in 12 and have it start at 144 inches.

Here is what the **Roof Section at Wall** dialog box for the two gable end walls should look like. The first pitch on a wall with a gable above it is always grayed out. The first pitch is set by the roof default pitch in the **Build Roof** dialog box.

Click the **Build Roof** tool to access the **Build Roof** dialog box. Click **OK** to build the half hip roof.

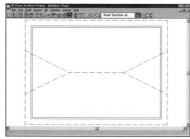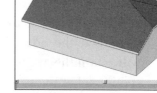

Half hip roof

Mansard Roof

A mansard roof is a hip roof with two slopes on the roof sections above each of the four walls. The second slope begins at the same height above each wall. Usually the lower slope is much steeper than the upper slope, with the upper slope being quite gentle. Let's convert the half hip roof to a mansard. The two vertical walls must no longer be designated as gable walls. We want the lower pitch to be 12 in 12 and the upper pitch to be 1 1/2 in 12. The upper pitch should begin at 144 inches (4 feet above the top plate).

Make the following changes to the roof sections over each wall by using the **Roof Section at** tool for the four walls.

- For the two vertical walls, clear the **Full Gable wall** box. Make the first **Pitch** 12 in 12. Make the **2nd Pitch** 1 1/2 in 12 and let it start at 144 inches.
- For the two longer walls, make the first **Pitch** 12 in 12. Make the **2nd Pitch** 1 1/2 in 12 and let it start at 144 inches.

Here is what the **Roof Section at Wall** dialog box should look like for all four walls.

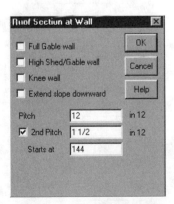

Click the **Build Roof** tool to access the **Build Roof** dialog box. Click **OK** to build the mansard roof.

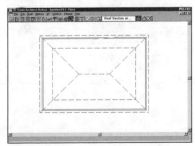
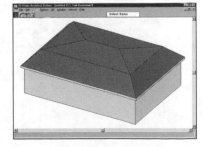

Mansard roof

Roof Type Quick Reference

The following chart provides a quick reference for building all of the previous roof styles. The chart shows which walls to change and what to change in the **Roof Section at Wall** dialog box for each wall. These parameters are based on a 34x24-foot model. When using different size plans, you will have to adjust these numbers.

Roof Type	Wall to Change	Set as Full Gable	Set as High Shed/Gable	Pitch	2nd Pitch	2nd Pitch Starts At
Gable Roof	Vertical Wall 1					
	Vertical Wall 2					
	Horizontal Wall 1	x				
	Horizontal Wall 2	x				
Shed Roof	Vertical Wall 1	x				
	Vertical Wall 2	x				
	Horizontal Wall 1		x			
	Horizontal Wall 2					
Salt Box Roof	Vertical Wall 1	x				
	Vertical Wall 2	x				
	Horizontal Wall 1			12 in 12		
	Horizontal Wall 2			3 in 12		
Gambrel Roof	Vertical Wall 1	x				
	Vertical Wall 2	x				
	Horizontal Wall 1			12 in 12	6 in 12	156
	Horizontal Wall 2			12 in 12	6 in 12	156
Gull Wing Roof	Vertical Wall 1	x				
	Vertical Wall 2	x				
	Horizontal Wall 1			3 in 12	12 in 12	114
	Horizontal Wall 2			3 in 12	12 in 12	114
Half Hip Roof	Vertical Wall 1	x			3 in 12	144
	Vertical Wall 2	x			3 in 12	144
	Horizontal Wall 1			6 in 12		
	Horizontal Wall 2			6 in 12		
Mansard Roof	Vertical Wall 1			12 in 12	1 1/2 in 12	144
	Vertical Wall 2			12 in 12	1 1/2 in 12	144
	Horizontal Wall 1			12 in 12	1 1/2 in 12	144
	Horizontal Wall 2			12 in 12	1 1/2 in 12	144

Gables over Doors and Windows

To create a gable roof over a door or window, use the **Roof Section at** tool to select the appropriate object. When a door or window is selected, the **Roof over Door/Window** dialog box will appear with a single check box for **Gable Over Door/Window**. If this box is checked, Automatic Roof Designer will place a gable over the object. Object size does not matter, the gable will be created with an overhang of one foot on each side of the object. To remove the gable, simply click the object again with the **Roof Section at** tool, and clear the **Gable Over Door/Window** check box. When you rebuild the roof, the gable will be removed.

Placing Dormers in a Gable Roof

Creating dormers in an attic is the most difficult roofing technique to master. It requires you to create a new floor for your plan, and modify this floor with knee walls and windows in order to form gables. We will start with a new 40x30' plan to demonstrate this technique. First use **Close All** to close any plans that you have been working on. Choose **New** from the **File** menu to begin a new plan. Choose **Move Out (x2)** from the **Window** menu. Draw a rectangular floor plan, about 40x30'. We will use this outline to design our gable roof with dormers. We need to create a second floor for this plan, but before *3D Home Architect Deluxe* will let us do this, we must first save the plan. Choose **Save All Floors** on the **File** menu and name the plan DORMER.PL1. Choose **Show Floors** on the **Window** menu; the **Show Floors** dialog box appears. In this dialog box, there are four **Build** buttons available; click the one that is under the column headed by **2nd**. The **New Working Plan** dialog box appears, with the **Derive new 2nd floor plan from 1st floor plan** option selected. Click **OK** to accept this option, and then click **OK** in the **Show Floors** dialog box to close it. We now have a second floor plan, which will house our dormers.

First, let's make the left and right walls have gables in them. Use the **Roof Section at** tool and click the left wall. Click the **Full Gable wall** box, and then click **OK**. Do the same for the right wall. In order to build a dormer, we must add two knee walls. (A knee wall is a short wall on an upper floor which is cut off by a roof section.) Click the **Wall Mode** button, and then click a point on the left wall about an eighth of the way up from the bottom wall. Create a new wall by dragging the pointer all the way to the right wall. Click the **Selection Mode** button, and then drag the new wall you just created until it is about 5' from the bottom wall. Using similar steps, make another wall about an eighth of the way down from the top wall. Make sure that both of the new interior walls are the same distance from their respective exterior walls. Click the **Dimensions** button and display exterior dimension lines for your plan. Your plan should now look something like this:

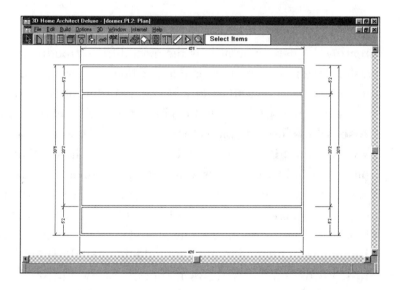

Now we must make the two new walls knee walls. Select the **Roof Section at** tool, and then click the top interior wall to reach the **Roof Section at Wall** dialog box. Check the **Knee Wall** box for this wall and click **OK**. Do the same thing for the lower interior wall. Click the **Selection Mode** button, and then double-click the new upper room. In the **Room Specification** dialog box that appears, set **Ceiling Height** to 4". Using similar steps, set the ceiling height for the new lower room to 4" also.

To continue, we must build the window boxes which will become our dormers. Click the **Wall Mode** button, and then "draw" two rectangular boxes on the outside of the lower interior wall. When this is finished, your plan should look something like this:

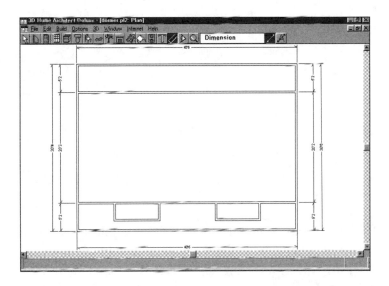

Click the **Selection Mode** button, and then drag each lower wall of the window box until it is 2' from the bottom wall. (The lower walls are the walls closest to and parallel to the bottom wall.)

Now we must use the **Break Wall** tool to delete the top portion of each window box you just created. Click the **Wall Mode** button, and then on the right-hand side of the toolbar, click the **Break Wall** tool. Click the lower interior wall in four places: the upper-left corner and the upper-right corner of each window box.

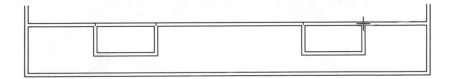

Click the **Selection Mode** button, click the upper, horizontal portion of one window box, and then press the **Delete** key. Do the same for the other window box. Your plan should now look something like this:

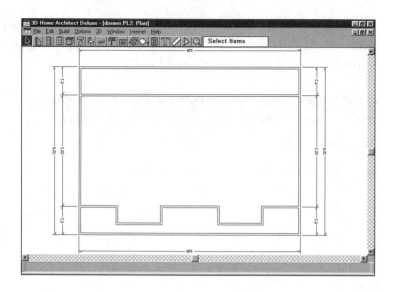

With the **Roof Section at** tool, click the left dormer's lower wall (the one closest to and parallel to the bottom wall of the plan), and then click the **Full Gable wall** box. Click **OK**. Do the same thing for the right dormer's lower wall. Now let's add a window to each dormer. Click the **Window** button, and then add a window to each of the lower walls in the dormers. (When you click to add the window, a warning box appears letting you know you are adding a window to an interior wall. Press **OK** to continue.) We are now ready to build the roof and see our dormers. Click the **Roof Mode** button, and then click the **Build Roof** tool. In the **Build Roof** dialog box, change the **Pitch** to 12 in 12. Click **OK** to build the roof. Click the **View Mode** button, and then click the **Full Overview** tool. Your full overview of the gable roof with dormers should look something like this:

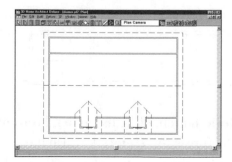

By moving the interior walls closer to or further from the outside walls, the dormers' elevation will change. Also, by changing the pitch for the roof, the dormers can be made longer. (Depending on the structure, there is a limit to how low the roof pitch can be set. Generally 9 in 12 is the lowest pitch that should be used.) You can play around with these settings and create just what you are looking for. Creating dormers in more complex plans can be done in the same way, although you will have to experiment with wall placement and pitch in order to achieve the desired effect.

Using the Break Wall Tool with Automatic Roof Designer

In certain circumstances, using the **Break Wall** tool will be necessary in order to build the roof you want. This will be especially true when designing full gable roofs for L-shaped homes. This example demonstrates the use of the **Break Wall** tool in a simple L-shaped home.

First, select **Close All** on the **File** menu, and then **New** on the **File** menu. **Select Move Out (x2)** on the **Window** menu. Now we are ready to design our floor plan. Let's start our L-shaped house with the upper wall 45' long. Make the left wall 30', and the right wall 18'. Start the lower wall from the left wall, and extend it out 20'. Now draw a 12' section upward from the lower wall. Finally, connect the middle and right walls with a 25' wall. Your plan should now look like this:

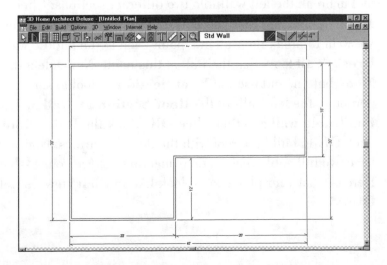

Now let's use a full gable roof for this plan. Click the **Roof Mode** button, then the **Roof Section at** tool to set the far right and left walls as full gables. Now click the bottom wall and set it as full gable. Click the **Build Roof** tool to bring up the **Build Roof** dialog box. We do not need to change any of the default settings, so click **OK**, and the roof is built. Your plan should now look like this:

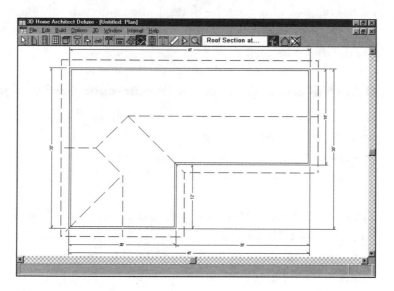

Notice, the full gable on the left wall is interfering with the full gable on the bottom wall. In order to correct this, we must use the **Break Wall** tool to break the left wall into two different sections. Click the **Wall Mode** button, and then the **Break Wall** tool from the right-hand tools. We want to break the wall at a point even to the middle wall. With the **Break Wall** tool click the wall at this point. Now select the **Roof Mode** button, and use the **Roof Section at** tool to select the lower portion of the left wall. In the **Roof Section at Wall** dialog box, clear **Full Gable wall** and then click **OK**. Click the **Build Roof** button, and click **OK** to build the roof with the default settings. Notice, you now have two full gable roof sections meeting to form your L-shaped roof. Here is what your plan should look like in **Plan** view, as well as in **Full Overview**:

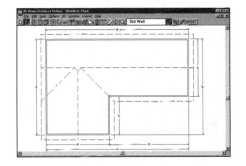 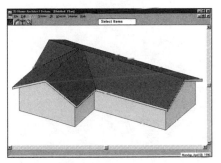

If your ridge line has a step in it, click the **Selection Mode** button, and then adjust each of the wall segments on the left wall. When you are finished, rebuild the roof. This example shows how a simple change affects the creation of a full gable roof. This technique will be useful in many such cases, as well as in creating other roof styles. Remember, you can always experiment with different techniques to see what they will yield.

This completes the tutorial on advanced roofing techniques. For a more complex model, you can combine any or all of these styles by controlling the parameters for the roof sections above each given wall, using the same techniques as above.

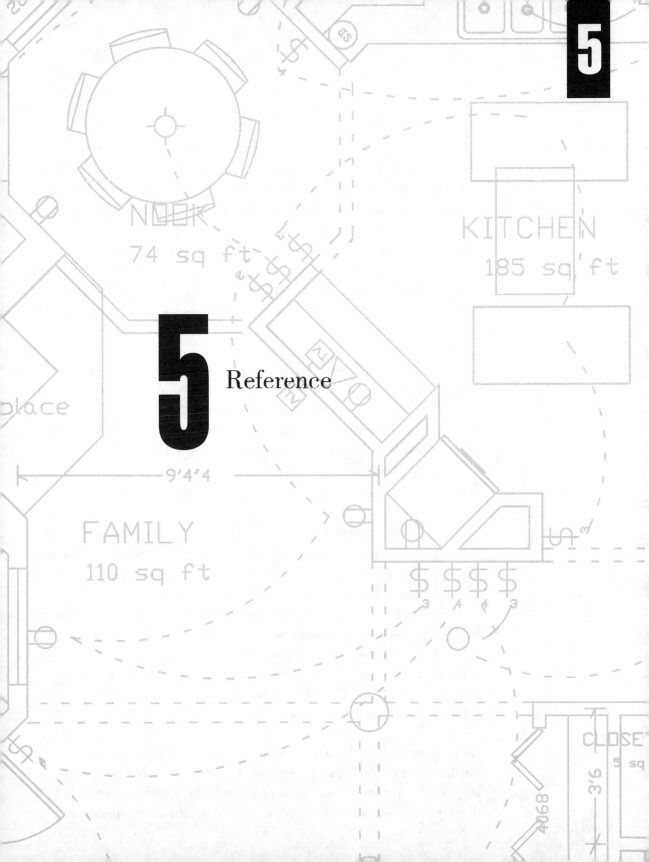

5 Reference

Chapter 5

Reference

The best way to learn **3D Home Architect Deluxe** is to use it, but there will always be some details you will need to look up. Having tried out **3D Home Architect Deluxe** in the tutorial, you can start right in on your own projects, using this chapter when necessary.

First, you will be presented with a description of the toolbar and the various commands it contains. These descriptions will be brief, however, as virtually all of these commands are also available from the menus. Second, each menu and its commands are more fully described, in menu order.

Two points to bear in mind about this reference section are that almost everything in it will also be in the online Help system in some form; this section mostly just explains how each command is structured. To see how to use the commands in practice, complete with special tips, refer to the index to find where they are discussed in the tutorials.

Toolbar Commands

The toolbar runs horizontally across the top of the program window, right under the menu bar. Toolbar buttons are shortcuts to the most commonly used, but not all, menu commands. The toolbar can be turned off and on using the **Hide Toolbar** command on the **Window** menu, or by pressing the **F5** function key. The toolbar has three parts: buttons on the left, buttons on the right, and a status box in the middle, which usually names the right-hand tool currently selected. A brief message explaining what each button does will appear in the status bar at the bottom of the screen when the pointer is positioned over it. To select any command, just click its button.

Buttons on the left side of the toolbar do not usually draw or create anything; they select the category of tools to be used (in other words, they set the mode). In most cases, clicking a button on the left side displays a tool on the right-hand side of the toolbar, like opening a particular drawer of a tool chest. For example, clicking the **Wall Mode** button brings up some tools for creating walls: the **Standard Wall, Railings, Hatch Walls, Break Wall, and Thickness** tools. Each of the buttons on the right side either selects a tool to be used or executes a command.

Some buttons on the left side of the toolbar behave differently. These are the **Fixture, Furniture, Outdoor Objects**, and **Outdoor Images** buttons (when you click these buttons, a dialog box appears) and the **Fireplace, Text** and **Stairs** buttons (after you click these buttons, you must click in the **Plan** window to add text, stairs, or a fireplace).

The toolbar changes when you switch from **Plan** view to other views. In the **Camera** views, all toolbar commands are on the left and affect the view's appearance by allowing you to select objects, zoom in and out, change the colors of objects, create an **Applied Materials** view, and create and control the recording of a 3D walkthrough. Note that commands related to moving a camera in the **Camera** views are available only from the toolbar, not from the menu. The navigation buttons are shortcuts that reposition and rotate the camera.

The following describes briefly all the commands available from the toolbar, with right-hand tools grouped with their corresponding left-hand tools. For the details on the command that a tool represents, refer to the corresponding menu command described later in this chapter.

Selection Mode

Selection Mode button

The first button on the left in the toolbar is the **Selection Mode** button. It lets you click and drag objects and their handles to select, move, resize, and rotate them. Note that the **Selection Mode** button is a bit of an anomaly in the toolbar, in that selecting it both activates the pointer and sets a mode which makes tools available on the right side of the toolbar when objects are selected. Also, you can use the different drawing tools to select objects of their own kind, so if you have just placed a cabinet and decide you want to move it, you can just select it with the **Cabinet** tool without first clicking the **Selection Mode** button and then clicking the cabinet. This is not true of furniture and fixture objects; to select them, you must first click the **Selection Mode** button and then click the object.

Note that for some items, such as foundation piers and lots, being in that tool mode is the *only* way to select that item; in other words, the **Selection Mode** tool will not select it.

Next tool

The **Next** tool is used for selecting objects that are stacked one on top of the other, like staircases or cabinets, and even some objects embedded in other objects, like component windows embedded in bay, box, and bow windows.

Open tool

The **Open** tool is used to display a dialog box for the object selected, where various characteristics can be set. These dialog boxes are very important, so double-clicking with the pointer can be used as a shortcut to access them.

Copy tool

The **Copy** tool simply copies the currently selected object to the Clipboard. To paste the copy, click the location where you want the copy to appear.

Delete tool

The **Delete** tool deletes the selected object. To delete more than one object at a time, use the **Delete Items** command on the **Edit** menu.

These tools will only display when an object has been selected, and even then not all will show up for all objects. A wall, for instance, cannot be copied, so the **Copy** tool is inappropriate and does not display when walls are selected. Likewise, when a room is selected, only the **Open** tool is shown, because rooms are not true objects, and cannot be copied, stacked (at least on the same floor), or deleted (except by deleting all the objects that make it up).

Wall Mode

Wall Mode button

The **Wall Mode** button activates **Wall** mode, which allows you to create a variety of walls using the tools you select from the right side. Besides the wall commands below, several others are available through the **Wall** command on the **Build** menu.

Standard Wall tool

The **Standard Wall** tool is used to create or select walls (and even delete them, by drawing over them).

Railings tool

The **Railings** tool creates special low walls for setting off areas like decks, porches, and stairs.

Hatch Wall tool

The **Hatch Wall** tool does not really make a wall; it simply adds hatch marks to an existing wall, to make it stand out better.

Break Wall tool

The **Break Wall** tool divides one wall into two independent walls. You will see a line where the break occurs; you can then select either of the walls. Selecting the **Esc** key while the **Break Wall** tool is selected returns you to the previous mode.

Thickness button

The **Thickness** button is not really a drawing tool, but rather a multiple toggle, which allows you to cycle through possible wall thickness settings (two, four, six, eight, and twelve inches) by clicking the button. All walls created afterwards will then have that thickness.

Door Mode

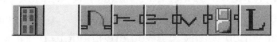

Door Mode button

When depressed, the **Door Mode** button allows you to place doors in the walls in your plan. To do so, select the appropriate door tool, then click a wall.

Standard Door(way) tool

The **Standard Door(way)** tool creates a doorway in a wall. To place a particular type of door, double-click on the doorway. To indicate the direction of the opening, click the doorway, grab one of its handles, and then drag in the direction that you wish the door to open. To create a double door, widen the doorway to 4 feet or greater.

Sliding Door tool

The **Sliding Door** tool is used to place sliding doors. These doors can be placed in both exterior and interior walls and have different features depending on the wall type.

Pocket Door tool

The **Pocket Door** tool creates pocket doors (doors that slide into a "pocket" in a wall). These are usually placed in interior walls, but can be set in exterior walls.

Bifold Door tool

The **Bifold Door** tool creates folding doors, again usually in interior walls. Depending on the width of the doorway, these will be single or double folds.

Garage Door tool

The **Garage Door** tool is used to place garage doors in exterior walls.

Doorway Library tool

The **Doorway Library** tool opens the Doorway Library to allow selection of shaped entryways and transoms.

Window Mode

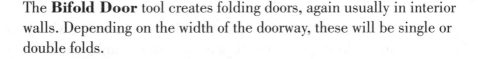

Window Mode button

Windows work almost exactly like doors. Clicking the **Window Mode** button selects the **Window** mode, and makes five window tools available. Clicking an interior wall with a window tool will cause a message to appear which warns that you are about to put a window in an interior wall. Interior walls in homes do not usually have windows in them, but you can override this warning to place a standard window in one if you like. Bay, box, and bow windows, however, can never be placed in interior walls.

Standard Window tool

The **Standard Window** tool creates just that, a standard window.

Bay Window tool

The **Bay Window** tool produces a three-sided, three-windowed bay window that projects out from an exterior wall. The bay is a structure comprising three standard windows: one in the center, and one on each side, angling back toward the base wall.

Box Window tool

The **Box Window** tool acts just like the **Bay Window** tool, except the two sides of the window projection are perpendicular to the base wall, instead of diagonal.

Bow Window tool

The **Bow Window** tool, like the **Bay** and **Box Window** tools, creates a complex window structure. The difference here is that the projection "bows" out from the wall, with each section of the bow being a standard window. Note that this particular bow window has five sections. Seven-, nine-, and eleven-section bow windows are also available, but only from the **Build** menu.

Within bay, bow, and box windows, you can select individual windows by clicking them using the **Standard Window** tool.

Windows Library tool

The **Windows Library** tool opens the Windows Library to allow selection of specialty windows.

Cabinet Mode

Cabinet Mode button

Clicking the **Cabinet Mode** button activates **Cabinet** mode, which lets you place cabinets using the following tools. Unlike doors and windows, cabinets are not openings in walls; they are their own kind of object. All can be placed in your plan away from a wall, but when placed near a wall they will snap to it and face out from it. When placed away from a wall, a cabinet will snap to the floor, while a wall cabinet will be placed at a default height of 54 inches. Placing a cabinet in a corner will create a special corner cabinet with two faces. (The arrow that displays when a cabinet is selected shows which way it is facing.) Also, cabinets come in standard modules which are usually meant to be attached to one another, so when you place cabinets side by side, they will appear to join and be one.

Base Cabinet tool

The **Base Cabinet** tool creates simple base cabinets. Usually, you will place these along a wall, but they can also be set out in the middle of a room to make an island. In addition, various fixtures, like sinks, can be placed inside cabinets.

Wall Cabinet tool

The **Wall Cabinet** tool produces a wall cabinet. It is usually positioned against a wall above a base cabinet, but it can also be located away from a wall and attached to the ceiling.

Full Height Cabinet tool

The **Full Height Cabinet** tool simply places full-height cabinets, like those in pantries.

Soffit tool

The **Soffit** tool produces a soffit which fills the void between a wall cabinet and the ceiling.

Shelf/Rod tool

The **Shelf/Rod** tool may seem odd here, but shelving is treated pretty much like cabinetry. This tool is intended for use in closets, but a single shelf can also be added to interior walls. To install multiple shelves, use furniture shelves or customize an enlarged cabinet.

Fixtures

Fixtures button

When you click the **Fixtures** button, a dialog box appears and shows a series of item groups. Clicking any of these will advance you to the next level of item groups; you can continue to click/advance until you finally reach specific fixture items. To add an item to your plan, click **OK**. The **View** button lets you get a preview of the fixture. If the fixture is of a type that must go in a cabinet (like a sink), then the preview will show the fixture in a cabinet. After you add a fixture, you can continue to click and add the same type of fixture as many times as you want. To place a different type of fixture, though, you have to go through the selection process again. Some fixtures are free-standing and can be placed anywhere in a plan, while others need to be placed in an object such as a cabinet, sink, or oven. Before you place a fixture in a cabinet,

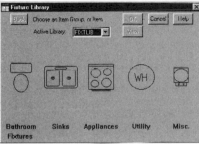

you must make sure the cabinet is big enough to hold the fixture. The fixture will be centered in the cabinet.

The Fixture Library contains 3D fixtures and appliances for both indoor and outdoor usage.

Top level of Fixture Library dialog box

Furniture

Furniture button

The **Furniture** button is exactly like the **Fixtures** button: it opens a library of objects organized in a hierarchical list, from which you select an object to place. The furniture includes beds, chairs, tables, and other movable things. (To switch to another library, click the text box next to Active Library, and then click a name in the list.)

The Furniture Library contains both indoor and outdoor furniture. Furniture objects can be manipulated in three dimensions.

Outdoor Objects

Outdoor Objects

The **Outdoor Objects** button is like the **Furniture** button—it opens a library of objects organized in a hierarchical list from which you can select an object to place. The Outdoor Objects Library includes fences, bridges, ponds, statues, mailboxes, and other objects that can be manipulated in three dimensions.

Outdoor Images

Outdoor Images button

The **Outdoor Images** button opens the **Select Image** dialog box, which allows you to choose outdoor trees, shrubs, flowers, statues, or rocks. These images appear as 2D bitmap images in the 3D views.

Fireplace

Fireplace button

Click the **Fireplace** button, and then click a wall or inside a room to place a masonry fireplace.

Stairs Mode

Stairs Mode button

The **Stairs Mode** button sets **Stairs** mode, but no right-hand tools will display. All you do in this mode is create built-in stairs and landings. To add stairs, click the spot where the bottom of the staircase begins, and then drag to the spot where the top of the staircase ends. To add a staircase starting from the top and ending at the bottom, hold the **Shift** key down while dragging. To make a landing, drag one set of stairs. Leave space for a landing, then drag a second stair section in roughly its intended location, and going in the appropriate direction. Then click in the space between the two stair sections, where the landing should be, and the landing will be created. Once created, the staircase (now comprised of the stair sections and landing) can be edited by double-clicking any part. Note that this tool is for creating built-in stairs; bolt-in circular staircases are really fixtures, and thus are selected and placed from the **Fixture Library** dialog box.

Roof Mode

Roof Mode button

The **Roof Mode** button sets the **Roof** mode, which will show three right-hand tools for building and editing roofs.

Roof Section at tool

The default tool is the **Roof Section at** tool. With this tool active, clicking on a wall yields direct access to the **Roof Section at Wall** dialog box. Clicking this tool on a window or door brings up the **Roof over Door/Window** dialog box. In these dialog boxes you can choose to have a gable roof built over either a door or a window.

Build Roof tool

The **Build Roof** tool brings up the **Build Roof** dialog box.

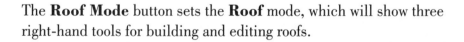

Delete Roof tool

The **Delete Roof** tool deletes the roof but not the roof-at-wall information for any of the walls or gable-over-opening information for any of the doors and windows in the plan. This information remains until you actually change it.

Electrical Mode

Electrical Mode button

The **Electrical Mode** button prepares the program to place a variety of electrical symbols into your plan. Outlets, lights, and switches can all be placed, moved, and rotated like cabinets. Other symbols can be obtained from the **Symbols Library** dialog box and placed like fixtures. Electrical symbols have no 3D representation.

110V Outlets tool

The **110V Outlets** tool places 110-volt outlets on walls. You can place 220-volt outlets by selecting them in the **Build** menu.

Lights tool

The **Lights** tool allows you to place lights, in both walls and the ceiling.

Switches tool

The **Switches** tool lets you place switches on the walls of your plan.

Connect tool

The **Connect** tool creates connections, a circuit, between the switches, lights, and outlets in your plan. Starting with one switch, click and then drag to each light or outlet, and finally to a second switch if you want a two-way circuit (resulting in 3-way switches) for turning things on and off at either switch. To disconnect items, click them again.

Place Outlets tool

The **Place Outlets** tool will automatically place a series of 110-volt outlets at standard intervals along the walls of whatever room you selected. It is best to name your rooms prior to using this tool, since a named room allows the program to place the outlets in special ways appropriate for the specific room.

Symbol Library tool

The **Symbol Library** tool opens the **Symbol Library** hierarchical dialog box, from which you can select special electrical symbols, like telephone jacks and smoke detectors, to place in the plan. Note that items in the Symbol Library will not be represented in 3D views.

Text Mode

Text Mode button

Clicking the **Text Mode** button will cause the **Edit Text** dialog box to appear whenever you click in your plan. After entering the text and clicking **OK**, the text will be placed into your plan, where it will be treated like any other object. Text is handled much as in a CAD program: it is drawn as a vector object on the plan, and is sized in plan inches, not points.

Dimension Mode

Dimension Mode button

Dimension tool

Exterior Dimensions tool

Once in **Dimension** mode, you can create dimensions for your plan in two ways.

The **Dimension** tool is a drawing tool that lets you create manual dimension lines between parallel walls, just like you build walls, by clicking and dragging. These lines update automatically to reflect any movement of the walls being relocated, and can themselves be selected and moved.

Clicking the **Exterior Dimensions** tool automatically creates exterior dimension lines for your plan. Unlike manual dimension lines, these will not always update automatically. If you change the exterior dimensions of the plan, exterior dimension lines will update accordingly. However, if you construct additional exterior walls, new exterior dimension lines will not automatically be constructed to encompass those new exterior walls. In that case, just reselect the tool; the current exterior dimension lines will be removed, and new lines drawn, which will then account for the new exterior walls.

View Mode

View Mode button

Selecting the **View Mode** button allows you to open new windows on your plan. When you open any of the following windows, the toolbar will change to reflect the tools available in that window. Up to ten windows can be open at once, and each of these views will automatically reflect changes in the others. To switch between windows, click the one you want active, press **Ctrl+Tab**, or pick a view from the bottom of the **Window** menu. A **Plan** view must be open before you can open any of these other views. Note that a seventh view, **Materials**, is available in the **Options** menu.

Plan Camera tool

The **Plan Camera** tool turns the pointer into a camera pointer. You click in your plan to place the camera, then drag a line of sight to point it. A **Camera** window then opens, displaying the portion of your plan you pointed at. Notice that the camera will appear in **Plan** view; it can be rotated and moved like an object to change the **Camera** window perspective. You can also double-click the camera in the **Plan** view to set, for example, the distance of the camera from the floor.

Tools available in the **Camera** window include the **Selection** tool, **Adjust Color** tool, **Rotate Camera** tools (Left and Right), **Move Camera** tool (In and Out, Left and Right) and **Zoom Mode** tool. The scroll bars can be used to move more of the view onto your monitor screen. You click objects in the **Camera** window with the **Adjust Color** tool to change the color of that class of objects, using the **Adjust Color** dialog box that will display. Note that these tools are fully described in the section on the **Camera** window. The **Wall Elevation** tool is used to

Wall Elevation tool

open an **Elevation** view by clicking and dragging toward a wall. Tools available are the **Selection, Adjust Color,** and **Zoom Mode.**

Overview tool

The **Overview** tool opens a window immediately when selected, providing a bird's-eye 3D view of the current floor. Besides the

Selection tool, **Adjust Color** tool, and **Zoom Mode** button, this window also features a **View Angle** tool, which opens the **View Angle** dialog box where you determine from what direction and distance your plan is seen.

Full Camera tool

The **Full Camera** tool provides a more realistic view of your home, showing a perspective view of an entire multistory model. Tools available are the **Selection** tool, **Adjust Color** tool, **Rotate Camera** tools, **Move Camera** tools, **Zoom Mode** button, the **Applied Materials** tool, and the **Walkthrough** tools.

Cross Section tool

The **Cross Section** tool produces a two-dimensional view, including roofs, in a vertical plane and shows width and height. You will find this view ideal for lining things up precisely, because you see them straight on and how high they are relative to one another. Tools available are the **Selection** tool, **Adjust Color** tool, and the **Zoom Mode** button.

Full Overview tool

The **Full Overview** tool provides a three-dimensional view of your entire multistory model including roofs. Tools available are the **Selection** tool, **Adjust Color** tool, **View Angle** tool, and the **Zoom Mode** button.

Zoom Mode

Zoom Mode button

Selecting **Zoom** mode provides you with tools for changing the magnification within the active window.

Zoom tool

The **Zoom** tool allows you to zoom in on your plan, by dragging a box around the area you want to zoom in on. When you release the mouse button, the area within the box will fill the window.

Undo Zoom tool

The **Undo Zoom** tool is an executing command that reverses the last zoom operation.

Move Out (x2) tool

The **Move Out (x2)** tool reduces the magnification of your plan by half each time you issue the command.

Fill Window tool

The **Fill Window** tool resizes your entire plan to just fit in the active window, thus "filling" it.

Reference tool

The **Reference** tool only appears if you have an additional floor loaded in memory as a Reference Plan in the **Show Floors** dialog box, in which case this tool causes an outline of that plan to toggle on and off "underneath" the current working plan.

Swap Work-Ref tool

The **Swap Work-Ref** tool also appears only if a reference floor is in use. This tool swaps the Working Plan and the Reference Plan with one another. Reference Plans are activated via the **Show Floors** dialog box.

Menus

In the preceding section you were presented summaries of the commands available in the toolbar. Now, you will be shown detailed descriptions of all these commands, plus all others, as they are ordered on the menu bar. Remember that besides the descriptions here, various parts of the tutorials will show more involved commands in actual use. Almost all of the program's commands are accessible from drop-down menus listed on the menu bar. To display any of the menus, just click its title, or press the **Alt** key and the first letter of the menu, or use the keyboard shortcut displayed to the right of the menu items. Each menu will then display a list of commands appropriate to it, some of which will bring up dialog boxes and submenus with their own commands.

File Menu

Commands for creating, opening, closing, saving, printing, exporting your plans and finding saved plans are featured in this menu.

New

The **New** command will open a new, untitled plan to give you a fresh start. Note that in *3D Home Architect Deluxe*, opening a new file does not automatically close all the currently open files. With this program, you can have up to ten files open at once (if your RAM allows). You can even have several copies of the same plan open at once, which can be handy for detail work on different parts of your plan.

The title bar of your new plan will read "Untitled: Plan," indicating the file is in fact new, and that the view is **Plan**. The **Plan** view alone is always what will be displayed for a new file. All the defaults for your new plan, such as the **Show Items** dialog box and **Plan Setup** dialog box settings and the window scaling and object colors, are loaded automatically from a special file called PROFILE.PL1. You can of course, change these settings. To change the default setup, you must open PROFILE.PL1, change its settings, and save it. Bear in mind any changes made to this file will show up in all files you create later, so be careful not to include unwanted objects or changes. If you used the default setup scheme, the profile plan will be located in C:\Program Files\3D Home Architect Deluxe 3.0.

Open

The **Open** command brings up the **Open Plan File** dialog box from which you can choose a file to open. The dialog box includes an edit box where you can enter the name of the file you want to open, and three list boxes, one for picking files to open, one for choosing file types, one for choosing a directory. To open files from different drives and directories, you can either enter the path name in the edit box, or just click in the appropriate list boxes. To open a file, enter or select it, then click **Open**, or just double-click it in the file list.

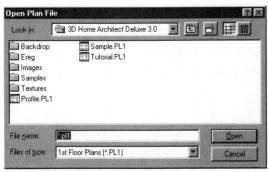

Open Plan File dialog box

The **Files of Type** list box lets you select the type of files displayed in the file list. **3D Home Architect Deluxe** really supports only one file type, a plan, but organizes and labels these differently according to function. Plan files are assigned the extension *.PLn. Automatic save files are labeled *.PAn, and back-up files, *.PBn. (The program produces automatic save files by constantly saving your plans as you work on them. Back-up files are temporary stores for the old contents of plans that have just been saved.)

What is the "n" all about? To keep the different floor plans for a given design together, the program uses one file name for all, but uses the letter "n" to indicate which floor of the design the file contains. The program will support up to four floors plus a foundation and an attic, so the extensions are *.PL0 for the foundation, *.PL1 for the first floor, and so on up to *.PL5. A first-floor plan, *.PL1, is the default. For more on working with different floors, refer to the section on **Show Floors** in the **Window** menu.

Change Units (Metric Dimensioning)

The **Change Units** command is only available from the **File** pull-down menu when no windows are open. To get there, select **File/Close All.** Selecting **File/Change Units** displays the **Change Units** dialog box, which sets the system units to imperial (feet and inches) or metric. If **New** is selected from the **File** menu, the new plan will be set to use the current system units, and this plan's units cannot thereafter be changed.

Whenever an existing plan is accessed, the system units are set to that plan's units. They remain at that setting, even if you terminate and restart **3D Home Architect Deluxe**, until a plan having different units is accessed. Thus if you open an imperial units plan, or just click in its already open window, the next new plan you create will have imperial units.

Close

The **Close** command shuts the active window. Note that you can close one view of a design and others will remain open. For instance, closing a

Plan window will not automatically close an open **Elevation** window associated with it.

For an existing plan, the **Save** dialog box will appear, asking you whether you want to save the changes. Clicking **Yes** will save the changes, **No** will disregard them, and **Cancel** will leave the file open. If the plan being saved is new, and **Yes** is selected, a **Save Plan File** dialog box will then appear. The **Save Plan File** dialog box looks and acts like the **Open Plan File** dialog box.

Save Plan File dialog box

Close All

Close All works like the **Close** command, but instead of only closing the active window, it will close all the open windows for all plans.

Save As

The **Save As** command brings up the **Save Plan File** dialog box, allowing you to enter a new file name and so save the current plan's contents to a different file, or the file to a different location. If you intend to open an existing file, then make changes and save the result to a new file, it is a good idea to use the **Save As** command right after opening the existing file, to make sure you do not accidentally replace the old file by saving over it.

Save All Floors

The **Save All Floors** command is a bit different from **Close All**, in that it does not save all the open files, but only all the files (floors, that is) that belong to the currently active plan that have been loaded into memory. Using **Save All Floors** will save changes in all the associated floors, but not in other plans that may be open.

To help prevent the loss of data, the program provides two kinds of backup files. The first, labeled *.PB1, is used as a buffer to store the previous contents of a file when you save a new version. Note that a PBn file is created for each plan you create, and remains in the directory with the original file until both are deleted. Each time you change the contents of a file and save it, the PBn file is updated also.

The second back-up file type is Autosave, labeled *.PAn. A blank Autosave file is created each time you start **3D Home Architect Deluxe**, and one such file is created for each floor you create for a given plan. The program automatically saves the contents of the design you are working on to Autosave files every five minutes. Should you suffer any system or program failure, when you next start the program a warning dialog box will appear, advising you of the failure and prompting you to open the Autosave files and save their contents to new files. You should do this right away, otherwise the old Autosave files may be overwritten. For example, if you had a plan, Home.PL1, which you had changed but not saved, and your system crashed, you would end up with the original Home.PL1 file, plus an Autosave version labeled Home.PA1, which would include at least some of the changes. If upon restarting the program, you did not open Home.PA1 and save its contents to a new file, but instead just opened the original Home.PL1, after five minutes the contents of Home.PA1 would be replaced by those of the old file, and all your changes from the first session would be lost. Autosave will only be written to the directory in the event of a crash.

Plan Finder
3D Home Architect Deluxe comes with a database of many plans that can help get you started. You can use any of these plans as a template as you begin to design your home. You can search this database for plans that match your search criteria. This saves you the time of having to create a desirable plan completely from scratch.

Note: If you choose **Minimal Installation** during installation, you can access this database through the CD-ROM. Otherwise, the database is located on your hard disk in the same directory as the *3D Home Architect Deluxe* program files.

To search for plans:

1. On the **File** menu, click **Find Plan**. If necessary, insert the *3D Home Architect Deluxe* CD-ROM in the CD-ROM drive.

2. The **Plan Finder** dialog box appears.

3. Enter criteria for your search (e.g., **Style of home, Number of floors,** etc.). Use these choices to limit your search to the homes that meet your needs. You may want to use larger numbers in the **Number of floors, Square feet, Bathrooms,** and **Bedrooms** categories to avoid overlooking flexible plans.

   Square feet is commonly equivalent to living space. That is, in most cases, the listed square footage will not include the space created by non-daylight basements or garages.

   Note that if you chose **Remodel** as **Style of home**, other criteria are unavailable.

4. Click **Next**. The **Select Plan** dialog box appears, listing plans that meet your criteria. If you do not find plans that match your needs, consider broadening the range of your search by increasing the number of square feet, or additional bedrooms, bathrooms, or floors. To change your search criteria, click **Back**.

5. To preview a plan, select a plan and click **Next**. The **Preview** dialog box appears, displaying an overhead view of the plan. To see the overhead view you must have the CD-ROM in the drive.

6. Click **Open Plan** to open the plan. Click **Back** to return to the previous dialog box.

Export

The **Export** command displays a menu from which you can choose a command for exporting data to other programs. The file formats supported are **DXF** (data exchange format) for exporting to CAD programs, **Bitmap** (BMP) for saving images, **Windows Metafile** (WMF) for word processing and publishing programs, and **TXT** (tab-delimited text file) for spreadsheet and database programs. (Note that *3D Home Architect Deluxe* cannot import any of these file types.) The export options available depend on the type of window active: DXF files can only be created from **Plan** view, while only a Metafile and Bitmap can be created from **3D** views, and only **Materials** view can create a TXT file.

DXF Current creates a DXF file for the current floor plan view, while **DXF All** creates a DXF file which encompasses all floors from **Plan** view. The **Write DXF File** dialog boxes opened by these commands look like the **Save Plan File** dialog box, only the file type is changed to *.DXF. In order to be included in the new DXF file, items in your plan must be turned on in the **Show Item**s dialog box, but need not be displayed in the current window.

Note that exporting all the floors of a plan sends them not to separate DXF files, but to a single DXF file. All the objects of each floor plan are then organized in the DXF file into layers, with a single layer for each floor and each type of object on that floor, labeled A-WALL-1, A-FURN-1, A-WALL-2, A-FURN-2, and so on.

The Bitmap (BMP) command is available in the 3D views and the **Applied Materials** view; it opens a **Save 3D Image** dialog box. Entering a file name and clicking **OK** creates a BMP file of the current view.

The **Metafile (WMF)** command will prompt you to drag a box around whatever you wish to export. Only the objects displayed within that box will be exported. Once you have dragged a box, a **Write Windows Metafile** dialog box will appear. When you have entered a filename and clicked **Save**, a final dialog box will appear. This **Metafile Size** dialog box contains settings controlling how big your Metafile will appear when imported into another program. Width will default to six inches, regardless of how wide your box was, but you can change this.

Write Windows Metafile dialog box

Height can also be changed here. **Wall Line Thickness** allows you to increase the thickness of the lines used for walls in the Metafile, so that they stand out better. The default setting is 1. Entering higher numbers will create thicker lines. While the number to use varies with the width of the Metafile and the size of the final picture, 6 through 8 usually works well for large plans.

The **Materials (TXT)** command, which is available in the Materials list, opens a **Write Materials Export File** dialog box. Entering a file name and pressing **OK** in this dialog box creates a TXT file containing the entire Materials spreadsheet. The extent of the exported file will depend on the spreadsheet, which in turn will depend on whether you created a Materials spreadsheet for an area, room, or the whole floor when you selected **Materials** from the **Option** menu.

Print

The **Print** command opens a dialog box in which you can specify what part of your plan to print, at what size, and how many copies. You can also select a printer from here. Only items selected in the **Show Items** dialog box will appear in a printout. (To view this dialog box, on the **Options** menu, click **Show Items**.)

The **Print** dialog box varies depending on the view. The **Wall Line Thickness** option is available only in **Plan** view. In 3D views, either the Shaded or Color option is available depending on whether the printer is black and white or color. In the **Materials** view, the **Print** dialog box is much simpler.

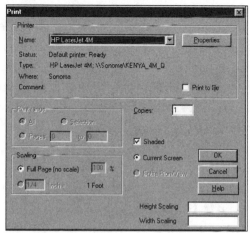

Print dialog box

Depending on the current view, options here include the printer to use, number of copies, the thickness of wall lines, whether to print the entire plan or only the current displayed screen, and whether the plan should be at full scale or some percentage, scaled to fill the paper (just like **Fill Window**), or printed at quarter-inch scale, commonly used in building plans (a quarter inch equals one foot). The **Color** check box enables color printing when checked, providing a color printer is installed. If a black and white printer is installed, the Shaded option enables the 3D view to be printed with shading. The **Properties** button here will open the standard Windows printer dialog boxes. The **Wall Line Thickness** setting here acts like that in the **Metafile Export** dialog box: you can alter the number to thicken wall lines so they show up better. Basically, leave wall line thickness alone unless you feel that the wall lines are too thin when printed on your printer. You can then experiment with increasing the wall thickness to achieve the desired print quality.

The **Print** command prints a Windows Metafile (WMF) that does not include any bitmap images you have added, such as trees, shrubs, or flowers from the Outdoor Images Library. To include bitmap images in your printout, choose the **Print Image** command

3D Home Architect Deluxe does not support printing on a page size greater than legal size. If you do print on a page larger than legal size, the image will be put in the upper-left corner of the page. You can reduce the size of the image in order to fit all landscape and electrical information on one page. If you want the image scaled down to half-size, change it to 50%. The percentage scaling will print single pages only, the image will just be smaller on that page. In order to get the plan spread out over multiple pages, you must select the **Inch = 1 Foot** setting.

Print Image

Choose the **Print Image** command when you want to include bitmap images in the printout. *3D Home Architect Deluxe* uses bitmap images to represent items from the Outdoor Images Library such as trees, shrubs, flowers, statuary, and rocks.

The **Print** dialog boxes for both the **Print** and **Print Images** commands are identical, with one exception: because the **Print Images** command generates a bitmap file, not a Windows Metafile, there is no **Wall Line Thickness** setting available when you choose **Print Images**.

Exit

The **Exit** command exits the program when selected, closing all windows, after first prompting you to save any open files that have changed.

The list at the bottom of the **File** menu shows the last four plans you used. By selecting any of these, or just typing its number, you open it immediately, bypassing the **Open** dialog box.

Edit Menu

The **Edit** menu contains commands for modifying existing objects in your plan. Most of these are standard Windows commands, but there are some commands unique to *3D Home Architect Deluxe*.

Undo

The **Undo** command reverses many previous operations. *3D Home Architect Deluxe* supports one level of undo. An **Undo enable** option in the **Plan Setup** dialog box of the **Options** menu lets you switch the command on and off. The program will run slightly faster when **Undo** is off. Note that even when **Undo** is disabled, you can still undo some commands, namely any changes made with the **Move Area**, **Delete Items,** and **Reverse Plan** commands. **Undo** does not work on most changes made within a dialog box (i.e., window resizing, building roofs, and other similar cases).

Cut, Copy, Paste, and Delete

Cut, Copy, Paste, and **Delete** are standard Windows commands. **Cut** removes the selected item from the plan to the Clipboard, **Copy** copies the item to the Clipboard, and **Paste** places an item from the Clipboard onto a plan. Note that pasting an object works only in **Plan** view. Both cut and copied items can be pasted into a plan. **Delete** deletes a selected item without storing it on the Clipboard, which means it works just like pressing the **Delete** key: a cleared or deleted item cannot be pasted back into a plan. All these commands work on all objects, and all except **Delete** work only in **Plan** view. **Delete** can be used in all views except the Materials list spreadsheet.

Delete Items
dialog box

Delete Items

The **Delete Items** command, available only in **Plan** view, opens a dialog box in which you can delete entire categories of objects from a single room or an entire plan. **Delete Scope** contains option buttons you select to determine whether you will be deleting objects from a specific room, or from all rooms. **Delete** contains check boxes for object categories, any number of which you can select. **Dimensions, Roof,** and **Outdoor Images** are only available if **Delete Scope** is set to **All Rooms.**

Selections made, you then click a room to delete its objects, or anywhere in a plan if you had checked **All**

Rooms. The dialog box will remain open, letting you go from room to room, until you click **Done**. Dialog box settings are not saved, so you must select them each time you use the command.

Note that walls cannot be deleted through this dialog box. They must be deleted individually by using the **Delete** tool, pressing the **Delete** key, or drawing over them again. Note also that manual dimensions cannot be deleted through **Delete Items** either. They too can be deleted individually like walls.

Select Items

The **Select Items** command activates the **Selection Mode** button, which lets you select individual items by clicking them. In most cases you can also select objects by clicking them with the tools used to create them. This is handy because you may want to edit an object as soon as you place it in the plan. This saves the step of selecting the **Selection Mode** button to double-click the object. Just double-click with the tool you used to create the object. Note that you need to be fairly accurate with the tool when you double-click, because if you miss the object, the tool will think that you want to place another of the same type of object. This works for all objects except furniture, fixtures, outdoor images and outdoor objects; for these, you need to use the **Selection Mode** button to select them.

Open Item

The **Open Item** command allows you to change otherwise unavailable aspects of a selected object by opening an object specification dialog box. Most objects have a specific dialog box containing options describing various detailed characteristics, like the height of a wall, the trim style of a window, or the size of a bed. You can also activate this command by double-clicking an object. The command applies to all objects, including walls, rooms, and cameras, and works in all views.

The options contained in each dialog box depend on the type of object, but all have basic dimension and style information, and most have a preview of the selected object. The dialog boxes for some objects (for example, windows) contain a **Default** tab or button which displays default values that you can change.

An explanation of the specification dialog box for each type of object will be included with the description of creating that object.

Move Area

The **Move Area** command moves an area and all objects within it at once. To use, select the command, click and drag a box around the area you want to move, then drag the area to its new location.

Build Menu

Build is the central menu in *3D Home Architect Deluxe*. It is from this menu that you select commands for creating and placing objects in your plan. Many of the selections in the menu bring up submenus with further selections, because many objects have several types from which to choose (like windows). Of course, you should already be familiar with most of them, since they are featured in the toolbar. The tools that appear on the right side of the toolbar (the tools in a mode) and the selections in a submenu work pretty much the same way, so that learning how to use one will help you learn all of them. Also, as you are working, messages will appear in the status bar, guiding your efforts.

Note that most of the mode and drawing tools will remain selected until you select another mode or tool, so to draw a series of standard walls, for example, you select **Wall** mode and **Standard Wall** only once, then just keep dragging walls.

Wall

Wall is the mode command to select when you wish to create and edit walls. The four different kinds of walls the program can create include Standard (Std), Railings, Invisible, and Beams. Once in **Wall** mode, all these can be produced by selecting the desired wall type tool, then clicking and dragging the wall to the location you want in your plan.

Walls can be drawn vertically or horizontally, or at any 15-degree angle. The end of the wall where you began the drag will remain fixed, while the other end will move about until you finish dragging. While you are drawing, the length of the wall will display in the toolbar's status box. Once you have finished a wall, you can move and resize it by selecting it, which will display its three handles. (Note that to select a wall, you must click in its "central area," which is everything not within six plan inches of an end. The "center," by which walls connect and are measured, runs the length of the wall, down the middle.)

Selected wall showing handles

To move the wall, just drag the center handle. The pointer will change to a double-headed arrow, which indicates in what direction you can move the wall. Walls can only be moved perpendicular to the direction in which they run; they cannot be moved lengthwise or rotated. To lengthen or shorten a wall, you can either drag one of the end handles, or simply draw a new wall of the same type. Drawing over a wall will erase it; drawing from one end out will extend it. To delete a wall, you can draw over it completely, or select it and pull one end to the other (essentially resizing it to nothing), or use the **Delete** key, **Delete** tool, or **Delete** command.

Drawing one wall close enough to the end of another of the same kind will cause the program to join the two (different kinds of walls will line up, but not connect). Connected walls will seem to be one piece, but you can still select the individual walls. The new wall may extend, contract, or move to meet the old wall accurately, and the old wall may extend or contract to meet the new. The program will try to make all the joins as smooth as possible by eliminating gaps and stubs. To do so, the program will adjust the end of a new wall if it approaches an old wall, and will adjust the end of an old wall if it is crossed by a new one.

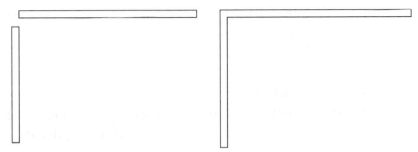

Second wall at 90°, being drawn close to first wall After walls have been snapped together and smoothed

This extending, contracting, and moving to make walls meet is called snapping, and the distance within which it occurs is called the snapping distance. The default snapping distance is one plan inch; to change it, go to the **Dimensions Setup** dialog box in the **Options** menu.

Once a wall has been connected to other walls, moving it will cause the connecting walls to extend or contract to keep them joined, if possible.

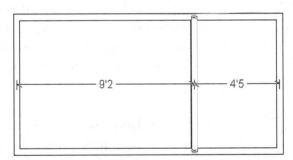

Basic four wall enclosure with dividing wall selected

Sometimes, however, you will be unable to move a wall, because it is connecting and snapping to other walls that are holding in place. This is a particular problem when a diagonal wall connects to horizontal and vertical walls to create a three-way corner, because with three walls connecting in one place, the program does not know which wall to adjust. To get around this, you should add diagonal walls last, or temporarily shorten one of the walls to break the three-way connection.

The length of new walls will be displayed in the status box in the toolbar as you draw them. When you move walls connected perpendicularly to other walls, temporary dimension lines will display locating the wall as you move it.

Standard Wall

The **Standard Wall** command creates simple, standard, exterior, and interior walls, the building blocks of the program, that define your plan by enclosing space. They are created and edited as described above. They can be located by dimension lines, both manual and automatic, define rooms, and have windows and doors placed in them, and cross-hatched.

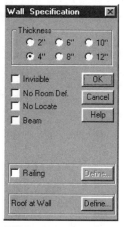

Wall Specification dialog box

All walls are basically the same and are standard. Special walls are just standard walls that have special characteristics assigned to them. To view and change these characteristics, double-click a wall to open the **Wall Specification** dialog box. Besides setting wall thickness, in this dialog box you can determine whether a wall will be invisible, define a room, be located by dimension lines, be a beam or railing, and specify roof settings for the wall.

A wall checked **Invisible** (shown with dashed lines) cannot be seen in 3D views, but can define rooms and align other walls; **No Room Def.** means that the wall does not define a room. **No Locate** means that dimension lines will not locate these walls, as long as the wall is not the endpoint for the dimension line. **Beam** marks the wall as being a beam, but will not show in a 3D view. **Railing** will produce a special kind of low-height wall. The settings in this dialog box both determine and are determined by the selected wall's type: a standard wall will have a thickness, usually four inches, but no other settings (at least by default), while a beam will of course have the **Beam** check box selected. This means that you can create a wall of a particular type both by using a specific wall tool, and by changing the characteristics in this dialog box. Clicking the

Define button leads to the **Roof Section at Wall** dialog box, used to set basic roof section parameters on a wall by wall basis. This dialog box can also be opened with the **Roof Section at** tool, which is available in **Roof** mode.

You can change the color of interior walls or apply material to them on a floor-by-floor or room-by-room basis, and then view your changes in 3D. To learn more, see "Changing the Color or Material on Object Surfaces," which is the last section in this chapter.

You can change the color of exterior walls or add a material to them on a floor-by-floor basis, and then view your changes in 3D. To do so, double-click just outside the wall you want to change to open the **Assign Colors** dialog box. For further steps in this procedure, see "Changing the Color or Material on Object Surfaces," which is the last section in this chapter.

Railings

The **Railings** command creates special walls that remain visible and define rooms, but do not affect plan dimensions. Their chief purpose is to define areas like balconies, porches, or decks, usually on the exterior of a plan, so that those additions can be created without changing the program's understanding of the structure of the house. Railings can also be used to mark off staircases and landings, and of course to simply divide a room.

3D interior railing defining a stairwell

A unique feature of railings is that their appearance can be changed by the settings in the **Railing Specification** dialog box opened by clicking **Define** in the **Wall Specification** dialog box. Options affect the type and size of vertical and horizontal pieces used in the railing, and the default colors assigned. (Selecting **Exterior Colors** will ensure that the railings defining an exterior room are different colors than interior walls, so they can be easily told apart.)

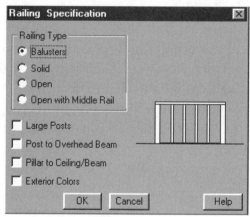

Railing Specification dialog box

Invisible

The **Invisible** command creates "walls" that define rooms, but are invisible and not located by dimension lines. These options will appear checked in the **Wall Specification** dialog box. Invisible walls are not physical walls; their chief use is to divide larger spaces into individual rooms, without using a physical member like a standard wall or railing. This permits defining a room area by double-clicking it and naming it, without having to have the area completely walled in by physical walls. In the program, Invisible walls act just like standard walls in every other way.

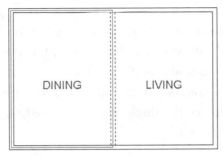

Invisible wall used to separate Living and Dining rooms

Beams

The **Beams** command creates a type of wall that has no siding. In this sense, they are kind of like invisible walls. In fact, like invisible walls, beams don't show up in 3D views. Their primary use is in **Plan** view for showing where a beam (a common construction item) is located.

Hatch Walls

The **Hatch Walls** command will not create a wall. Rather, it marks an existing wall with hatching, diagonal lines. This is commonly used in drafting to make walls stand out better, particularly their thickness. To hatch a wall, select the command then click a wall. The entire wall will fill with cross-hatching, but will be affected in no other way. You would use wall hatching to mark a wall for a special purpose, such as a wall intended to be removed in a remodel.

Break Wall

The **Break Wall** command simply breaks one wall section into two when you select the command then click a wall. A thin line will indicate the break; clicking either side with the pointer will display the resulting wall on that side. Note that this is not the command to use for a doorway. Instead of breaking walls to make openings, just place a door into a wall.

This wall has been broken in two, and the right wall is selected.

To exit the **Break Wall** mode and return to the previous command mode, press the **Esc** key.

Wall Thickness Settings

2, 4, 6, 8, 12 Inch Walls are options for setting the thickness of any wall you create later. All wall types can have any of these thicknesses. Note that there are three ways to specify the thickness of a wall. You can either use this menu selection, or you can use the **Thickness** button in the toolbar, or you can change the thickness for an existing wall in the **Wall Specification** dialog box.

Walls of different thicknesses can be joined together. If they are running in the same direction, a step will be created on either side, as the thinner wall meets the thicker. This is because all walls are joined at their center lines. Moving one wall sideways to align it flush with the other wall on one side will have no effect, because the join will always snap back to the center. To make the two walls flush on one side, intersect them with a third wall, making a cross. This will free the two wall ends to slide along the third wall, preventing them from snapping to each other's center. If you like, once the walls are flush on one side, you can then delete part or all of the third wall. You will probably only delete one arm of the cross, however, since two walls of different thicknesses seldom meet without a third intersecting them.

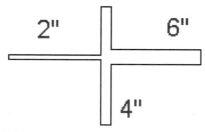

To join two walls of different thicknesses evenly, use a third wall. After the walls are joined, you can then delete the third wall (in this case, the 4" wall).

Door

The **Door** command sets the program to **Door** mode, and opens a submenu featuring the different types of doors the program can create. These include **Standard Door(way), Sliding Doors, Pocket Doors, Bifold Doors,** and **Garage Door**s. Also on this submenu is the **Doorway Library** command, which opens the Doorway Library.

Doors and windows are treated by the program as openings in walls. To create a door, you must first have a wall to place it in. Once you have your walls, set the program to **Door** mode, choose the type of door you want, and click the wall where you want the door. A doorway will appear, centered where you clicked. If you click the doorway you just created, it will select the doorway, and display dimensions and handles for resizing or moving the doorway.

2668

Door placed in wall with 4 digit dimensions showing door to be 2'6" wide by 6'8" high

The size of the door opening will be indicated either with four digits, like 2668, showing width and height in feet and inches (so 2668 means two feet, six inches wide, and six feet, eight inches high). When you first place a door, its size will be determined by the default for that type, and the room available. (The program will narrow a door to fit a tight space, but when the space is too tight, a warning dialog box will appear.)

Once a door has been placed, you can edit it by selecting it, then manipulating its handles. As with a wall, dragging the end handles of a door will resize it, and dragging the center handle will move it. A door can only be moved sideways in a wall, as the arrows of the center handle will indicate. Unlike a wall, however, when a door's end handle is dragged, both ends move, to keep the door centered. The movement will be somewhat constrained, to make sure the door uses a standard size. To delete a door, select it and press the **Delete** key, or click the **Delete** tool, or resize it to nothing.

3868

The numbers change as the door is widened.

In addition to resizing and moving a door, you can determine how it will open. While this is different for each type of door, basically you click one of the three handles and mimic how the door should open by dragging the handle. Note that until you do this, or change the door specification, standard doors are really just doorways. Dragging a handle creates a door and pulls it open. A doorway four feet wide or wider will automatically became a double door.

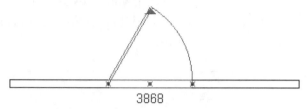

3868

The rotation handle is used to set the angle of the open door.

As with most kinds of walls, you can select different kinds of doors in your plan with the pointer, the door tool used to create it, or even another door tool.

Double-clicking a door, or selecting it then using the **Open Item** command (or the **Open** tool), will bring up the **Door Specification** dialog box. Here you can set both major characteristics of the door, such as style, type, and size (height, width, and thickness), and minor ones, such as trim and frame dimensions, by choosing from list boxes and entering dimensions in edit boxes.

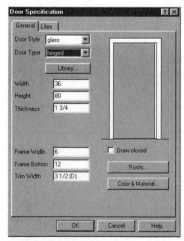

Door Specification dialog box

To choose a door style, click the box next to **Door Style** and then click a name in the list that appears. (Your choices are **default, slab, glass,** and **panel**. If you click library, you are asked to click the **Library** button in the dialog box to access library doors.) **Door Type** is a list box that lists all of the possible door types **(doorway, hinged, slider, pocket, bifold,** and **garage)**. Door dimensions can be changed by simply entering new values in the dialog box. **Trim Width** (the door sills and moulding), **Frame Width** and **Frame Bottom** (for glass doors) dimensions can also be entered. Note that these settings are interdependent: a slab door will have frame dimensions of 0, because it has no frame, while a glass door does have a frame, and so will have dimensions here. If you have chosen a glass door you can dress up your door with muntin bars and user-definable lites (from 1 over 1 to 8 over 8) in the **Lites** tab. Many different glazing options are available (including normal, diamond, prairie, and craftsman). Besides the object preview, which shows what your door will look like, this dialog box also gives you the option of seeing the door opened or closed in the preview and 3D views.

You can change the color of doors or apply material to them, and then view your changes in 3D. To learn more, see "Changing the Color or Material on Object Surfaces," which is the last section in this chapter.

Although you can create doors only in **Plan** view, you will find it helpful to edit them in other views, or at least have other views open. The **Elevation** view is especially good for changing doors, because you can change width and height by dragging, and get a better sense of how your doors fit with your windows and cabinets.

Standard Door(way)

The **Standard Door(way)** command creates both single doors and double doors. While other commands create doors that always have actual doors (even garage doors), standard doors are just empty doorways until you select a handle and drag it from the wall, mimicking how the door should open. This makes a door appear, opening in that direction. To eliminate the door (but not the doorway), pull it "shut," back into the wall. To create double doors, place a standard door, then widen it, and finally drag the center handle out to place and open the doors themselves. Doorways will display in your plan as openings in the walls, while the doors themselves will be shown as "swings," a line and arc swinging out from the doorway. To adjust the angle of the open door, make the door active, then position the pointer over the triangular rotation handle at the edge of the door. The pointer will change into a circular arrow, and you can then adjust the angle of the door swing.

The program will place doors of a default size, depending on type and location. Standard exterior doors are usually 36 inches wide, while interior doors are 30 inches wide. Doors in exterior walls will also have sills added automatically.

Sliding Doors

The **Sliding Doors** command creates both exterior and interior sliding doors. They are placed and edited like standard doors. To determine which of the two parts slide and in what track it sits, drag the end handle on that side in the appropriate direction. For example, dragging the right handle down would make the right half of the door the moving part, and place it in the lower track. Exterior sliding doors always have the moving part on the inside. Sliding doors default to a width of five feet and must be at least four feet, but otherwise can be resized.

Pocket Doors

The **Pocket Doors** command creates doors that slide into wall "pockets." These are usually placed in interior walls, but can be set in exterior walls also. They are especially useful for creating sliding doors in spaces narrower than four feet. Dragging an end handle determines on which side the door fits into the wall.

Pocket doors default to 30 inches wide, but can be resized up to 72 inches. To make a pocket door wider than this, use the **Width** option in the **Door Specification** dialog box. This will make it a double pocket door. You may also create a double pocket door by clicking the **Selection Mode** button then making the door wider by dragging the end handles. When the width exceeds 44 inches, the pocket door will become a double pocket door.

Bifold Doors

The **Bifold Doors** command creates folding doors, again usually in interior walls, and usually for closets. Dragging a side handle out will determine which way the fold faces, and from what side the door opens. The default size for a bifold door is 30 inches, as with all primarily interior doors, but widening one beyond 32 inches will make it a double door.

Garage Doors

The **Garage Doors** command places garage doors in exterior walls. The default width is eight feet and cannot be narrower than six.

Doorway Library

The **Doorway Library** command opens the **Doorways Library** dialog box, which allows you to select shaped entryways and transoms.

Window

The **Window** command sets the program to **Window** mode, and opens a submenu featuring different windows. The submenu contains commands for **Standard Window, Bay Window, Box Window**, and several kinds of bow windows, and includes a command which lets you access the Windows Library. Each window type acts a bit differently due to different construction methods and constraints, as explained below. All windows are placed just like doors: you pick the window type you want (either through the menu or with one of the window tools in the toolbar), then click a wall where you want the window to be placed. Just like doorways, windows can be moved back and forth along a wall by clicking it and then dragging from the center, or widened and narrowed to standard sizes by dragging the side handles, or deleted by pressing the **Delete** key or **Delete** tool (or resizing to nothing). Moving the center handle perpendicular to the window will also change the window's configuration, depending on direction and window type. Of course, if you try to place a window where it will not fit, an error message will come up.

Windows are placed and act like doors because they are the same kind of objects—openings in a wall. Because of this you can even edit doors in **Window** mode, and vice versa (clicking on a door with a windows tool will select the door). As with placing doors, it is a good idea to wait until you have drawn all your walls before placing windows, so the program will know what to do. For instance, until you have enclosed your house with exterior walls, and so defined an inside and outside, you can put windows anywhere. Once the house is closed, however, placing a window in an interior wall will bring up a warning dialog box because interior walls do not usually have windows. (You can override this, however. No warning comes up if the adjoining room is labeled Porch, Deck, Balcony, or Court.)

As with doors and other objects, you can fine-tune a window by opening a specification dialog box for it. To do so, just double-click the window, or select it and then click the **Open** tool. The **Window Specification** dialog box appears, which contains settings for the type of window material, window dimensions (including the height of the moving piece), and frame and trim dimensions. There is also a tab for **Lites,** which allows you to have "leaded glass" in your window, also known as muntin bars. You can dress up your plan with muntin bars and user-definable lites (from 1 over 1 to 8 over 8) on windows. Many different glazing options are available (including normal, diamond, prairie, and craftsman). If you check the shutters box, shutters will be placed next to this window. The default width for **Shutters** is half the width of your window, but you can also set the width to 15" wide by checking the **Narrow Shutter** box. The dialog box includes a preview showing what the window will look like.

Window Specification dialog box

Clicking the **Default** tab displays default settings for window styles and dimensions. The default settings are the same for all types of windows, but bay and bow windows alter them automatically to take into account their oddities of construction. You scroll through an option list for **Window Type** and enter values for the other options.

Default tab in the Window Specification dialog box

You can change the color of windows or apply material to them, and then view your changes in 3D. To learn more, see "Changing the Color or Material on Object Surfaces," which is the last section in this chapter.

About Default Settings

For most object types, the default settings are derived from the plan-wide defaults for that object type. The plan-wide defaults for a particular object type are accessed by clicking the **Default** tab in the object's specification dialog box. This will display a dialog box where you can change the defaults. Some of the defaults are initial values—the value at the time of the object's creation—but defaults can be changed independently for each object. Other values are "dynamic" defaults, which means that if you change them for one object, all the objects of that type will change to have the same values. For windows, for example, the height, width, and distance from the floor are initial values, so all windows have these values when first created. If you change those defaults, then new values will only apply to windows created subsequent to the defaults being changed. Changing dynamic defaults, on the other hand, will affect all windows that are mapped to the default. You can tell which settings are mapped to the default because they will have a **(D)** next to the value. Pressing the letter **D** in an option box will revert the setting to the default, after leaving that box.

Why is it necessary to have two types of defaults? The reason is that they serve two different but equally valuable purposes. Initial values are useful because, in the case of windows, you usually (but not always) want them to be the same size. Initial values ensure that all windows are the same dimensions when first placed. You can tweak them individually, of course, because you may need one window to be a special size. Dynamic defaults let you change settings on a plan-wide (i.e., current floor) basis. For example, if all the windows in your design use the plan default type, then you can easily change the type for all of the windows in your plan by changing what type of window the plan default is set to. Note that there is no central location in which to set the plan defaults. The defaults are accessed by opening the specification dialog box for any example of particular objects in your plan, and then clicking the **Default** tab or button.

Although you can create windows only in **Plan** view, you will find it helpful to edit them in other views, or at least have other views open.

The **Elevation** view is especially good for changing windows, because here you can see how high and wide the window is, what the frame and trim look like, and how the window relates to the wall and other plan elements. Even better, you can see what you are doing while changing the height, width, vertical, and horizontal positions of the window.

Standard Window

The **Standard Window** command creates standard windows, basically any window not a bay, box, or bow. Besides the usual placing, moving, resizing, and delete commands, standard windows can also be edited in the following two ways.

First, when dimensions are shown with four-digit numbers, the height of the window from top to bottom can be increased or decreased by dragging the center handle in or out, perpendicular to the window surface. The window dimension will display the changing height. When resizing with this command, the top of the window remains at the same height; it is the bottom that moves up and down, like a window shade.

Second, the top of the window (that is, how high it is on the wall), its height top to bottom, width, style, and other characteristics can be changed using the **Window Specification** dialog box described above. All the items in this dialog box can be changed for standard windows, and defaults for all are set in the **Default** tab.

Although you can only use the listed window style, you can use almost any dimensions you want for your windows. Be careful, however, that your window designs are practical. For example, you can draw a single twenty-foot wide picture window, but a single piece of glass that big, and the wall construction it would require, would be far more expensive and complicated than most homeowners and builders could handle. You would be better off with six three-foot windows, or several sliding doors. Likewise, you can set the window separation to zero and place several windows side-by-side, but actually building these without structural supports in between would be difficult.

The program defaults for standard windows assume that windows will be 80 inches high at the top, three feet wide and high, double-hung, with standard-sized frames and trim, and that windows will not be closer than two inches to each other.

Bay, box, and bow windows are created "structurally," that is, built from standard windows and structural members. Prefabricated bays and bows are available from numerous manufacturers and have the advantage of being slightly less costly and more refined, in that they usually have more glass compared to frame, and more elaborate frames and trim. Structural bays, boxes, and bows, however, offer more flexibility for features like floor-to-ceiling openings and built-in seating, are easier to repair, and are built from standard materials on site. If you are going to install prefabricated windows, you can approximate them using the **Bay, Box,** and **Bow Window** commands, or just indicate the opening using a standard window. Check with your builder and suppliers to see what will work best.

Besides the structural windows available on the **Build** menu, you can always create custom windows by building them yourself from walls and standard windows. For example, if you want a bay window with three windows across the front instead of just one, you can create the wall structure then add the five component windows. (Placing a standard bay window structure and adding extra windows will not work, because the program will allow only one window per side in a defined bay window.) You can use similar tricks for creating recessed windows for herb gardens and interior courts (and have to, because the defined windows all project outward).

Bay Window
The **Bay Window** command creates a bay window out of three standard windows, with one at the front parallel to the wall and two on either side at angles. To create a bay window, just select the command and click the appropriate wall; the bay structure will be created automatically, and can be moved and resized like a standard window. Notice that three dimensions are displayed: the width of the bay at the wall, at the front

window, and the depth from front to wall. If **Opening Size** is checked in the **Show Items** dialog box, the width of all three windows will also be shown.

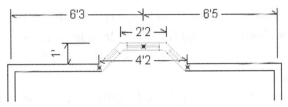

Bay window selected to show dimensions and handles

You will see that the center handle of a bay window is in the front window. Besides dragging this side to side to move the bay along the wall, you can also drag it in and out, within limits, to decrease or increase the depth of the bay.

While changing the depth, you will also be changing the width of the three windows. This is because it is assumed you want the windows to resize with the bay; to treat the individual windows separately, click each while in Standard Window mode. Once you have resized a component window this way, it will stay that size regardless of how you change the bay, except to become smaller to fit a smaller bay. For the component to resize automatically again, you have to recreate the bay. To change component window specifications, first select a component window, then open the dialog box by double-clicking or clicking the **Open** button. The dialog box will show how the standard window defaults have been adjusted to accommodate the bay window configuration.

Bay windows by default are 1 foot deep, 2 feet 2 inches wide at front, and 4 feet 2 inches at the wall, with the center window 1 foot 6 inches wide and the side windows 10 inches.

Box Window
The **Box Window** command creates a special version of a bay window, with the front window parallel to the wall and the two sides

perpendicular. You create and change box windows just as you do bays, including editing the component windows. To make a dormer window, just create a box window and delete the two side component windows.

Box windows default to 4 feet 2 inches wide, 1 foot 6 inches deep, with a 3-foot wide center window and 8-inch wide side windows.

Bow Window

Bow, 5 Section (and **7, 9**, and **11 Section**) commands create a more complicated version of a structural window. Essentially, this is just a series of identical standard windows arranged in an arc. Bow windows usually have an odd number of sections (component standard windows) so that there will be a window rather than a divider in the center. All the bow windows are alike, only the number of sections changes. The procedures for changing bow windows and bay windows are similar, with some notable differences.

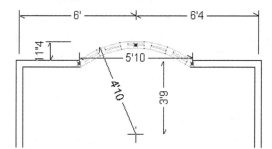

Bow window selected to show dimensions and handles

The most noticeable difference is that bow windows have four dimensions: the width along the original wall, the distance from the center of the bow to the outer edge of the wall, the distance the bow projects from the outer edge of the wall, and the distance (radius) from the center of the bow to an outer corner. All four dimensions are needed, because while the middle two will add up to the last for a bow with an even number of sections, for an odd number they will not. This is because the depth of the bow is measured to the flat center of a window, while the radius extends all the way to a corner.

Window opening dimensions are given for only one component, because all are the same in a bow. Which brings up the second exception: because all the component windows of a bow must remain the same, you cannot selectively change them individually as you can with bay windows. Changing the specifications of a single component window will change all other components within that bay window.

A five-section bow window defaults to 5'10" wide, 4'10" in radius, 3'9" from the bow center to the wall, with windows 3 feet high and 10 inches wide.

Window Library

The **Window Library** command opens the **Window Library** dialog box, which allows you to select specialty windows not available from the **Standard Window** dialog box. These include round and oval windows.

Cabinet

The **Cabinet** command activates **Cabinet** mode, and displays a submenu listing the available types of cabinets. These include **Base Cab, Full Height, Wall Cab, Soffit,** and **Shelf/Rod** (which are treated like cabinets). Cabinets are unlike walls, doors, and windows in that they are not part of the structure of a plan, but rather are independent and movable. They can be placed and moved about freely, and do not affect the basic plan. Cabinets can, however, attach to walls, and cabinets of the same kind can be attached to one another.

Beyond their mobility, cabinets have three other special attributes: they are modular, they face a direction, and some can have fixtures placed in them. Being modular simply means that cabinets of the same type (and often size) are usually placed together to form a single unit, like a set of cabinets in a kitchen forming an island. The program reflects this modularity by snapping cabinets together into constructions that display like a single piece. Because cabinets have distinct fronts and backs, they have a direction. The program indicates direction with an arrow, and will only attach cabinets by their backs and sides to each other and walls, and will only attach cabinets that face the same direction. Cabinets' ability to contain fixtures is discussed in the fixtures section that follows.

To create a cabinet, just select the mode and type (either through the menu or via the toolbar), and click your plan. Notice that if you place a cabinet with its back or side to a wall, the cabinet will snap to the wall, attaching itself (pretty much like walls snap together). If you click close enough to a wall, the program will automatically turn the cabinet to face the proper direction; clicking a corner will create a special corner cabinet. (Note: "corner cabinet" is not a type of cabinet, just a regular cabinet, either base, wall, or full-height, that faces two directions; if you want a regular cabinet in a corner, place it elsewhere, then drag it into the corner.) Cabinets will contract automatically to fit a constricted space, down to the minimum width allowed. Also, placing a new cabinet next to an existing one of the same type will cause the two to snap together.

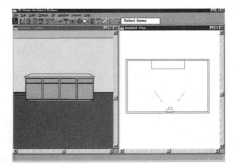

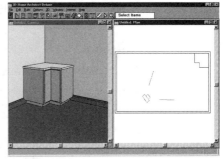

Row of cabinets forming single module against wall

Corner cabinet

When you place a cabinet, and then select it, its outline and direction arrow will display. Notice that as long as you hold the mouse button down, you can move the cabinet about orthogonally (only horizontally or vertically), not in any direction. To move the cabinet (or other objects) freely, hold the **Ctrl** key down while dragging the object.

Once selected, a direction arrow, three side handles, a center handle, and one triangular rotation handle will display. To move the cabinet, drag its center handle; to resize it, drag the side handles. To rotate, drag the triangular rotation handle, at which point the pointer will become a circular arrow. Note that you can select any cabinet with any cabinet tool, or with the **Selection** tool, but be careful—clicking a base cabinet with the **Wall Cabinet** tool will not select the base, but will create a wall cabinet above it, and vice versa. When selected, the width of the cabinet will also display. Cabinets can be deleted using the **Delete** tool, **Delete** key, or by resizing to zero.

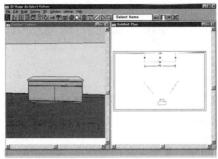

Widened cabinet

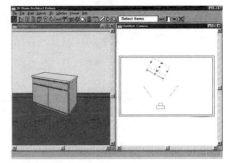

Rotated cabinet

Cabinets attached to one another will display as a single piece unless the **Module** option is checked in the **Show Items** dialog box, in which case the boundaries and directions of all cabinets will be shown. An individual cabinet can always be selected, even if attached to others. Attached cabinets can be moved sideways at once by "pushing" with the cabinet at the end. Likewise, cabinets attached to a wall will move with the wall. Note that to attach cabinets to a wall, you must move the cabinets to the wall. Moving the wall to the cabinets will not attach them. (Running PlanCheck will attach the cabinets to the wall, though, because the program wants to keep things tidy.)

The **Cabinet Specification** dialog box displayed by opening a cabinet allows you to change the size of the cabinet, and both the size and nature of its parts. You can even add items such as drawers and shelves. The defaults for a cabinet are set in the **Cabinet Defaults** dialog box, and depend on the type of cabinet. Options in this dialog box include the type (**base, wall,** and **full-height**), face styles, and dimensions, including settings for counter thickness and overhang, and the separation between panels. Because cabinets come in standard sizes, a minimum width and width increment are included. Changing settings in this dialog box will affect only this plan; to change the settings for all subsequent plans, change the defaults in the PROFILE.PL1 plan.

Cabinet Specification

Face Style	plain doors ▾
Special	normal ▾
Item Type	▾
Item Height	

[Add New] [Delete]

Cabinet Height	36
Width	24
Depth	24
Floor to Bottom	0

☐ Roll out shelves
☐ Glass doors
☑ Flat sides

Materials list: BDR2436

[Color & Material...]

[OK] [Cancel]

[Default...] [Help]

Cabinet Specification dialog box

In addition to those offered in the default dialog box, the **Cabinet Specification** dialog box furnishes options for customizing a cabinet by changing its color, shape, material, and components. The **Special** list box lets you determine the shape of an end cabinet, for instance. An end cabinet will angle off instead of coming to a square corner, while a radius end will be rounded off. A peninsula radius will create a half-round end cabinet, provided the cabinet has nothing on either side.

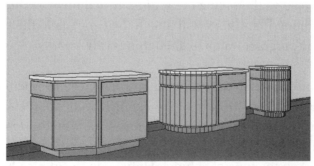

3D view of end, radius, and peninsula radius cabinets

Besides displaying options, the preview in this dialog box will also let you choose items to change. Clicking part of a cabinet in the preview will cause the **Item Type** and **Item Height** list boxes to list what the part is and how tall it is, in inches. Also, you can select a part and use the **Add New** and **Delete** buttons to edit it. For example, if you wanted to change a single drawer to a double drawer, double-click the cabinet to display the **Cabinet Specification** dialog box. Then click the cabinet drawer in the preview in the dialog box, and finally change **drawer** to **dbl drawer** in the **Item Type** list. Note that some options will change depending on the type and location of a cabinet. For instance, only wall cabinets have a **Floor to Bottom** height by default, and regular cabinets have a **Roll-on shelves** option, while corner cabinets can have a **Lazy susan**.

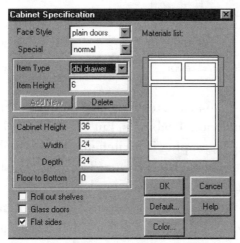

Cabinet Specification dialog box changing drawer to double drawer

You can insert new items into the cabinet. The point of insertion is between other items. If you click between two items on the cabinet, two arrows appear to the side marking the insertion point. You can then select the type of item that you want to insert from the **Item Type** list box. Items below the insertion point will move down toward the bottom of the cabinet. If insufficient room exists at the bottom of the cabinet to accommodate the movement, a warning dialog box will appear. If that happens, you will either have to delete one or more of the existing items, or increase the height of the cabinet to make room. By raising the height of the cabinet, and then changing the cabinet to contain just shelves, you can create convincing built-in bookshelves, and other custom storage items.

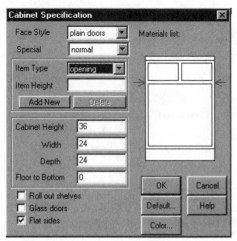

Insertion point marked between two drawers on cabinet

Cabinets being modular, you can create custom cabinet configurations not only by changing individual cabinets, but by arranging cabinets in special groups. One such grouping is a kitchen island, which comprises a number of carefully aligned base cabinets. To create an island, create a series of cabinets attached side by side (and so facing one direction), then create another series facing the other way. The program should determine which way each cabinet should face, but if not, just rotate each until it faces the right way and attaches. When completed, your island should display as a single piece. If lines still show between cabinets, even when the **Module** option in the **Show Items** dialog box is off, the cabinets are not attached properly and need adjusting. The same technique can be used for creating a group of wall cabinets hanging from the ceiling above the island.

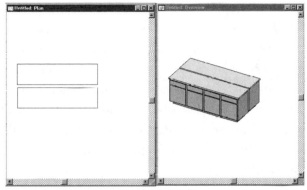

Two rows of four cabinets facing opposite directions

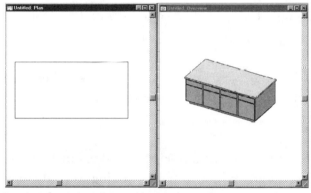

Rows brought together to form a cabinet island

Another special cabinet configuration is used for designs with inside corners, like a U or L, to allow a continuous countertop along the shape of the cabinet configuration. The easiest way to build such a shape is to put together a line of cabinets down one side, then place a corner cabinet, and finish with another line. This will result in what looks like a single, continuous piece. If the corner is away from a wall, so a corner cabinet cannot be used, the program will allow a "blind" cabinet, or even create a filler space in the inside corner, so long as the two neighboring cabinets are within nine inches. Note that a continuous top can only be stretched across an inside corner, that is, where the cabinets are facing one another across the gap. If the cabinets on either side of the corner are facing apart, they will not attach, so the top will not stretch.

Base Cabinet

The **Base Cabinet** command creates cabinets that sit on the floor, and are usually, but not always, set against walls. Fixtures like sinks and ovens can be placed in them, from the top or side depending on the fixture. Since the cabinet must be big enough to accommodate the fixture, it is a good idea to plan ahead, before carefully arranging elaborate cabinet designs. Default dimensions for base cabinets are 36 inches high, 24 inches wide and deep, and a minimum width of 9 inches and width increment of 3 inches.

Full Height Cabinet

The **Full Height Cabinet** command places full height cabinets, like those used for pantries.

Full-height cabinets are 84 inches high and 24 inches wide and deep by default. Minimum width and increments are 9 inches and 3 inches.

Wall Cabinet

The **Wall Cabinet** command produces wall cabinets, which can be positioned on a wall, or hung from the ceiling. Usually they are set above base cabinets, but they do not have to be.

Wall cabinets default to 24 inches wide, 12 inches deep, 30 inches high, and 54 inches from the floor to the bottom of the cabinet. Minimum width and increments are 9 inches and 3 inches.

Soffit

Interior **Soffit** is created in **Soffit** mode. A soffit fills in the area between a wall cabinet and the ceiling. Soffits move and resize the same as wall cabinets. The soffit default depth is one inch greater than the default depth for wall cabinets.

Shelf/Rod

The **Shelf/Rod** command produces shelving that is treated and displayed in **Plan** view much like cabinetry. This command places a single shelf only.

Shelves are 12 inches deep, 24 inches wide, and 69 1/4 inches from the floor by default. Note that there are several furniture items in the Furniture Library which feature shelving, such as bookcases. For custom shelves, try using base cabinets which contain shelves.

Fireplace

The **Fireplace** command activates a special mode for creating fireplaces. The mode is special because it creates two kinds of fireplaces. Both kinds are built-in masonry fireplaces, but those placed in walls act like doors and windows, while those placed in the middle of a room act like cabinets. The two kinds differ in the way that they are placed and moved.

All masonry fireplaces have three components: the hearth, which projects out from the rest of the fireplace, the firebox, and the surrounding walls. Dimensions and other settings for these pieces can be modified in the **Fireplace Specification** dialog box, which appears by double-clicking the fireplace (or using the **Open Item** command on the **Edit** menu). The height, width, and depth of both the fireplace and firebox can be set, as well as the depth of the hearth. The **Left** and **Right** option buttons, with **Firebox Offset**, determine how far left or right the fire box is off center within the fireplace. Masonry fireplaces, while they lack a default dialog box, do have default sizes which also act as minimums, and which are shown in the specification dialog box. Resizing below a minimum in the dialog box is not allowed. Default dimensions are 48, 48, and 31 inches for fireplace height, width, and depth, and 25, 24, and 18 inches for the firebox. The hearth depth can be set to zero. When selected, the fireplace's width, and that of the firebox, will be displayed.

You can change the color of fireplaces or apply material to them, and then view your changes in 3D. To learn more, see "Changing the Color or Material on Object Surfaces," which is the last section in this chapter.

Wall fireplaces are created by selecting the **Fireplace** command, then clicking a wall where the fireplace is to be located. If it is an exterior wall, the new fireplace will automatically face inwards. If it is an interior wall, click the side of the wall in the room into which you want the fireplace to face. Once placed, wall fireplaces can be widened by dragging the side handles or moved by dragging the center handle along the wall. Dragging the side handles inward toward the center will delete the fireplace; you can also delete a fireplace using standard delete commands. Dragging the center handle perpendicular to the wall will move it in and out. A wall fireplace can be set in so the box is flush with the wall, or pulled out so that the back is flush with the back of the wall. For example, for fireplaces on exterior walls, dragging the center handle of the fireplace out and away from the house will move the fireplace further into the wall, so that the chimney is external and runs up the outside of the structure. To increase the chimney height, click the **Selection Mode** button, and then double-click the chimney. In the **Fireplace Specification** dialog box, change the number in the box next to **Height**. You can also change the height in a **Full Camera** view—press the **Ctrl** key, then click the upper handle on the chimney and drag it upward. (Using this method, you can move the chimney through upper floors, the ceiling and the roof.)

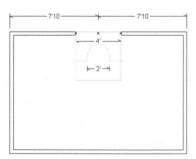

Exterior wall fireplace with chimney inside

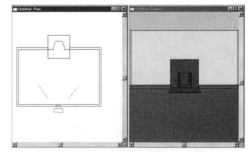

Same but with chimney outside wall

Free-standing fireplaces can be placed and edited just like cabinets— moved by dragging the center handle, resized by dragging the side and front handles, and rotated by dragging the rotate handle. Unlike wall fireplaces, they cannot be fully set into a wall, but can be placed against one (but will not attach). Also, free-standing fireplaces can be deepened by dragging the front handle. Note that most residential houses feature wall fireplaces.

A third kind of fireplace is available, but not under the **Fireplace** command. These are prefabricated fireplaces, which are listed in a number of styles and sizes in the **Fixture Library** dialog box. These are treated like fixtures because, unlike masonry fireplaces, they are not built on site, but prefabricated and then built into the structure. To choose one, click the **Fixture** tool (or use the **Fixtures** command on the **Build** menu), then work through the dialog boxes by choosing **Utility**, then **Metal Fireplaces**, the type of fireplace. When you have the item you want, click **OK**, then click your plan to place the fireplace.

Once placed in your plan, prefabricated fireplaces will display movement and rotation handles and width when selected. Drag these to move or rotate the fireplace. These fireplaces can be deleted using the **Delete** key and commands, and also can be opened. The specification dialog box will not be for a fireplace, however, but rather for a Fixture/Furniture, because prefabricated fireplaces are considered to be fixtures.

These metal fireplaces are not meant to be free-standing, but built into special wall designs. To place one of these fireplaces, it is best to first create a three-wall niche behind the wall into which the fireplace will be placed. Make sure the niche is larger than the fireplace to be installed, then use the **Fixture** command (or tool) and click the back wall of the niche to place the fireplace of your choice. This will attach the fireplace to the wall, like a cabinet, so that moving the wall will move the fireplace. Next, drag the side walls against the fireplace, then "push" it forward by dragging the back wall to which it is attached forward. This will cause the fireplace to "punch through" the wall, assuming it is a four-inch wall. If the wall is thicker, replace the wall section in front of the fireplace with a 4"-thick section using the **Break Wall** command.

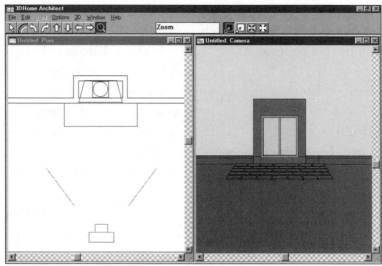

Metal fireplace boxed in by walls, placed against back wall

Remember, masonry fireplaces in walls act like openings, so they make their own space. Prefabricated fireplaces are fixtures, so cannot be placed in a wall; instead, they are basically walled into their own "room." But for the fireplace to show in the next room, a hole needs to be opened in the wall between. To project a prefab fireplace into a room, you must draw its own "room" behind the larger room.

Fixtures

The **Fixtures** command does not set the program to a mode. Instead, selecting this command will display a dialog box of labeled fixture symbols that are "item groups." Clicking any one displays the next level in that item group, continuing until the bottom level, at which point clicking the item selects the item for placement in the plan. This level will be distinguished from the other levels in the hierarchy because the items will be labeled as individual pieces instead of groups, and when you click one, it will be outlined. Selecting an item and clicking **OK** loads that item, so that when you click your plan, it is placed in the plan. Note that you can double-click the item in the dialog box to bypass the **OK** button and go directly to placing the item in the plan. When an item is loaded and ready for placement in the plan, the pointer changes to the **Fixture** pointer (a toilet) to remind you that you are placing a fixture.

The dialog box is called the **Fixture Library**. To use this library, click an item group in each dialog box to reach the next item group, as described above. For example, clicking **Bathroom Fixtures** will display a second item group, featuring **Toilets, Bathtubs, Shower Tubs, Showers,** and **Mirrors**. Clicking any of these will display another item group, this time either all toilets, or bathtubs, or showers, and so on. Clicking **OK** is only available if an item has been selected. If you decide you want to retrace your steps without exiting the library, click the **Back** button. This will return you to the previous item group. The **Active Library** box will display the fixture collection being used. (There are two collections currently available, which contain both indoor and outdoor fixtures.)

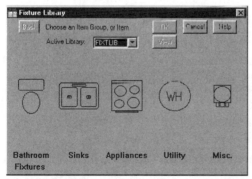

Fixture Library, top level

Selected items can be previewed in 3D by clicking the **View** button. To load the item that you are previewing for placement in the plan, click **OK**. To return to the hierarchy, click **Back**. You must go through the entire selection process for each item, and once loaded, an item must be placed immediately, or you will have to go through the hierarchy again to select the fixture. You cannot select a fixture for placement, then draw walls, and then return to the **Fixture Library** and expect that the fixture that you selected earlier will be ready for placement. You will have to go through the entire selection process again. Once you have selected a fixture, however, you can place multiple copies of the same fixture by simply clicking the plan as many times as needed.

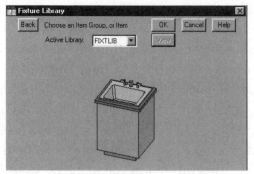

Fixture Library dialog box, preview of sink placed in cabinet

Fixtures behave differently according to whether they are free-standing or not. Some fixtures, like toilets and water heaters, even prefabricated fireplaces and stairs, can be placed anywhere in a room and so are considered free-standing. Others, like kitchen sinks and ovens, must be placed on or in a cabinet. You can discern whether a particular fixture is free-standing or not by previewing the fixture by clicking the **View** button. If the preview shows the fixture set in a cabinet, then the fixture is not free-standing, and requires that it be placed into a cabinet.

Free-standing fixtures are simple to use: just pick one, and click where it goes. When selected, the fixture's width will display, plus a center handle and a rotating one. To resize, open the **Fixture/Furniture Specification** dialog box by double-clicking the item or using the **Open** commands (you must first have enabled fixture and furniture resizing in the **Plan Setup** dialog box). The dialog box will show the item's height, width, depth, and distance to the floor, along with a preview. To change dimensions, just enter new values. If you decide you prefer the first version, click **Reset**. Some free-standing fixtures will attach themselves to walls, so that moving the wall will move the fixture.

You can change the color of free-standing fixtures or apply material to them, and then view your changes in 3D. (Fixtures that have been added to cabinets cannot be changed this way.) To learn more, see "Changing the Color or Material on Object Surfaces," which is the last section in this chapter.

Fixture/Furniture Specification ☒

Standard Toilet

Item Height	28
Width	31
Depth	28
Floor to Bottom	0

Color & Material...

Reset | to original size | OK | Cancel | Help

Fixture/Furniture Specification dialog box for a toilet

To place a fixture in a cabinet, the cabinet must first exist in the plan. If it does not, you have to place the cabinet first. The cabinet also has to be big enough to take the fixture; if it is not, a warning dialog box will display. Once placed in a cabinet, a fixture will move with the cabinet. It cannot be edited by itself. To change the fixture to another, just click the existing fixture/cabinet with the **Fixture** tool with the new fixture loaded. The new fixture will replace the current fixture in the cabinet. Since the fixture and cabinet behave like a single object in the plan, deleting will delete both the fixture and the cabinet together. You can't simply delete the fixture from the cabinet; both will be deleted, and you will need to create a new cabinet to replace the old one.

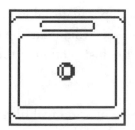 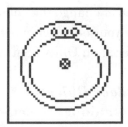

Placing a cabinet fixture into an existing cabinet fixture replaces the fixture.

Furniture

The **Furniture** command acts just like the **Fixtures** command. When selected, it opens the **Furniture Library** dialog box, organized into item groups and items. To use, click item groups until you reach actual items, click the desired one, then click **OK**, and finally click your plan to place the furniture item. Note that you can bypass the **OK** button by simply double-clicking the item. Clicking **Back** will take you back one step in the hierarchy. Clicking **View** when an item is selected will bring up a three-dimensional preview. To exit the preview and go directly to place the furniture item, click **OK**. To exit the preview while remaining in the dialog box, click **Back**. When placing furniture, the pointer turns into a chair to remind you that you are placing furniture items. By clicking again and again, you can place multiple copies of the same furniture item in the plan. The active library menu will display the furniture collection being used. (Both indoor and outdoor furniture items are available.)

Furniture acts like a free-standing fixture. It can be placed anywhere in a plan big enough to hold it, then can be moved and rotated. To change dimensions, first open the **Plan Setup** dialog box, enable fixture/furniture resizing, then open the **Fixture/Furniture Specification** dialog box by double-clicking the item or by using the **Open** commands. A dialog box will display the height, width, depth, and distance to the floor of the object, and allow you to enter changes. Clicking another entry box will update the preview to show the effects of your changes. **Reset** will change the dimensions back, and **OK** will accept the changes and close the dialog box.

You can change the color of furniture or apply material to it, and then view your changes in 3D. To learn more, see "Changing the Color or Material on Object Surfaces," which is the last section in this chapter.

Outdoor Objects
The **Outdoor Objects** command opens a hierarchical library which allows you to place three-dimensional outdoor objects in your plan. The objects include fences, bridges, ponds, and other outdoor items which are not considered furniture or fixtures. The **Outdoor Objects Library** dialog box behaves like the **Fixtures Library** dialog box, which is described earlier in this chapter.

Outdoor objects can be viewed and changed in three-dimensions. If you want to change an outdoor object, you must first click the **Selection Mode** button and then click the object. To change the object's size, click one of the red squares on its outer edge, and then drag to resize. To move the object, click the red square in the object's center, and then drag to the location you want. You can also double-click the object, and then change its properties in the **Image Specification** dialog box.

Outdoor Images

The **Outdoor Images** command allows you to place outdoor images such as plants, trees, and rocks in your plan. After you click this command, the **Select Image** dialog box opens; it contains a hierarchical list format that is similar to the **Fixture Library** dialog box described earlier in this chapter. However, unlike three-dimensional objects such as fixtures and furniture, outdoor images are bitmap representations that can only be changed in two dimensions (height and width). When you change the height, the width changes proportionally, and vice versa.

Outdoor images are visible in the **Applied Materials** view and any of the 3D views. Double-clicking the image opens the **Image Specification** dialog box, which contains a description of the image and options to change the image's transparent color. This may be desirable if part of the image appears to disintegrate due to the color of the surface behind it. When you choose black as the transparent color, every black pixel of the image becomes transparent; choosing white causes white pixels to be transparent.

Stairs

Like fireplaces, stairs come in different types. The **Stairs** command creates built-in stairs that are placed and edited somewhat like cabinets. Prefabricated stairs (circular staircases), on the other hand, are created using the **Fixtures** command. Built-in staircases have a number of special characteristics. Staircases can be placed inside or outside of a home, can be set to go up or down from the current floor, and can have several sections, even connected by landings. These features will all be covered below, and extensive examples are featured in the tutorial in chapter 3. ***3D Home Architect Deluxe*** makes building staircases easy, but still you must use some forethought when placing and sizing these complicated structures to make sure they work well when actually built.

To create a single-section staircase, select **Stairs**, then click and drag the staircase, starting where the bottom will be and dragging "up" to the top of the stairs. The program will use default settings for the dimensions of the staircase components. How high and long the staircase will be, and whether it reaches the next floor, will depend on how far you drag.

Once placed, staircases can be moved and resized in a way similar to cabinets, by dragging their center handles to move them, and dragging their side handles to change their length (and therefore, height), and width. Unlike cabinets, they will not attach to walls and cannot be rotated. Staircases, like other objects, feature a specification dialog box that can be opened by double-clicking a staircase, or selecting them and using the **Open item** command. These dialog boxes will be covered in more detail below. To delete a staircase, resize it to nothing, or use the **Delete** commands.

To make a staircase that goes "down" from the current floor rather than up, hold the **Shift** key while dragging. Although easy to do, and useful for things like decks and balconies, down staircases are trickier to plan and execute, so take care when using them. In general, you always want to create an up staircase, unless you are building a staircase off of a deck or porch.

To make a multiple-section staircase with landings between staircases, it is helpful to have a clear picture in your mind of the positioning of the stair sections. First, drag out the stair sections, leaving space for where the landing(s) should be. Make sure that the stair sections are oriented such that the arrows on the stair sections indicate the proper path up the stairs. Then click, while in **Stairs** mode, between the stair sections. A landing sufficient to link the two will be created, much like fillers are created in interior corners for cabinets. Note that you can create a staircase with a maximum of four stair sections only, which is enough to do even complicated staircases. The sections can point in different directions, as in the example below. The program will let you create very elaborate designs, in fact, probably more elaborate than you really want to build. Multiple-section staircases move as one piece, but the individual sections can be selected and edited independently.

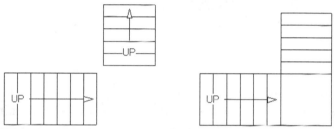

Place stair sections first, then click between sections to create a landing.

In the above example, the first stair section was dragged out, and then the second stair section was dragged out, leaving space for the landing.

Note that the beginning of the second section is near the end of the first section, and that the arrows indicate a logical path up the stairs. This is the way you want to orient the stair sections. Imagine yourself going up the stairs, and position and drag out the sections in the order that you would climb them. Once the sections are dragged out, click the space that you left for a landing and a landing will be created between the stair sections, linking the sections and creating the staircase. In addition to the L-shaped staircase shown above, here are some other common staircases:

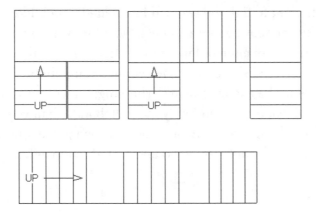

In case you are wondering, landings are really just custom treads that the program shapes and sizes automatically. Once created, however, they can be resized independently of the stair sections by clicking and dragging their handles. This allows you to extend a landing into a small balcony or mezzanine. (Try it out and see what you get in a **Camera** window.)

Although easy to take for granted, staircases are really quite elaborate constructions. In order to be effective and safe, the design must balance three factors: the height of the individual stairs (the risers), their width (tread width), and their number. When you drag out a staircase, you are really just telling the program how many steps to use. It will use default settings for the width and height of each stair, which means your staircase may not reach the next floor. This happens because the program cannot tell whether you are trying to build a single- or multiple-section staircase. Once you have set the length, indicated in the status box, the program adjusts the risers and treads to fit the length as well as possible.

To see all the factors involved in staircase building, place one, then open it to reveal its **Staircase Specification** dialog box. The first line will indicate whether the staircase reaches the next floor; if it does not, clicking **Make Reach** will automatically calculate stair dimensions and number. The top left will show how many sections and landings are in the whole staircase, how many risers are in the current section, and the height of the risers and the "best" value for the tread. (Note that building codes do not permit risers to vary by more than an eighth of an inch, so the program keeps them all the same.) On the right-hand side of the dialog box, the number of risers of a recommended height to reach the next floor are displayed. Clicking **Make Reach** will feed these values to the program, which will then "stretch" your staircase.

Stairs Specification dialog box

The **Make Reach** button is the easiest way to set up your staircases, but if you are experienced or confident enough, you can provide your own settings in the edit boxes at the bottom of the dialog box. This section of the dialog box will display which stair section you are working on, and will let you adjust the tread width and number, and length of the staircase. Of course, these settings are interdependent, so altering one will alter the others (to see the change, click another edit box). If after making changes, you change your mind, click **Revert**.

Clicking the **Style** button in the **Staircase Specification** dialog box will open a second dialog box, called **Stair Style**. Here you can check options that will determine the appearance of your staircase. **Open Underneath** removes the wall beneath a staircase. **Open Risers** actually eliminates the risers (the vertical part of a step), leaving each step lying on an open pair of stringers (the side pieces of a staircase that stretch diagonally and actually support the individual steps). **Large Stringer Base**, when checked, makes that first step a bit larger.

Railing will add two- or four-inch rails to your stairs. **Use Exterior Colors** will apply these to your staircase, useful for when you make a staircase off an outside deck.

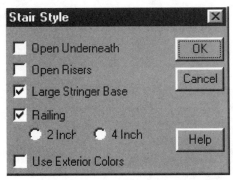

Stair Style dialog box

Although you cannot add staircases or edit them by dragging when in views other than **Plan**, the **Camera** and **Elevation** windows are invaluable for determining how your stairs look, and even how to make them. One example is drawing staircases next to walls. Being next to a wall, you can see the staircase in the **Elevation** view while editing it in **Plan** view. Even more useful, or at least fun, is to view different elevations of multiple-section staircases.

About Down Staircases

As noted above, you should always try to use "up" staircases if possible in your plan. There are certain times, though, when a "down" staircase is preferable. These are staircases that go down from a deck or porch. An example of how to create those types of stairs can be found in the comprehensive tutorial in chapter 3.

Probably the only reason that you would want to do a "down" staircase in an interior room is to see how it will look in one of the 3D windows (**Camera** or **Overview**). There is a simple, but important, step that you need to do in order to see a staircase go down to the floor below, and not appear to be fused into the floor. That step is to put the down stairs in their own little room. In essence, you want to create a stairwell for your down staircase. Here's what you do: drag out railings (you can also use standard full-height walls, but railings are more common) to define the stairwell. This is exactly like creating a room that has railings for walls. If the staircase is against a wall, you only have to drag out three railings, because the room wall proper will act as the fourth wall and thus complete the enclosure. We advocate using railings instead of regular walls because that is the way most staircases are built; a safety railing surrounds the opening in the floor.

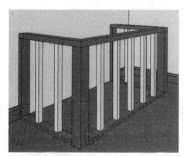

Railings used to create a stairwell against wall

The final step is to double-click the little room that you have created and select **Open Below** for the **Room Name** in the **Room Specification** dialog box. The **Open Below** room just defines the "hole" in the floor through which the down staircase passes from below. When you view from the upper floor, the staircase will be labeled Down, although it is still the Up staircase from the lower floor.

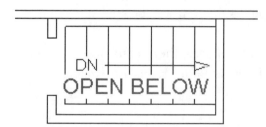

Stairwell has to be declared Open Below to show stairs coming up through the floor.

Here is the previous staircase in a Camera view.

Circular Staircases

Prefabricated, metal circular staircases are available in the **Fixtures Library**. These are treated like fixtures because unlike the staircases above, they are not built on site, but are prefabricated then simply placed in your design.

To choose one, select **Fixture** mode, then work through the dialog boxes by choosing **Utility**, then **Circular Stairs**, then select the size you want.

Once placed in your plan, prefabricated staircases will display central and rotation handles and show width when selected. Drag these handles to move or rotate the staircase. These staircases can be deleted using the **Delete** key and commands, and also can be edited using the **Fixture/Furniture Specification** dialog box. The staircase's height, width, and depth, plus a preview will be shown.

Unlike prefabricated fireplaces, there is no need to build walls around these staircases to frame them in. Everything needed is included with the staircase.

Foundation Piers

The **Foundation Piers** command is comprised of two options: **Round Pier**, and **Square Pad**. Both are really appropriate only to a foundation floor, but the program provides these commands for all floors. To use them, select the appropriate command and then click the foundation plan along the foundation outline (or along a wall) to place the pier or pad.

Round piers are a type of foundation where holes are drilled several feet into the soil with augers, and then concrete is poured into the holes. Framing above the hole extends the pier above ground level. The structure is then attached to these piers, which are often reinforced with rebar. This type of foundation is considered a friction foundation, because the load on the round piers is taken up both by the bottom of the pier, and by the side surface in contact with the soil.

Square pads are most often associated with footing foundations. In this type of foundation, a shallow but wide trench is dug into which concrete is poured, leaving a flat surface upon which the structure rests. The idea is to spread the load out over a wider surface. Square posts are used to augment this type of foundation.

The type of foundation required depends to a great degree on local soil conditions. Round piers are more expensive to construct, but they are better for areas where the soil is weak or prone to movement. The type of foundation that is most suited to your project is something that you definitely need to discuss with a licensed contractor.

Electrical

Clicking the **Electrical** command displays a submenu with commands for placing different electrical items. The first four of these commands, **110V Outlets, 220V Outlets, Lights**, and **Switches**, once selected, let you place any number of the items featured by the command in your plan, just by clicking. The item will be placed in a wall, floor, or ceiling as appropriate. Selecting an electrical item with the **Selection** tool lets you move and rotate it like a fixture, but you cannot open one, since there are no electrical specification dialog boxes. Electrical items are deleted by using the usual **Delete** commands. The **Symbol Library** dialog box is used to place other electrical items, and is organized as a hierarchical library, much like the fixtures and furniture libraries. The **Connect** command is used to create circuits between the different symbols. The **Place Outlets** command automatically places electrical symbols in your plan.

110V Outlets

The **110V Outlets** command produces 110-volt outlets wherever you click in your plan. Clicking near a wall will place the outlet in it.

220V Outlets

The **220V Outlets** command also produces outlets in a wall, but the outlets are 220 volt.

Lights

The **Lights** command enables you to place lights in your plan. Clicking near a wall will place the light in the wall, and clicking away from a wall and toward the middle of the room will place the light in the ceiling.

Switches

The **Switches** command places switches in your plan. They are allowed only in the walls.

The **Symbol Library** command works like the **Fixtures** and **Furniture** commands, in that it opens dialog boxes from which you pick symbols for various electrical items, like telephone and television jacks. As with the other libraries, this library is organized into items within item groups, creating a hierarchy of choices. The top-level item groups are **Electric Outlets, Lights & Fixtures, Switches**, and **Special Symbols**.

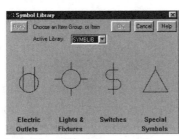

Symbol Library dialog box

The symbols in this library act like the other electrical items; the only difference is how they are placed. To obtain a special electrical symbol, select **Symbol Librar**y, then click through each item group until you find the item you want. Items, as opposed to groups, will be outlined. To place the item in your plan, click **OK** then click your plan.

The **Connect** command creates circuits between switches and other symbols. To use, first place the switches and symbols, then select the command and proceed to click and drag between objects to be connected, starting with a switch. For multiple-switch systems, start with one switch, drag to the symbols, then end with the other switches. To disconnect an item from the circuit, just click it.

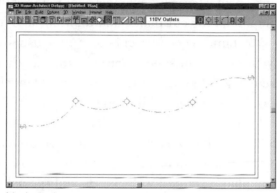

A basic circuit

The **Place Outlets** command allows you to turn over the placement of electrical symbols to the program. It is an executing command that will automatically place outlets, and some lights, according to standard practice. To use, select the command, then click a room. To employ this command most efficiently, use it after you have finished the rest of your plan, and named your rooms.

In addition to outlets being placed automatically by the **Place Outlets** command, the **PlanCheck** command of the **Options** menu will redesignate existing outlets to fit the rooms they are in, and will prompt you to add special symbols as required by standard practice, such as telephone and television jacks, fans, and smoke alarms.

Although the **Place Outlets** and **PlanCheck** commands will handle much of your electrical system design, there is still plenty for you to do in deciding where to place switches and lights, what special features to include, and how to connect them. When placing electrical symbols, use common sense and standard designs as much as possible. Custom arrangements should be carefully planned to avoid costly construction and materials, and just plain clumsy arrangements. After all, there is a reason light switches are on the wall on the opening side of doors.

Note: Electrical items do not have representation in any of the 3D views.

Two things to think about when placing electrical items is that they are not structurally important to your plans, and their use and location is largely prescribed by building code regulations. It is usually best to wait until the rest of your plan is finished before placing electrical items. Because their use is regulated, the program automates much of the placement process. For instance, while you place plain 110-volt outlets, the program will determine, based on location within rooms and circuits, whether the outlet should be waterproof (exterior), or ground-fault interrupt (bathroom), or more than one-way. Likewise, the program uses standard heights to place symbols: wall outlets and special symbols are 12 inches from the floor, wall switches are 48 inches, wall lights are 72 inches, and ceiling fans and lights are the ceiling height. Outlets above a cabinet are six inches up, unless the cabinet contains a sink, in which case the outlet is placed behind the cabinet. The difference may not be immediately apparent because only waterproof and interrupt outlets are labeled in the plan (as WP and GFI, respectively), and the program may not update the symbols until the **PlanCheck** command is used.

Because their placement is largely automatic, electrical symbols will display only in **Plan** and **Materials** views, and no specification dialog box is provided for them. A description of each is provided in the Materials list, however.

Roof

The **Roofs** command displays a submenu with commands for **Roof Section at, Build Roof,** and **Delete Roof**. The **Roof Section at** tool allows you to click a wall with the pointer, and change its properties via the **Roof Section at Wall** dialog box. You can also click a door or window and edit the **Roof over Door/Window** dialog box with this tool.

The upper section of the **Roof Section at Wall** dialog box allows you to declare the type of roof section that the wall will support. The lower section allows you to determine the roof section's pitch as well as where a second pitch begins (for a gambrel roof, for example).

Roof Section at Wall dialog box

Full Gable wall

If you wish to place a gable above the wall, the **Full Gable wall** check box must be selected. The wall section will be extruded up into the gable. If this check box is left clear, a hip is placed above the wall. This should be used where you wish a full gable to be placed. If you wish a half gable, for example at the side of a sloping roof section whose top hits a higher wall, select the **High Shed/Gable wall** check box. If two full gable walls meet at a corner, a valley is produced. This is necessary in order to obtain full gables on either side.

High Shed/Gable wall

Select this check box if a sloping roof section is not to rise from this wall. For example, for a shed roof, the wall under the high side of the roof as well as the half gable walls to either side of it would have this box checked. When you need a gable and are in doubt as to which type (full or this normal type) to use, you will usually want to use this type.

Knee wall

A knee wall is a wall shortened by being cut off by the underside of the roof. Normally, Automatic Roof Designer produces roof sections sufficiently high that all walls underneath can end at the room's ceiling height, or higher if **Ceiling over this room** is not checked in the **Room Specification** dialog box. Selecting **Knee wall** tells the roof designer that it need not allow for the height of the knee wall, but can determine the roof structure from the other walls, then cut off the knee wall as needed to fit under the roof. Knee walls are often exterior walls, but they must be inset from walls below, since the outer wall below will determine the sloping roof section that rises to cover the knee wall.

Extend slope downward

This check box allows Automatic Roof Designer to ignore the height of this wall in determining the roof section over it. The roof section is instead determined by other walls and just extends down over this wall.

This is like the knee wall except that the roof section that covers a knee wall is usually determined by a parallel wall from the story below, which is further out from the center of the building, whereas the roof section covering an Extend Slope Downward wall is usually determined by a parallel wall on the same floor that is nearer to the center of the building.

The two connecting walls to the Extend Slope Downward wall must be gables. This function is ideal if you wish to bring a roof section out over a small jog or alcove in an outer wall so that the roof line remains the same down the run of a wall.

Pitch

The default value for pitch is set in the **Roof Section at Wall** dialog box. Pitch is entered in the standard X **in 12** measure, which represents rise to run (X" rise to 12" run). You may enter a fractional pitch in the form of 3 1/2 or 3.5. The smallest pitch that may be entered is 1/2 **in 12**, and the largest 48 **in 12**. If there are two pitches in the roof section above this wall, such as in a gambrel roof, this box controls the first, or lower pitch.

2nd Pitch

Select this box if you wish a second pitch on the roof section above this wall. The second pitch is the upper pitch on the roof section, as in the higher portion of a gambrel roof. The **Starts at** box indicates the height above the floor at which the **2nd Pitch** begins.

Roof over Door/Window allows you to place a gable over the object. To later remove the gable, simply click the object again with the **Roof Section at** tool, and remove the check. When the roof is rebuilt, the gable will disappear.

Build Roof displays Automatic Roof Designer, which will design your roof based on the values you have provided. (See chapter 4, "Advanced Roofing Techniques" for more information on these dialog boxes.) **Delete Roof** removes the current roof from your plan, but leaves any settings you have made intact. This may be helpful when editing your plan.

To change the color of the roof or apply material to it, click the **Color** button to open the **Assign Colors** dialog box. For further steps in this procedure, see "Changing the Color or Material on Object Surfaces," which is the last section in this chapter.

Dimension Lines

The **Dimension Lines** command displays a submenu with two commands for creating dimension lines in a plan. The first of these, **Dimension**, will set the program to a mode and let you draw manual dimension lines by clicking and dragging them like walls. The second command, **Exterior Dimen**, will also create dimension lines, but will do so automatically. These will be drawn only around the exterior of your plan.

Dimension line between walls

Dimension lines on a bow window

Dimension lines are treated like objects in **3D Home Architect Deluxe**, but do not have any physical existence, so they can be created and moved mostly like walls. They will display only in **Plan** view. Their purpose is to locate walls and openings in walls by showing how far one wall is from another, or how far an opening is down a wall. (Note that temporary dimension lines will display for specific, selected objects, like openings, fixtures, and furniture, in all views in which the objects can be selected.)

Dimension lines are always drawn perpendicular to the walls they are locating. Like walls, dimension lines can be drawn at any angle, in 15-degree increments. As for openings in walls, dimension lines can be parallel to these and still locate them. To do so, a line is extended to the center of the opening from the dimension line. This is called "reaching." The line is called a "mark." The same dimension line may locate several walls and openings, with marks extending to each item. In this case, the portion of the entire dimension line between marks is called a "section."

The numbers in a dimension line show length in feet, inches, and eighths of an inch. A 12-foot distance would be shown as **12'**, 12 feet 4 inches as **12'4**, and 12 feet 4 1/2 inches as **12'4"4** (four eighths equaling a half inch). The size of the numbers themselves is fixed, to make sure they can always be read.

Unlike other objects, dimension lines have no specification dialog box for controlling their appearance. Instead, the **Dimension Setup** command in the **Options** menu opens a dialog box for setting defaults for your entire plan.

Manual Dimensions

The **Dimension** command is used when you wish to create manual dimension lines. To do so, select the command, then click and drag in your plan, starting at a wall and dragging a line perpendicular to it to a facing wall. You can also drag a line to or from an opening, by starting or ending your drag close enough to the center of it. You can even drag a line between two openings. The **No Locate** wall attribute prevents dimension lines from locating a wall in most cases. Automatic dimension lines do not locate a wall with this attribute set. A manually drawn dimension line can locate such a wall, but only if it also locates no more than one normal wall. If it locates two or more normal walls, any

No Locate walls are ignored. A dimension line that extends past several interior walls or openings will locate all of them by using a mark for each item, and so creating a series of sections.

Once placed, dimension lines can be selected and moved like walls. They will display three handles and can be moved sideways by dragging the center one, and resized by dragging the ends in and out. You will notice that actually dragging an end handle is difficult because it cannot be selected if a wall is present. This is because the ends will move automatically as the items they locate move.

Although dimension lines expand and contract automatically, they will not move sideways to accommodate changes. For this reason, it is a good idea to place them only after you have arranged your walls and openings. Another reason to wait is the effect that diagonal walls can have. Although dimension lines and numbers will automatically adjust to changes, diagonal walls can cause slight errors in measurement. If you have had to make changes after placing dimensions for diagonal walls, select each possibly affected line. This will cause the lines to update.

While all the sections of a dimension line are treated as one when creating and editing them, individual sections can later be deleted, by simply drawing over them. (As with walls, the whole line can be deleted this way also.) Adjacent sections will not be affected.

Exterior Dimensions
When selected, the **Exterior Dimen** command immediately creates a comprehensive set of exterior dimension lines all around your plan. These lines will locate all exterior walls and openings, interior walls (as long as they are not non-locating), like beams, and end on an exterior wall. Of course, exterior dimensions can be placed only if your plan has an exterior, and for this the plan must be completely enclosed in walls.

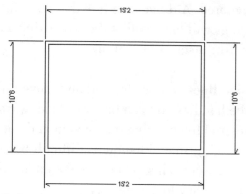

Basic enclosure with exterior dimension lines

Executing this command will always create at least four lines, one for locating the exterior walls of each side of a plan. Up to three separate dimension lines can be created, however. The first, closest to the plan, locates openings and interior walls; the second, just interior walls; and the third, just exterior walls.

Once created, automatic dimension lines are treated just like manual ones, but the program does remember which is which. Each time you execute the **Exterior Dimen** command, all the automatic dimensions will be deleted and redrawn. As with manual lines, it is a good idea to wait to position automatic lines until after you have finished placing walls and openings. Still, if changes occur, selecting this command should correct everything. (One thing that will not update is how your lines affect the legibility of your plans. To neaten things up, you will often need to move dimension lines around, and you will need to do this each time you refresh your automatic lines.)

Ground Covering
The **Ground Covering** command allows you to apply a covering such as grass, cement, gravel, or stone to a section of the ground outside your plan. The first step to adding ground covering is building the lot your plan resides on. On the **Build** menu, click **Build/Move Lot**; this places a 50'x100' lot. To see the boundaries of the lot, click the **Zoom Mode** button, and then click the **Zoom Out** tool. Click the **Zoom In** tool

when you are finished to reset the view.

To add a ground covering, go to the **Plan** window if you're not already there. On the **Options** menu, click **Show Items**, and then click **Beam/Soffit** if it's not already selected. Next, on the **Build** menu, click **Ground covering**. In your plan, click the desired location to add the ground covering. It has a default size of 3'x3'; at this point, you may want to move or resize it. If so, click the **Selection Mode** button, and then click the ground covering. To move it, click the center red square, and then drag to the location you want. To resize the ground covering, click one of the red handles on the boundary of the ground covering, and then drag to resize.

You can also change the size and other properties of the ground covering in the **Ground Cover Size** dialog box. With the **Selection Mode** button selected, double-click the ground covering, and then make the changes you want in the dialog box. This is also where you determine the material that you want to apply to the ground covering. Click **Color**, then **Material**, and then **Choose Material**. In the **Select Image** dialog box, click the category of material you want (typical ground coverings are located under **grnd_cvr**), then click a subcategory, and then click the actual material you want. Click **OK** to choose that material. (You can also double-click the material to choose it.) Click **OK** two more times to exit the dialog boxes and apply the material to the ground covering.

To view the ground covering with applied material, click the **View Mode** button. Click and drag to create a **Camera** view that includes the ground covering. (Adjust the view after creating, if necessary.) On the **3D** menu, click **Setup Applied Materials View**. In the **Applied Materials View Setup** dialog box, under **Color Model**, click **Color** if it is not already selected, and then click **OK**. On the **3D** menu, click **Applied Materials View**.

Keep in mind that the **Applied Materials** view is like a snapshot, except for resizing its window, you cannot change its view in any way once it is generated. Since the **Applied Materials** view is based on the **Camera** view you create, you may need to make several adjustments to the **Camera** view to get the exact **Applied Materials** view you want.

Text

The **Text** command places the program in text entry mode, meaning that you can click anywhere in your plan and a text dialog box will appear in which you enter text to create labels and comments for your plan. To create a label, click the **Text** button, then click the area of your plan where you want the top center of the text object to be. The **Edit Text** dialog box will appear, in which you type your text.

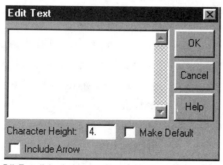

Edit Text dialog box

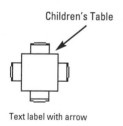

Children's Table

Text label with arrow

You can type normally, but do not use hard returns. (You can also press **Ctrl+Enter** to go to the next line.) Besides entering text, you can also determine its size with the **Character Height** edit box, and make this size the default by clicking the **Make Default** check box. Selecting the **Include Arrow** check box will attach an arrow to your text object, which you can then drag to the object to be labeled. To place the text object in your plan, click **OK**. The arrow can be repositioned by clicking it and dragging the handles.

Text in *3D Home Architect Deluxe* is treated like an object: each entry can be moved, resized, and deleted like other objects. To do so, just select the text object with the **Selection** tool. Three handles will appear, the center for moving the label, the sides for changing the line length. To change the size of the text, you must use the **Edit Text** dialog box, which can be reopened by double-clicking on the object or using the **Open** commands.

Note that **Character Height** is expressed in inches. This means that unlike dimension numbers, text will often be illegible on screen because it will be too small to read. The important thing is that it be legible when printed. Usually, five plan inches at quarter scale (a quarter of an inch equals one foot) will work well. For other scales, you will have to experiment. Arrows can have one bend, and will always join to the associated label. Arrows cannot be edited separately from their text. Even though treated like objects, labels can only be seen in **Plan** view, and while they have size, in that they are displayed in scale, they do not occupy space, so they can be placed on top of other objects. As with electrical symbols, it is best to place labels only when your plan is finished.

Also, like electrical symbols, text can be created automatically. One way to do this is to select a room label from the **Room Specification** dialog box, which appears when you open a room. Another way is to run PlanCheck, which will determine the names and functions of rooms based on contents and configuration, and then place labels automatically. In either case, the labels can be edited.

Build/Move Lot

With the **Build/Move Lot** command, you add boundary lines to the property your plan is on, and then move those boundary lines if desired.

To add a lot, on the **Build** menu, click **Build/Move Lot**. To view the boundary lines of the lot, click the **Zoom Mode** button, and then click the **Zoom Out** tool until the lines become visible.

To change the size of the lot, on the **Build** menu, click **Build/Move Lot** again. Click one of the boundary lines, and then click and drag one of the red handles on a boundary line while in **Build/Move Lot** mode, to resize the lot, or click and drag the centered red square to move the lot. You can also double-click a boundary line while in **Build/Move Lot** mode, and then change one or more of the numbers in the **Lot Size** and **Height** dialog boxes.

About Rooms

Four-wall enclosure defined as a bedroom

Rooms are not listed on the **Build** menu, and there is no tool you can use to create them. This is because they are not really objects, but instead collections of objects, something like your whole plan. In fact, you can think of rooms almost as if they were plans within plans, because what a floor plan does is define a space, by surrounding it with walls so that you can tell what is inside and what is out, and that is exactly what rooms do. You define a room as you do a house, by enclosing it in walls. Once so enclosed, the room can be considered apart from the rest of the rooms, and treated as such. This is why rooms are so important in *3D Home Architect Deluxe*. They let you divide your plan into separate areas, and let you treat each area separately, so what you do in one area does not affect the other areas.

To create a room in your plan, wall off an area so that it is completely separate from the rest of the plan. Once walled in, the program will recognize it as a room without you doing anything. Clicking within a room (but not any of its objects) will cause it to be outlined, which is one way of determining whether you have a room or not. Another way is to run PlanCheck. *3D Home Architect Deluxe* uses room definitions, based on the contents of rooms and names you give them, to determine which rooms are which, and what should be in each. Based on its understanding of what rooms should contain, the program will assign names to rooms it understands, and will ask you to define the rest.

This study's left wall is an Invisible wall.

For example, if you create a two-room plan, and one room has a kitchen sink, when you run PlanCheck the program will automatically label the room with the sink Kitchen and will prompt you to name the other room. PlanCheck will also use the names you give to rooms to determine what they should have. For instance a good-sized room without windows will cause PlanCheck to advise you to add windows, unless you have named the room Closet.

Archways are created
using wide doorways.

To create a room, all you have to do is subdivide your plan with walls of any type: standard walls, railings, beams, or invisible walls. Of course, you need to be able to get into your room, so if the wall is a standard wall or railing, you need to place a door in it. Beams and invisible walls will define a room, but will not close it off in any way, leaving the room open, which is pretty common, especially where a sense of spaciousness is important. (Many dining rooms, for example, are not completely enclosed by walls). Another method is to create a real wall but place a large doorway in it, which creates a kind of arch to divide the rooms.

Delete Items
dialog box

A room cannot be deleted in the sense that a piece of furniture can be. The contents of a room, though, can be deleted using the **Delete Items** command. On the **Edit** menu, click **Delete Items**. Under **Delete**, click one or more categories of items you want to delete, and then in your plan, click the room(s) containing the items. Click **Done** to exit the **Delete Items** dialog box.

Another way to affect a room is to open its **Room Specification** dialog box. To do so, click a room, and then on the **Edit** menu, click **Open Item**. You can also open the dialog by double-clicking the room. The dialog box features a list box, Room Name, and there are check boxes for enabling the ceiling and roof displays. You can change the ceiling height and the width of various moulding pieces; the **Color** button gives you access to color and material choices for walls, floors and moulding on a room-by-room or floor-by-floor basis, and ceilings on a floor-by-floor basis. (To learn more about colors and materials, see "Changing the Color or Material on Object Surfaces," which is the last section in this chapter.)

![Room Specification dialog box showing fields for Room Name, Floor Height 0 (D), Ceiling Height 96 (D), Color and Floor Defaults buttons, checkboxes for Ceiling over this room and Roof over this room, and moulding settings: Crown Mould. Width 0 (D) Height 96 (D), Chair Rail Width 0 (D) Height 36 (D), Base Mould. Width 5 1/2 (D), with Ok, Cancel, Help buttons]

Room Specification dialog box

Base, chair rail, and
crown mouldings

Room Name is limited to those listed. It tells the program what kind of
room the space is, and therefore what it should have. Most of the names,
like Living, are obvious. One is not: **Open Below**. This is a standard
name for an opening in the floor, which is used to leave a hole in the
floor for down staircases, and the like. The **Ceiling over** and **Roof
over** check boxes allow you to determine if a certain room will have a
flat ceiling or a vaulted ceiling, or no roof at all. If both boxes are
checked, the room will have a roof with a flat ceiling. If the ceiling box
is not checked, the room will have a roof with a vaulted ceiling. If
neither box is checked, the room will not have a roof or ceiling. You
cannot check only the ceiling box, you must have a roof in order to have
a ceiling. **Floor Height** specifies the ground level of the floor. This is
useful in designing split-level homes. **Floor Height** defaults to 0, but
you can specify a negative number, and cause the floor to be lower in
one room than another. When you set this value, the **Ceiling Height**
value automatically updates to keep the ceiling level across the plan. If
you want the ceiling to be 96", but the floor to begin at -36", you will
also need to reset the ceiling height to 96". You can use stairs to join the
two different levels. **Ceiling Height** controls the height of your walls in
the room. **Base Mould. Width** sets the width of the moulding around
the floor, and **Chair Rail** and **Crown Mould.** set the width and the
distance top to bottom and floor to bottom, of strips of moulding that run
around the walls and the wall/ceiling junction, respectively.

To set defaults for ceiling heights, mouldings, colors and materials on the current floor, click **Floor Defaults**. The default dimensions are 96" (8') for ceilings, with a base moulding of 5 1/2". Chair rails and crown mouldings will not display as long they have the default setting of 0. As with other defaults, changing these in this dialog box will only affect your current plan; to change the program defaults, change and save the settings in the PROFILE.PL1 plan.

Room names and sizes can be displayed automatically depending on the **Show Items** dialog box (accessed from the **Options** menu) settings. Note that the names will be only those assigned in the dialog box; simple text labels will be ignored. Rooms affect and are affected by several other commands, and this is noted in the discussion of each such command. A last consideration is that room information will not always update automatically. To make sure all room information is up to date, run PlanCheck.

Options Menu

Options is the menu used in *3D Home Architect Deluxe* to determine how your plans will look and how they will be put together. Most of the commands in this menu open dialog boxes in which you make choices about which objects will display, and how they will act in your plan while you are drawing.

Most of the dialog boxes will feature some default values. Remember that if you want to change these for only one plan, you can make the changes in that plan alone, but if you want the changes to affect all of the plans you draw later, you should make the changes to the PROFILE.PL1 plan that contains the program's defaults.

Show Items

The **Show Items** command opens a dialog box containing options that determine which objects will display in your plan. Objects can still be drawn and will remain in the plan even if their display is turned off; they just will not be visible. All objects, regardless of whether or not they are

Show Items
dialog box

being displayed, will be saved to files and included in the Materials list, but only those being displayed will be included in **DXF** and **WMF** files created using the **Export** command on the **File** menu, or printed using the **Print** or **Print Image** command on the **File** menu.

Most of the options in this dialog box are obvious, but some are less so. For instance, **Opening Size** refers to the width of doors and windows. When selected, a figure will appear in each opening, giving its width in feet and inches. The exact format of the number will depend on settings in the **Dimensions Setup** dialog box.

The two check boxes under **Room Labels, Area** and **Size**, determine what numbers are attached to room labels. Checking the first will cause the area in square feet to be displayed, while the second will display the room's overall width and length.

The **Modules** check box, under the **Cabinets** option, shows the individual cabinet modules of a cabinet structure by drawing lines between them. You can also see the separate cabinets by just selecting them. The **Modules** option does not affect the editing of cabinets, just the display.

Plan View Colors
dialog box

Notice that walls cannot be hidden, but beams and walls defined as "invisible" in their **Wall Specification** dialog boxes can be. If their display is not turned off, these special walls will display with dashed lines.

Plan View Colors
The **Plan View Colors** command opens the **Plan View Colors** dialog box, which controls the colors used to make the different objects in **Plan** view stand out. These are not the colors the objects will be in 3D views; they are just used in **Plan** view to make objects

easier to see. While you can change all these colors, it is a good idea to keep your scheme simple, to avoid a cluttered and confusing display. With this in mind, the dialog box defaults use black for all structural objects, muted colors for labels and furniture, fixtures, and cabinets, and vivid red for electrical items.

PlanCheck

The **PlanCheck** command invokes a process that automatically checks your plan for compliance with standard building practices by going through every room and determining whether there are adequate windows, doors, electrical systems, and so on. When the analysis is complete, the **PlanCheck** dialog box opens displaying the total number of questionable items, the number of the current item, and a message area explaining it. Clicking the **Hold** button will exit the dialog box and return you to the plan, so that you can fix the problem (it's a good idea to have the whole plan visible on screen). After fixing the problem, if you select the **PlanCheck** command again, the **PlanCheck** dialog box will reappear with the next problem in the list displayed. If you want to skip over a problem that PlanCheck reports, click the **Next** button. Finally, if you want to exit PlanCheck, click **Done**. How you address the problems that PlanCheck finds is up to you: you can either review all of the problems and then fix them at the same time, or place PlanCheck on hold while you fix each problem, working your way through the list one at a time.

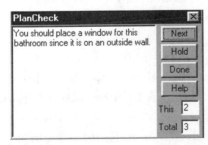

PlanCheck dialog box

In addition to highlighting questionable areas in your plan, PlanCheck will also fix some things automatically. Rooms without names will be assigned them if the program can ascertain what they are. For example, if an unnamed room has a toilet in it, PlanCheck will label the room Bathroom. (You can assign names yourself using the entry box in the **Room Specification** dialog box, opened by double-clicking a room or using the **Open** command. Room names are important for PlanCheck because it looks for different things in different rooms. For example, a small room labeled Closet will not need windows, but a bedroom will.) Cabinets that have been detached from walls during editing will be reattached, and any doorways that have been changed from exterior to interior will have their exterior thresholds removed.

Many of the messages in PlanCheck are just suggestions: you do not have to do everything PlanCheck says you should. Still, you should be sure you understand the question and know that what you are doing makes sense. For example, PlanCheck may suggest that the inside door to your garage is too narrow. You may decide to leave it as is to accommodate your kitchen design, but you should realize that too narrow a door could be a nuisance when carrying groceries and laundry back and forth from your car.

Keep in mind that this is not a legal or adequate check of your plans. Just because the plan "passes" PlanCheck does not mean it will pass an official inspection, qualify for a building permit, or be buildable. Be sure to consult local builders and officials before you begin designing, and throughout design and construction. Find out from people who know what is required and what works best in your area.

Materials

The **Materials** command opens a submenu featuring three commands for building a Materials list: **Build All Floors, Build from Area,** and **Build from Room.** Selecting any of these will cause the program to open a Materials list for the chosen area. **Build All Floors** creates a Materials list for the whole floor plan. **Build from Area** will prompt you to drag out a box on the plan, and a Materials list will be created for all objects fully enclosed within the box. **Build from Room** creates a Materials list for a room that you have selected by clicking the room before invoking the command.

The Materials list is a spreadsheet listing each kind of material item needed to build your plan. You enter your own cost in the price column, then a cost for that item will automatically appear in the **Tot. Cost** column.

Materials list

When a Materials list is opened, you will be able to export its contents using the **TXT** command in the **Export** submenu on the **File** menu. Remember that all objects in the selected area, whether displayed or not, will be included in the Materials list. Also note that electrical symbols will be explicitly described here, so you can check the exact characteristics of outlets and switches.

How extensive is the Materials list that *3D Home Architect Deluxe* generates? It is actually quite thorough in listing major components. Here is a basic list of what is contained in the Materials list:

- Cabinets, fixtures, and furniture objects.

- Electrical fixtures, outlets, and switches. Electrical wiring is not included.

- Wall framing with studs at 16" intervals, and double plating on the top of the frames. Also, square footage of wall board required. Decks are constructed with 2x6" redwood decking planks unless another material is selected.

- Flooring is constructed with 2x10" joists set at 16" intervals.

- Roofing materials including roof sheathing, rafters, gable fascia, eave fascia, and gutters.

- For foundations, the Materials spreadsheet lists cubic yards of cement needed for the foundation wall and concrete footing. Drilled pier holes and concrete support posts are also listed.

- Carpeting and other flooring materials are as defined in the **Room Specification** dialog box for a particular room.

- Interior wall material as defined in the **Room Specification** dialog box for a particular room.

- Exterior wall material as defined in the **Assign Colors** dialog box, which opens when you double-click just outside an exterior wall.

- Roof materials as defined in the **Build Roof** dialog box.

- Ground covering in square footage.

- Landscaping items from the Outdoor Image Library.

What is *not* included are the materials needed to connect all these components together, such as nails, staples, etc., and of course, the labor required to put it all together.

Keep in mind that the Materials list calculates the exact amount of materials needed. Especially for walls and floors, you need to "budget to fudge it." You always need a little bit more material than is theoretically required. You should adjust the figures for base materials (like studs, joists, wall board, carpet, etc.) upward by 10%. If the Materials list says you need 1000 square feet of wall board, budget for 1100. You are not bound to use the materials listed—you can make substitutions in the **Quantity, Unit,** and **Price** columns. If you wanted to use 2x12" joists instead of 2x10" joists, you can specify this change in the appropriate box in the **Comment** column, instead of the **Size** column. The idea here is to get a list of materials that you can take to your local supplier and get an estimate of how much the materials alone are going to cost you.

Finally, the Materials list only lists materials, not the hours of labor required to make your plan come true. The cost of quality labor can exceed the materials costs for many aspects of building. If you plan to do the work yourself, know beforehand what you are getting into. Likewise, if you are going to have others do the work, make sure to include those labor costs in your budget.

Disclaimer: Brøderbund Software makes no guarantees regarding the completeness of the **Material** list, since additional materials may be required for your plan.

Plan Setup

The **Plan Setup** command opens the **Plan Setup** dialog box, which contains settings that control how the program works for your plan file. Four check boxes at the top enable the program **Undo** command, resizing of furniture and fixtures by dragging their handles, setting whether the boundaries of windows and doors are the trim or the frame, and restricting of the camera to a room. Remember that the **Undo** command, found on the **Edit** menu, can reverse only the very last operation, and that even when disabled, you can still use the command to undo the last **Move Area**, **Delete Items**, or **Reverse Plan** command. By default **Fixture/Furniture resize enable** is selected. This causes fixtures and furniture to display with side handles, allowing you to resize them like cabinets. Clearing this option causes fixtures and furniture to display with only a center handle for moving and a rotation handle for turning. Note that any such resizing, though, will not be reflected in the Materials list. This is because the Materials list refers to items by their label, not by their physical dimensions. Once you start resizing objects, the correlation between the object label and its actual physical dimensions are no longer accurate.

Plan Setup dialog box

Casing is the trim that surrounds a door or window. When you resize a door or window, the sides of these openings are kept away from an intersecting wall by the width of the trim or casing. There may be times when you want the casing to be ignored so that you can move or resize a door or window flush against an intersecting wall. When this is the case, select **Ignore casing for doors, windows**.

The **Restrict Camera to Room** check box allows you to restrict camera view to one room only. This way you no longer have to wait while the system sorts and redraws portions of your model that you do not need for a particular view.

The edit box for **Unconnected wall min. length** simply sets the length of the smallest wall you can draw. The default is 18 inches, which keeps you from drawing little stubs by accident. The **Inches scrolled by arrow key** setting affects how far your plan will scroll in its window when you press an arrow key. The default is 12 inches.

Dimensions Setup

The **Dimension Setup** command opens a dialog box which affects how dimensions are displayed. The **Dimensions Setup** dialog box contains three check boxes that determine how dimension line numbers look: the first places numbers above, rather than on, dimension lines; the second allows eighth-inch fractions to display rather than being rounded off, and the third allows dimension lines to locate doors and windows along a wall.

Dimensions Setup dialog box

The **Interior Wall** option buttons determine whether walls are measured from their centers, which is the default, or from their outer surfaces. (Exterior walls are always measured from their outer surfaces.)

Number Height determines how big dimensions will display, in scale inches. Unlike text, dimensions will display at this size at any magnification level, to make sure you can read them.

The last options determine the minimum movement for walls and openings snapping to another wall, or to a standard, even opening size. With a default 1-inch snap, walls will never be resized less than an inch, while openings will not resize less than an inch on each side, which will keep the opening centered and to a standard, 2-inch increment. Selecting **Unrestricted** will allow a snap of any length, even fractions of an inch.

Reverse Plan
Reverse Plan is a simple executing command that flips your plan over left to right, so what was on one side is now on the other. Top and bottom are unaffected. This change will be reflected when you save the plan.

3D Menu

The **3D** menu commands open different views of your plan and allow you to make changes within those views. You can open several views in the same plan at once, and switch back and forth by either clicking the view you want active, or entering **Ctrl+Tab** to cycle through the views.

You can even display multiple views of the same kind. The commands that open new views, **Plan Camera, Full Camera, Plan Overview, Full Overview, Wall Elevation,** and **Cross Section**, must all be selected with the **Plan** view active. Other commands in the menu are available only for the appropriate views.

Note that when 3D views are created, the program calculates the floor and ceiling areas, which results in the creation of an "attic."

Plan Camera tool

Plan Camera

The **Plan Camera** command allows you to locate a "camera" in your two-dimensional plan and point it at the view you want by simply clicking with the camera pointer where you want the camera and dragging a line of sight in the direction you want to look. (The lines angling out from the camera show how far left and right you will be able to see.) After you release the mouse button, a **Camera** view opens, showing a three-dimensional display of the view you selected.

Camera object in the
Plan Window

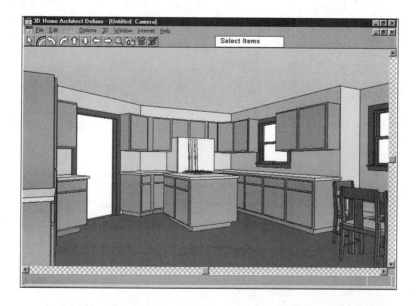

Once the **Camera** view has opened, besides a three-dimensional color display of your plan, you will see that the toolbar has changed. Instead of the usual commands, it will now feature the **Selection, Adjust**

Color, **Zoom Window**, **Applied Materials**, and **Walkthrough** tools, plus six arrows. The **Selection** and **Zoom Window** commands work as usual, and **Adjust Color** is covered below.

Toolbar in Camera view

The six arrows are camera movement tools. Clicking these arrows changes the position and/or horizontal line of sight (or angle) of the camera, allowing you to alter your perspective. The first two tools turn the camera left and right, changing its angle without changing its position (also called panning). The next two tools move the camera forward and back, changing the camera position but keeping the same angle (dollying in or out). The last two tools move the camera position left and right while keeping it pointed straight ahead (tracking left and tracking right).

The horizontal scrollbar in the **Camera** view lets you see that part of the view beyond the bounds of the computer monitor display. If, using the arrows and sliders, you move too far to one side, the image begins to go blank. This just means you have gone beyond the frame created when you first positioned the camera and its line of sight. To get a complete view, just reposition the camera again using the **Plan Camera** command.

Camera Setup	This Camera	Default
Inches each move	12 (D)	12
Degrees each rotate	10 (D)	10
Height above 1st floor	60 (D)	60
Clip Surfaces within	24 (D)	24
Remove Wall within	48 (D)	48
☑ unless opening		
OK Cancel		Help

Camera Setup dialog box

Notice that when you place a camera in your plan, it displays like a fixture rather than a pointer. Like a fixture, it will have two handles, with which you can move and rotate it. Double-clicking a camera or using **Open** commands on a camera opens a **Camera Setup** dialog box, where you can set how far the camera moves and rotates, and how high it is above the floor.

The **Clip Surfaces within** and **Remove Wall within** options determine whether object surfaces and walls within the set distances will show in the **Camera** view. The defaults are 24 and 48 inches, which ensure a relatively unobscured view.

Unlike other specification dialog boxes, all the defaults for this one are shown in the dialog box itself. Changing numbers in the first column will affect only the current camera, while changing the defaults will affect every subsequent camera placed in this plan. To change the program defaults so that cameras in all plans are affected, use the PROFILE.PL1 plan.

The **Applied Materials** view generates a version of the existing **Camera** view in which surfaces are rendered with their actual materials applied to them. The **Walkthrough** tool is available through two buttons; the first starts recording a walkthrough, and the second allows you to stop the recording when you're done.

Full Camera

The **Full Camera** command gives another three-dimensional camera view of your plan, showing you how it will look when finished. Besides providing a more realistic view of your home, **Full Camera** view also shows a perspective view of an entire multistory model, including the roof, when the camera is positioned outside.

Plan Overview

The **Plan Overview** command opens a three-dimensional, bird's-eye view of the currently active floor plan. Selecting the command displays the overview immediately.

Direction tool in
Plan Overview view

The toolbar in the **Plan Overview** view is like that in the **Camera** view, except that, instead of arrows, it has a single **Direction** tool which lets you determine from what angle you can view your plan. That tool is covered below. The scroll bars in the **Plan Overview** view allow you to view that portion of the overview which is beyond the bounds of the monitor screen.

Full Overview

The **Full Overview** command opens a three-dimensional, bird's-eye view of the entire plan, including multiple level designs with roofs. This makes it ideal for determining how your whole plan is coming along, especially since the view angle can be rotated all around the plan. While you can edit objects in this view too, the angles usually make it less easy than in other views.

View Angle

The **View Angle** command allows you to control the overview by opening the **View Angle** dialog box. This dialog box contains three slider bars: one for circling the camera around the house vertically, one for moving the camera toward and away from the house, and one for circling the camera around the house horizontally. The camera always remains pointed at your house, because you are changing its position and angle, not just angle.

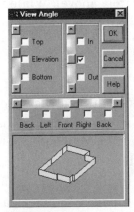

View Angle dialog box

The vertical position can be changed by either moving the slider or checking one of three options, **Top, Elevation,** and **Bottom,** which will move the camera right above, beside, or below, the house. For moving in and out, the options are **In** and **Out,** plus a check box in the middle for restoring the initial vertical position. The slider controlling horizontal position has option boxes, showing how far in front, behind, left, or right the camera is. To make it easier to see how all three settings are working together before actually changing the overview, the dialog box includes a preview window.

Wall Elevation

The **Wall Elevation** command opens to a two-dimensional view of a selected wall. To open an elevation, just select the command and click and drag toward the wall you want to see. As with the other views, the **Selection, Zoom,** and **Adjust Color** tools are included in the toolbar for the **Elevation** view. Because elevation shows only width and height, no view controls are featured other than the **Zoom** command and horizontal and vertical window scroll bars. Although you cannot add objects in this view or change walls (as in any view other than **Plan**), you can change objects like doors, windows, cabinets, and furntiure.

The **Elevation** view is used to show the exact vertical arrangement of objects in your plan as viewed straight-on (whereas the **Plan** view shows horizontal arrangement viewed directly from above). While not as fun as the three-dimensional views, elevations are crucial for lining up all the objects in your plan.

Cross Section

The **Cross Section** view gives a three-dimensional view including roofs, but of the vertical plane so width and height can be inspected. Along with **Plan** view, it provides information crucial for actual construction of your design. Just like **Elevation** view, you cannot add objects in this view or change walls (as in any view other than **Plan**), but you can still change objects like doors, windows, cabinets, and furniture. You will find this view ideal for lining things up precisely, because you see them straight on and compare their relative heights.

Applied Materials View

The **Applied Materials View** command allows you to view your home in three dimensions with applied materials, shading, backdrops, and images. This will help you obtain a visual sense of what your home will be like. This command is available in **Camera** or **Full Camera** view.

To save the view, on the **File** menu, point to **Export,** and then click **Bitmap** file. To print the view, on the **File** menu, click **Print Image**.

Setup Applied Materials View

Click the **Setup Applied Materials View** command to choose the settings for the view that appears when you click **Applied Materials View** (see above). These settings include color, type of shading, images shown, texture, color, and lighting.

Under **Color Model,** select **Ramp** or **Color**. Color gives you the most detailed display, but demands more computing power and may slow you down. If this occurs, choose **Ramp**. You are encouraged to try both options to see which one gives you the best results; also, a number of other factors affect the behavior of these options, including monitor setting, resolution, number of bitmap images displayed, the amount of applied materials used, presence of a backdrop image or color, amount of VRAM (video memory), and presence of hardware acceleration.

Under **Shade,** select **Flat Shade** or **Gouraud Shade**. Flat Shade gives curved surfaces a faceted effect, while Gouraud Shade makes them look smooth.

Other Options:

Show Images: turns the display of bitmap images (such as trees and shrubs) on or off.

Ambient Light: turns ambient light on or off; the amount can be adjusted in the adjacent scroll bar.

Default Lights: these are created based on camera position and varied automatically to display edges and contrast different surfaces. Select or clear this option to turn default lights on or off.

Backdrop: you can choose a new color or add a bitmap image as a backdrop. Click **Backdrop**, and then to change the color, click **Select Color**, and then choose a color in the **Color** dialog box. To add a bitmap image, click **Colors**, and then click **Select Image**. Click the image you want, and then click **OK** twice to return to the **Set Up Applied Materials View** dialog box.

Adjust Color

The **Adjust Color** command allows you to change the color of any class of objects in the active window by selecting the command, then an object. These colors are unrelated to those used in the **Set Plan Colors** dialog box, and are intended to help you with interior design.

Opening the **Adjust Color** dialog box by clicking an object with the **Adjust Color** tool (also known as the "Rainbow" tool), shows you the kind of object you selected, the current assigned color and its class in the bottom bar, and a series of sliders for changing that color. A color matrix with 16 colors allows you to pick a color. The matrix colors are just shortcuts to get you to the color you want quickly. Pick the color from the matrix that is close to what you want, and then use the sliders to adjust the color to your taste.

The RGB sliders let you create custom colors by changing the amount of red, green, and blue in each. Since this RGB model uses "additive" color, 100 percent each of red, green, and blue will be white, and 0 percent will be black. The numbers at the bottom of each slider can range from 0 to 255, because the program accepts that many distinct values for each.

Note that if you have an SVGA graphics card, the object's color will change as you manipulate the sliders. With a VGA card, the object's color will not be updated until you exit the **Adjust Color** dialog box. The color swatch at the bottom of the dialog box enables you to monitor the new color as you manipulate the sliders, though, even in VGA.

Equal values for each primary color will create shades of gray as you change them. This is basically what the **Brightness** slider affects, how dark or light the color seems, by moving all three primary color sliders at once. The **Contrast** slider will not affect the color directly, but will set the light-to-dark range of the color used for shading objects. Moving the slider will change the range of shades shown in the color swatch.

As with other dialog boxes, to have the program accept your changes, click **OK**. To go back to the original colors, click **Revert**. The **Copy** and **Paste** commands let you copy colors between object classes, and even to different floors. To do so, open a dialog box for one class, click **Copy**, then open a dialog box for the other class, and click **Paste**. The second class of objects will now have the same color as the first. You can use **Copy** and **Paste** to copy colors across floors using the same technique.

Note that you can click any object displayed in a window even if, like walls, you cannot actually select them. You can even click items that are not usually treated like objects, like the base moulding on a wall, or the frame of a window. Whatever you select with the **Adjust Color** command will be identified in the dialog box. Also, certain types of objects will have the **Use Second Color** check box. Clicking this box applies an alternative color to an object, so that you can allow objects of a similar kind to have different colors.

The default colors for object classes, and their second colors, are set in the PROFILE.PL1 plan. Changing the **Adjust Color** dialog box will affect only your current plan.

Plan Default Colors

The **Default Colors** command opens the **Plan Default Colors** dialog box, which allows default colors to be selected and adjusted for many different types of items. The colors selected in this dialog box are applied to the items in the 3D views. (Note: **Plan** view colors are set by selecting **Plan View Colors** on the **Options** menu.) Default colors are applied per floor; in other words, each floor (First, Second, Foundation, etc.) has its own default colors. The numbers next to the object categories represent the corresponding color in the color palette; for example, **walls** has color **1**, which is the first color in the palette (light yellow).

To change a default color for an object category in the **Plan Default Colors** dialog box, click the number next to the category. The current color for that category is highlighted with a dark outline in the color palette. Click the color you want, and then click **OK**.

Remove 3D

The **Remove 3D** command simply closes the three-dimensional and elevation views while you are in **Plan** view. This will neaten up the workspace and speed up the program.

Working with different views in ***3D Home Architect Deluxe*** can be very useful, and certainly fun, but the **Plan** view is the most important for both designing and building your plan. This is where you can create, position, and change all the objects that make up your plan. You can add and see all the details, like dimensions, text, and electrical features in **Plan** view.

Still, other views are important too. (In fact the program is named after the three-dimensional **Camera** view.) All the views have been carefully integrated, so that all can be visible at once for a given plan, and changes in any one view will automatically be reflected in all the rest. Also, more than one window of a given type can be open at once, which, for example, could allow you to see three different perspectives of a given room while you design it.

Show Walkthrough

The **Show Walkthrough** command allows you to show a 3D walkthrough of a plan. A walkthrough is a 3D representation of what your finished house would look like if you walked around or through it. Click this command, then open a walkthrough file (for example, MYPLACE.WLK). The application plays the walkthrough.

Record Walkthrough

The **Record Walkthrough** command allows you to record 3D walkthroughs of your plan. You record your walkthrough much as you would film your house, moving from area to area to show different perspectives. You save the walkthroughs as files that you can show later.

Stop Recording

Click the **Stop Recording** command to end a recording session that you started by clicking **Record Walkthrough**.

Window Menu

The **Window** menu features commands that control the size, magnification, arrangement, and features of the different windows on your desktop. Most will be familiar to experienced Windows users. Remember that these commands affect only the display of your plan; the plan itself remains at the same scale at which you created it. In other words, all these commands change just the view of your plan, not the plan itself. Another important point is that most of these commands will work in all views. Standard Windows commands can be used to resize and move the current window, and scroll bars can be used to change the position of the plan within the window. This menu also allows easy navigation when several views are open.

Zoom

The **Zoom** command allows you to zoom in on part of your plan, by selecting the command then dragging a box around the area in which you are interested. The program will then change the magnification so that the selected area fills the screen. Being a mode command, you can continue zooming until you select another command.

Undo Zoom

The **Undo Zoom** command simply reverses the last zoom. It does not reverse other **Window** operations. Note that the **Undo** command in the **Edit** menu does not affect **Window** commands either.

Move Out (x2)

The **Move Out (x2)** command reduces the current view by half, therefore showing twice as much of your plan. The command executes immediately.

Fill Window

The **Fill Window** command is also an executing command; it resizes the display of your plan so that the entire plan, regardless of scale or size, fits in the window. Some decks and balconies may be cut off, however, because they may not be counted as exterior dimensions, and the program cuts them off.

Color On/Off

The **Color On/Off** command toggles the display of colors on and off.

Show/Hide Toolbar

The **Show/Hide Toolbar** command is also a toggle. This determines whether or not the toolbar is displayed. Note that the toolbar can be turned on and off, but not moved.

Reference Toggle

The **Reference Toggle** command, together with the next two commands, controls the display of multiple floor plans. Since almost any design will have at least two floors, a foundation and a first floor, and only the plan for one floor can be displayed in a single **Plan** view, these commands are included to help you coordinate the different floor and foundation plan files needed. **Reference Toggle** is a toggling command that lets you turn on the display of a "reference" file, which when on is superimposed over the current plan. You cannot edit the contents of the reference plan, but you can use them to line up walls, stairs, and other items in your plan. You can even derive the basic plan for one floor from another automatically, as shown below.

Swap Work-Ref

The **Swap Work-Ref** command works with **Reference Toggle** to simultaneously change the working plan into the reference plan, and the reference plan into the working plan.

Show Floors

The **Show Floors** command opens a dialog box that you can use to build additional floors and keep the different floor plans for a given design organized. You can choose which floor plan will be working, reference, or in memory. Remember that *3D Home Architect Deluxe* uses one file per floor in your design, and gives all the files for all the floors the same name, but tells them apart by using the extension. For instance, PLn, where PL indicates this is a plan file, and "n" indicates the floor, with "0" for foundation, up to "4" for the fourth floor. (Check the **File** menu section for more details.)

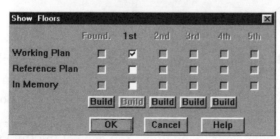

Show Floors dialog box

When opened, the dialog box will display a table of check boxes, with six columns, one for each possible floor, and three rows, labeled **Working Plan, Reference Plan,** and **In Memory**. Check boxes will show the status of each floor plan; those not yet existing will be unavailable. Only one file can, and must, be selected for **Working** and **Reference**, but all files may be checked **In Memory**. To change the status of each file, just click the appropriate boxes. (Note that files are held in memory so all the files of a given design can be renamed at once using **Save As**, or exported to a **DXF** file using **DXF All** on the **File** menu.)

At the bottom of each column is a **Build** button, which is unavailable if the floor already exists. Clicking this button will open a **New Working Plan** dialog box, in which you can build a new plan by tracing the exterior walls of the current working plan, opening a blank file, or simply changing the existing plan's name so that it becomes the plan for a different floor.

Note that if a 3D view has been previously generated, an attic will have been created and will be listed in place of the floor above the last built floor. Clicking the **Build** button under the attic heading will build the next floor.

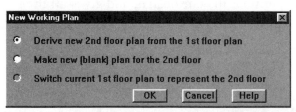

New Working Plan dialog box

Clicking the **Build** button under the foundation column will display the same dialog box, but selecting the **Derive** option will then make foundation the working plan in the **Show Floors** dialog box. Click **OK** twice to cause a **Foundation Setup** dialog box to appear; it contains boxes for specifying your foundation. You can set the thickness and height of the foundation walls, and decide whether footings or piers should be used, with edit boxes for the dimensions of each.

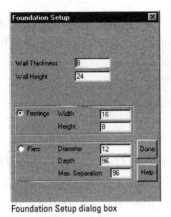

Foundation Setup dialog box

Walls will display with solid lines, while footings, the horizontal section under a foundation wall, and piers will be shown with dashed lines. Foundation walls can be selected and edited like standard walls, but piers and footings cannot. (They will attach to the foundation walls, however.) Foundation walls default to 8 inches thick by 24 inches deep, footings to 18 inches thick, and piers to 12 inches in diameter, 96 inches deep, and 96 inches apart.

While these options will be adequate for most designs, extreme conditions like unstable soils, steep slopes, or unusual designs will require more work. You should definitely check with local builders and officials before proceeding with building a foundation plan.

Tile, **Cascade**, and **Arrange Icons** are standard Windows commands for rearranging the windows and icons on your desktop. **Tile** arranges the windows side-by-side, **Cascade** staggers them one on top of the other, and **Arrange Icons** straightens them out. (As independent windows you can minimize any *3D Home Architect Deluxe* window to an icon, then restore it to full size when you need it.) The final item in the **Window** menu lists the windows open in the program and lets you change the active window by selecting it.

Internet Menu

The **Internet** menu features commands that allow you to access the *3D Home Architect Deluxe* Web site. At this site, you can upload and download plans and find lots of useful information on home design.

The first time you use any command on the **Internet** menu, *3D Home Architect Deluxe* asks you to configure your Web browser for use with the application. Follow the on-screen instructions to configure your Web browser to work with the program.

You can visit the *3D Home Architect Deluxe* Web site directly from your Web browser for help and useful tips concerning the use of the application. You can find this Web site at:

http://www.TotalHomeNetwork.com/

Go Online

To access the Internet from within *3D Home Architect Deluxe*, click the **Internet** menu, then click **Go Online**. This command only works if you have a Web browser (such as Netscape® Communicator® or Microsoft® Internet Explorer®) installed and have Internet access from your computer. The first time you click **Go Online**, the program asks you to configure your Web browser for use with the program. Follow the on-screen instructions to do this.

If you cannot find your Web browser, in Windows Explorer, click the **Tools** menu. Click **Find**. Click **Files or Folders**. Search your hard drive for NETSCAPE.EXE or IEXPLORE.EXE.

If you are using a browser other than Internet Explorer or Netscape you may experience problems connecting to the *3D Home Architect Deluxe* page. If you experience difficulties, you can connect directly to the site by launching your browser from outside *3D Home Architect Deluxe* and entering the following address in your Web browser:

http://www.TotalHomeNetwork.com

Note: If you do not have a Web browser installed, the **Go Online** menu command appears, but it does not function. Once you add Internet access and a Web browser to your computer, you can use this command.

Download Plan

The *3D Home Architect Deluxe* Web site offers many plans that you can use as you begin to design your home. With *3D Home Architect Deluxe*, you can download these plans from the Web site. To do this, click the **Internet** menu. Click **Download Plan**. Your Web browser starts and takes you to the **Plan Finder** page on the *3D Home Architect Deluxe* Web site. Follow the directions on this page to download plans.

Once you have downloaded a plan, you can open the plan from the Downloaded Plans directory.

Upload Plan

Have you created a plan you are proud of? You can share your plans with other *3D Home Architect Deluxe* users by uploading your plan to the *3D Home Architect Deluxe* Web site. To upload your plans:

1. Click the **Internet** menu. Click **Upload File**.
2. Navigate to the file you wish to upload.
3. Click **Yes**. Your Web browser starts and takes you to an upload page on the *3D Home Architect Deluxe* Web site. Follow the instructions on this page to upload your plan.
4. Once the application has uploaded your plan, a confirmation dialog box appears. Click **OK**.

Help Menu

The last menu item in *3D Home Architect Deluxe* is **Help,** which contains commands for accessing the online Help system that accompanies the program. The **Help** menu follows Windows conventions, meaning that it can be reached by selecting commands in the **Help** menu, or by clicking **Help** in some dialog boxes, or by simply pressing **F1**. The Help system is contained within independent windows that can be moved, resized, and minimized and maximized like any other, so you can view a help topic while working on your plan.

The Help system is organized so you can search it by index for commands, or topic, or key terms. Once in a topic, you can skip to other, related topics by clicking on "jumps," which are the green, underlined words. You can also move backwards through your search using the **Back** button, or go to topics by entering a search term.

The **Help** menu features four commands that allow you to enter the Help system: **Index, Basics, Current Mode, Using Help**. All open the Help system; the only difference is where you start.

Index
The **Index** command opens an index section in which you can view the topics covered and select ones to read in more detail.

Basics
The **Basics** command opens a help topic that covers all the basic commands, and includes jumps to more detailed discussions. This is the command to use for a quick tour of the program.

Current Mode
The **Current Mode** command, also activated by using **F1**, will always open a help topic relevant to whatever dialog box or command you are selecting. This is the context-sensitive portion of the Help system, and the command to use when stuck in a specific area of the program.

Using Help
The **Using Help** command opens a help file that contains topics about using the Help system.

About
The **About** command tells you the version and date of your program.

Changing the Color or Material on Object Surfaces
You can change the color or material for most of the objects in *3D Home Architext Deluxe*. Click the **Selection Mode** button, and then click the object you want to change to open its specification dialog box. Click **Color & Material** to open the **Assign Colors** dialog box. If you want to change the color, click a color in the color palette, and then

click the **OK** button twice to exit the dialog boxes and apply the color.

If you want to apply a material, follow the steps above until you have opened the **Assign Colors** dialog box. Once there, click **Material**, and then click **Choose Material**. In the **Select Image** dialog box, click the category of material you want. At this point, you will either see the selection of materials or a subcategory leading to the materials (it's different for each category). If you see a subcategory, continue to choose until you reach the selection of materials, and then click the material you want. (The material will be surrounded by a box after you click it.) Click **OK** two or more times to exit the dialog boxes and apply the material.

Even though a color or material has been applied, you can't see them in the **Plan** window. To view them, click the **View Mode** button, and then click inside the window and drag toward the wall. This opens a **Camera** window and shows you an applied color. To see a material, on the toolbar, click the **Applied Materials** tool (which looks like a camera). An **Applied Materials View** window opens, displaying the material you chose.

6

Introduction to Residential Design

Chapter 6

Introduction to Residential Design

This chapter looks at each step you encounter as you design your home or addition. This is not a complete account. There is much more to building a home than you will find here. Many books are available that cover the basics of building a home; if possible, try to get one that focuses on your locality since building practices and local ordinances vary. Your best source of information is your architect or builder, if you hire one. If you are going to do it yourself, find others who have recently completed a similar project. Many areas have owner-builder associations or programs through local junior colleges. Ask around. Now that you are interested in planning and building, you will be amazed at how many other people are as well.

Why Do You Need a Floor Plan?

A floor plan is the most basic part of the design of a new home or new part of a remodeled home. You have desires and hopes for your home that, while they mean a great deal to you, can easily be misunderstood by someone else. You may want a spacious master bath with plenty of counter space around the sinks. The floor plan will show the builder of the home exactly what you mean by "spacious" and "plenty," as well as how your bedroom, closets, and other rooms relate to the size of your master bath.

When you put your ideas for a room into a floor plan they become very specific. You and others can see how much they will cost, how much space they require, and whether they really fit in with the rest of the house and the building site.

Stop and think of all the parts and details that will make up your home, or addition. It can be overwhelming to think of all these things at once, but you can learn how to work with them one at a time. Each step can be interesting and enjoyable. You can learn about yourself and your family members as you discuss and decide how you will live in your home and what changes and benefits you will get from it. You may be surprised at what you find out.

Perhaps you have always wanted a large, impressive living room with a two-story glass wall and a balcony. However, you also know that the best times you have had with friends and your family have been in more intimate rooms that were cozy rather than impressive. The Filoli mansion, which is located in the San Francisco Bay Area, is a very large and beautiful house with magnificent rooms. Where did the family that built this house put up their Christmas tree and spend most of their time? In a small study. That was where they were comfortable.

This is just an example, not a recommendation for small houses instead of large ones. The important thing to think about is what will make you really happy and comfortable. Features that impress your friends, or even just yourself, may not be worth pursuing if they don't satisfy your real living needs.

This is your chance to organize the thoughts and desires you may have had for many years so they can become really clear. Find out which ones are important (and possible), and which ones are not. Start with your dreams. Think each step of the way. In the end you will get what you really want.

Who Else Needs Your Plans?

Your local planning department or building inspector will require one or more copies of your plans before you can begin construction. Your lending institution requires them before approving a construction loan. Your builder needs several sets of your plans: one to refer to at the office, one at the job site, and one for each of the electrical, plumbing, and other subcontractors. Before submitting your plans to these agencies, find out which format the plans must conform to. It may be that the plans you print out from *3D Home Architect Deluxe* look beautiful but do not conform to the requirements of a specific agency. For example, special paper or printing processes may be required.

The Building Site

The very first consideration is the building site. If you are building an addition, this includes the existing structure your addition will be added to. Your home must fit on the site, and usually must also satisfy setbacks required by your city or county building department. For example, common suburban setbacks allow the front of the house to be no closer than 20 feet from the front or back property line and no closer than 5 feet from a side property line. On a corner lot you must find out which property line is considered front and which is considered side. Setbacks vary from place to place. Make sure you or your builder knows and has satisfied the requirements for your locality. Don't start building until you are absolutely certain! If your house will come close to a setback and you are not sure exactly where it is, hire a surveyor and find out. The expense of the surveyor is nothing compared to tearing out your favorite sunroom because it is six inches too close to the property line.

Once you have satisfied the legal requirements, think about the orientation of your home on its site. Walks and driveways must meet their destinations in some reasonable way. If you are on a busy street, you may want a turnaround space in the driveway to avoid backing out directly onto the street. There may be one place that is particularly suited for a garden. How should the house relate to this? The family room could have sliding glass doors and an adjoining deck that look out on the garden. If the morning sun warms that area, a breakfast nook with a bay window might afford a pleasant view of the garden.

Often a house will be directed toward one part of the site more than others. If your side yards are narrow, you will want to orient your rooms and views toward the front and back of the building site. A large front yard facing a tree-lined street is an invitation to place the living room in the front of the house. If the street is closer, and much of the area is occupied by the garage and its driveway, perhaps the living room should face a garden area in the back.

Many parents want to be able to watch their small children at play in the backyard. A window over the sink or other kitchen work area that faces the back satisfies this and has become an American tradition in many homes.

Perhaps one side of your house can be made to face toward the south or nearly so. This southern exposure can be useful. Many homes have large windows protected by an overhanging roof on their south wall. In addition, deciduous trees are placed to the south of the house. In the summer when the sun is high, the roof overhang will block much of it from entering the windows. The tree leaves can filter most of the rest of it, leaving a pleasant house with light from the outdoors, but less heat from direct sunlight. In winter, the lower sun passes beneath the overhang and the leaves are off the trees, so the sun comes through and warms the house. However, it can also fade your furniture. You must decide what you want.

The Cost of Your Home Can Determine Its Size

The second thing to find out is how large your home should be. Many factors influence this size, but your budget places an upper limit on it. These are some of the expenses you will encounter as you plan and build your home.

Even if you do all of the planning and design yourself, you may need an architect or civil engineer to help you with your foundation or to ensure that your home's supporting structure is adequate. Many localities require the signature and stamp of an architect or engineer to approve foundations and large supporting beams. Be prepared for higher engineering costs if you are building on a steep hillside.

You may need a construction loan while the house is being built. If possible, get the kind that can be easily converted to a standard mortgage when construction is complete.

There will be fees for building permits, sewer hookups, and perhaps hooking up to other utilities. Check with your town or county building department for more information on these. While you are there, find out any other information you can about building and building costs in your area. Some building departments, especially in smaller towns, can be very helpful.

Site preparation can include surveying, grading, excavating for a basement, and running electricity, sewer, water, and other utilities from the street. If you don't already own your building site, remember to add in that cost!

Landscaping can be put off until the money is available, but you may still want to get an idea of what you will eventually spend on this. Check with your local government. You may be required to do a certain amount of landscaping before you can move in.

The largest single cost will be building the house itself. The basic way to estimate this cost is to multiply the total number of square feet in all the living areas by a *cost per square foot* number. This number depends on where you build. The types of materials used also account for variations in the square foot price. For example, ceramic-tile countertops, brass fixtures, and hardwood floors cost more than plastic laminate, standard fixtures, and vinyl floor covering. The amount of work you do yourself, and the difficulty of a particular building site also can change this cost factor.

When you have estimated the cost per square foot, divide it into your budget, or what's left of it after you have subtracted the other costs already discussed, and you will have an idea of the overall size of your house.

Arranging the Rooms

Laying out a really good floor plan from scratch can be difficult even for an experienced designer. It is not as simple as it looks. It is easier to start from a design you like and modify it to fit your needs. ***3D Home Architect Deluxe*** includes 350 sample plans for you to start with. Additionally, books of house plans can be found in any bookstore. You might get ideas for your master bedroom from one plan, the entry and main stairway from another, and so on.

Don't continue to read these books until you feel you know exactly what you want, though. This is definitely a "learn by doing" situation. Draw your plan into the computer. You may not be satisfied with your initial effort, but keep working with it. The system will help you as you change one area and then another. You should soon be able to see if it is going in the direction you want, or if you should really start over.

In addition to the room locations, think about how you will get from one room to another. Ideally you should be able to walk from the front door to any main room in the house without passing through any other room. (A main room would include a living room, kitchen, bedroom, or a bathroom meant for use by anyone; it would not include a bathroom or closet meant for use only by the occupants of a particular bedroom.) To accomplish this, the front door in your plan should open into an entry hall, and this or a connected hallway should connect the other rooms. While this ideal is not practical for a very small house or a guest cottage, it is the standard way to plan a larger home. Of course there will be exceptions to this rule, but the larger the home, the more strictly it should be followed.

Here are some tips to keep in mind as you lay out your plan. First, don't consider hallways as wasted space, so that you make them as narrow as possible, using the space you save elsewhere. This makes them cramped and unpleasant. Hallways are living areas too, and you can be in them a lot more than you realize. The features you design into a room will give that room its character and appeal. The features you design in your hallways add character and appeal to your home as a whole. In a two-story plan, try to combine an upstairs hallway with the stairway, so that they share a larger open area. Widen the hallway a little, raise the ceiling and place a skylight or chandelier over this area, and you may create a place where family members meet and talk and children play.

Special Rooms in Your Home

Have you ever walked through a recently completed house for which you could get no feeling at all? The rooms were ample in size, with sufficient light from the windows. There was adequate closet and cabinet space.

The kitchens and baths were correctly designed. There was just nothing special about it. A room needs more than four walls, a door, and a few windows to be special. A dormer window projecting from a sloping wall in an upstairs bedroom adds interest. Put in a window seat and you have something special.

Richly finished bookcases on either side of the fireplace may make the difference in providing a cozy end of a living or family room.

If you are fortunate enough to have exterior walls on two sides of your breakfast nook, fill them with windows and plant a garden outside. If not, perhaps you can extend the nook outward from the house and put windows on three sides.

If you have a wide opening to a dining room with additional wall space on either side, add double doors. Since you did not really need doors in the first place, you can keep them completely open, against the walls on either side. A rich finish and brass hardware on the doors will add interest, but the real gain is a change in the character of the dining room. The wide open doors are inviting—a signal to people that they are welcome to come in. This type of ambience makes a room special, which is more meaningful than making it impressive, or even beautiful.

Instead of a window over the kitchen sink looking out on the backyard, put windows above the countertop across that entire wall. You will lose some wall cabinets, but these could be moved elsewhere or replaced with a pantry closet. If you have a cooktop or range against that wall, get one with a built-in exhaust. Don't place curtains above a cooktop! Use venetian blinds or something that you know is nonflammable.

It takes time to think of these things. If you have run out of ideas, look at magazine pictures and friends' houses. Try to remember what was special about the house you grew up in, or your grandparents' house. Perhaps you can add a fireplace or a bay window, but remember—these things can add to the cost of your home, so there will be tradeoffs.

Rules Your Plan Must Follow

You must deal with building codes and building inspectors in just about any location you build in. While these can restrict your freedom to build exactly what you want, their primary purpose is to ensure that the house will last for many years in good condition, have adequate services for modern living, and be a community asset rather than an eyesore.

Certain notations may be required on your plan before it is approved. For example, a note about the size and location of crawl space vents around the house perimeter may be required. A door between a garage and the rest of the house may have to be designated as solid core (for fire protection). Studying another set of plans that has already been approved is the best way to find out about most of these things. After that, simply submit your plans. When you get them back they will either be approved or you will know what has to be done.

Be sure to find out how long it takes for the building department to review your plans. This could cause a major delay if you start this process too late. Also, you should allow time to resubmit your corrected plans once or twice. The building inspectors are there for your benefit. They will protect you from bad construction caused by your own mistakes, or by the shoddy workmanship of others. One owner-builder working on his first house hired a subcontractor to install all the wallboard. He was concerned that the job did not appear to be done well, but was not sure of this since he was not an expert. The building inspector came in while the subcontractor was there, took one look and started pointing out all the areas the owner was concerned with. The subcontractor had to redo some areas and fix others, until the job was done right, much to the relief of the owner.

Make a list of what the building inspector will inspect, and then make sure nothing prevents these inspections. Do not cover this work until it has been inspected! If the nailing of the subfloor to the joists must be inspected, don't install the hardwood floors before the inspection. You may have to take them back up.

A

Questions and Answers

Questions and Answers

Following these questions and answers, you will find Brøderbund Technical Support information. Please read through these questions and answers first and see if they address your problem. Note that Brøderbund Software cannot answer specific questions about your building project, only questions related to the features of *3D Home Architect Deluxe.*

Q. I have created a two-story house with a fireplace, but when I view the house in **3D** view, the fireplace does not extend above the first floor. How can I fix this?

A. While in **Plan** view, select the fireplace and move it into the wall by clicking the center of the fireplace and holding the **Ctrl** key down. Position the fireplace so that the edge of the firebox lines up with the wall, leaving only the hearth protruding from the wall. Then double-click the fireplace to get to the **Fireplace Specification** dialog box. Change the height of the fireplace so that it extends past the highest point of your roof.

Q. I can't figure out how to add elements to cabinets in the **Cabinet Specification** dialog box. How do I insert a shelf between two drawers?

A. Click between the two drawers, or whatever the items are, and two arrows will appear on the side of the cabinet. Pick the type of object that you want to insert from the **Item Type** list box, then click the **Add New** button. The item below the insertion point will be "bumped" downward, and the new item inserted. If there is not enough room, you will get a warning and will have to delete something from the cabinet to make room for the new item.

Q. Why do room labels not display centered in some rooms?

A. The room label is put in the center of the bounding rectangle of the room. For some rooms, such as L-shaped rooms, this results in the room label sometimes not being automatically put in the best place. It's easy to reposition the label: just click and drag it with the **Selection** tool.

Q. I have made a bay window, and I want to place some furniture inside the window alcove, but the program won't let me. How do I do this?

A. The alcove of a bay, box, or bow window is technically not "in" the room, and the program wants to keep the objects in the room. Click the room with the **Selection** tool and you will see an outline along the wall of the room. Whatever is contained within the outline is in the room; note that an alcove is not. You can still place furniture objects within the alcove, but you need to hold down the **Ctrl** key while you do so. Note that for large bay or box windows, you may find it better to construct them with standard walls and windows instead. That way, the resulting alcoves will be within the room.

Q. I put a down staircase going down to a lower level, and the stairs are just going straight into the floor.

A. You probably didn't create an opening in the floor through which the stairs could pass. Refer to chapter 5, "Reference" on down staircases for information on how to create a stairwell by creating an Open Below room with railings.

Q. None of the lights, switches, or outlets that I have placed from the **Electrical Symbol Library** show up in **3D** views. Is there something wrong with the program?

A. Objects from the **Electrical Symbol Library** do not have **3D** representation and won't show up in the **3D** views. They will, however, be present in any Materials list that you create, and PlanCheck checks electrical circuits and the presence of certain electrical items.

Q. I want to create a cabinet island in the middle of the kitchen with overhead cabinets hanging from the ceiling. How do I create ceiling cabinets?

A. Use wall cabinets, placed away from walls, in **Plan** view. When placed near a wall, the wall cabinets will attach to the wall, but if they are placed away from the wall, they attach to the ceiling and become ceiling cabinets.

Q. What font does the program use for text objects?

A. The program uses Arial, which is included with Windows. If you have removed Arial from your system, you should reinstall it.

Q. I placed a masonry fireplace in my living room, but I can't get it to go through the wall so that the chimney is outside. What's the trick?

A. While in **Plan** view, select the fireplace and move it into the wall by clicking the center of the fireplace and holding the **Ctrl** key down. Position the fireplace so that the edge of the firebox lines up with the wall, leaving only the hearth protruding from the wall.

Q. I'm a big fan of shuffleboard, and I'm sad to see that there is no shuffleboard table in the **Furniture Library**. Is there any way I can create my own?

A. Yes, but maybe not the way you think. You can't create a shuffleboard table to add to the **Furniture Library**. You can, however, make creative use of cabinets to create a quite realistic shuffleboard table, and many other types of objects. Place a base cabinet, then click the cabinet and use the handles to stretch it to the desired length. Double-click the cabinet to get the **Cabinet Specification** dialog box, and remove the doors and drawers. This will give you a long, flat surface, with smooth sides. For more detail, you could add cabinets of the same length to the sides, and make them thin. By making these side cabinets a little higher than the main table, you can create a "rink." You'll be surprised by the kind of things you can do with cabinets; you just need to use your imagination!

Q. Using the **Plan Finder**, I cannot seem to find the plan I want. How can I do this?

A. If you do not find plans that match your needs, consider broadening the range of your search by increasing the number of square feet, or additional bedrooms, bathrooms, or floors. Also, by using larger numbers in these categories, you will avoid overlooking flexible plans that you can alter later.

Q. Can I access the ***3D Home Architect Deluxe*** Web site directly from my browser?

A. Yes. Visit the ***3D Home Architect Deluxe*** Web site at http://www.TotalHomeNetwork.com. At this site, you will find information and useful tips concerning the use of the application.

Q. Can I edit a walkthrough after I have recorded it?

A. No. If you want something different, you must record another walkthrough.

How to Contact Technical Support

If you have worked through these troubleshooting suggestions and still need assistance, you can contact Brøderbund Technical Support by using the options listed below. It will be very helpful if you can tell us your computer make and model, and the brand names of both the video card and sound card you are using. If possible, have the computer both positioned near your phone and turned on. Please also be prepared to give us a detailed description of what happens when you try to run the program.

You can contact us in any of the following ways:
- Internet – Online support is available through our World Wide Web site at http://www.broderbund.com/support
- America Online® – Use the Keyword: BRODERBUND
- Mail – Send your questions to Brøderbund Technical Correspondence, 9715 Parkside Drive, Knoxville, TN 37922.
- Phone – Call us at (423) 670-2020 from Monday through Friday between the hours of 9:00 a.m. and 9:00 p.m., Eastern Time.

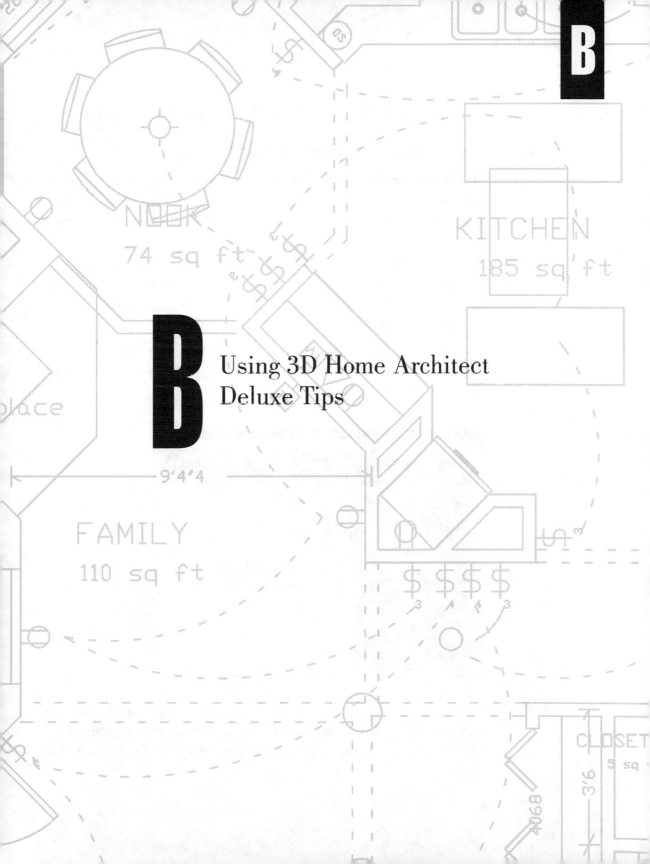

B

Using 3D Home Architect
Deluxe Tips

Using 3D Home Architect Deluxe Tips

Running 3D Home Architect Deluxe Tips

***3D Home Architect Deluxe* Tips** is a separate module that you can run as a separate application. It gives you access to over 100 articles from *American HomeStyle* magazine, as well as 50 video tips from Gerry Connell, The Home Pro™.

To load ***3D Home Architect Deluxe* Tips** double-click the **3D Home Architect Tips** icon in the program group. Note that while **Tips** requires the CD-ROM to be in the CD-ROM drive, the ***3D Home Architect Deluxe*** application itself does not.

The first screen that you will encounter when running ***3D Home Architect Deluxe* Tips** is the **Contents** screen. This is where you pick the topic area that you want more information on:

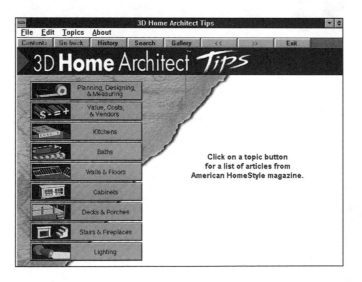

When you click one of the topic buttons, the list of articles for that topic category (culled from *American HomeStyle* magazine) appears to the right. You can then click one of the article titles, and a new screen will appear:

Video display area   Text display area

There are three display areas: The text area, the graphic area, and the
video area. The text area displays the text of the article that you
selected. The graphic area displays the graphic images, one at a time,
that are associated with the article. Finally, the video area is where The
Home Pro video clips are displayed.

Making Your Way Around Tips

Button Bar

The button bar at the top of the window allows for easy navigation
through *3D Home Architect Deluxe* **Tips**. The button bar is
available at all times in the program, although some buttons may be
grayed out, if they are inappropriate for a particular place in the
program. Here's what each button does:

Contents: The **Contents** button brings up the screen where you select
the topic area for *American HomeStyle* magazine articles.

Go Back: The **Go Back** button returns you to the previous screen.

History: The **History** button brings up a list of the most recent places that you have been in the program, so you can get to them quickly.

Search: The **Search** button lets you search through articles and video titles for keywords. The **Search** dialog box allows you to narrow your search to specific topic groups and allows for the use of logical operators to create a very powerful search engine. Be sure to click the **Hints** button in the **Search** dialog box for information on how to use logical operators.

Gallery: The **Gallery** button accesses the Video Gallery, where you can view any or all of The Home Pro videos.

<< and >>: These buttons are the "browse" buttons, and they bring up the next or previous article in a topic group. The browse buttons will automatically load the next topic group if necessary, thus enabling you to step through every article in order.

Exit: This button exits the program.

Menus

The menus in *3D Home Architect Deluxe* duplicate the functionality of the buttons described above. They also present standard Windows commands for printing, copying, and pasting the text articles. The **Topic** menu commands are shortcuts to accessing any topic group, as well as the Video Gallery. Please refer to the **About** menu for information regarding copyrights on the material presented in *3D Home Architect Deluxe* Tips.

Information in 3D Home Architect Deluxe Tips

Text Articles

The text articles are the principal of the three media types, because all of the graphic images and video clips are associated with a specific article. Graphic images are represented in the text as captioned icons. Use the scroll bars to move through the article, if necessary.

Viewing Graphics

Graphic icon

Clicking the icon or the caption displays the graphic in the graphic display area. To enlarge any graphic to full screen, simply click the graphic. To shrink it back down, press the **Esc** key, or click anywhere outside the image.

If an article has one or more graphic images associated with it, then the first graphic will be automatically displayed in the graphic area when the screen appears (some articles don't have any accompanying graphics, in which case a generic ***3D Home Architect Deluxe* Tips** graphic is displayed instead). As you work your way through the article, you may encounter more graphic icons. The graphic icons are arranged in the article by context, so that you see graphic images in their proper textual context.

Viewing The Home Pro Videos

If The Home Pro has a video on a topic similar to the text article, then The Home Pro logo automatically appears in the video display area at the bottom-left portion of the screen. To view the video, click the triangular **Play** button beneath the "video screen" (you can use the other controls there to pause the video, and to find specific portions of the video).

Location Slider   Backward/Forward/Stop/Pause/Play

Two Ways to View The Home Pro Videos

There are two ways to view The Home Pro videos. The first way is in conjunction with viewing an article, as described above (note that a few articles may have more than one video associated with it). The second way is through the Video Gallery, accessed by clicking the **Gallery** button. You can then click any of the titles and then play the video. The video player works the same as described above.

Copying and Annotating Articles

The **Edit** menu has two very useful commands: **Copy** and **Annotate**. If you are viewing an article, the **Copy** command will copy the text of the article to the Windows Clipboard. You can then bring that text into another program if you wish (please be mindful of the copyright on the articles, though).

The **Annotate** command is a way for you to make notes on articles. When viewing an article for which you wish to add a note, select the **Annotate** command. A dialog box will appear in which you can write your note. When done, click the **Save** button and your note will be attached to the article. A small paper clip will appear at the top left of the article. Clicking the paper clip will bring up the dialog box, displaying the annotation. You can use the other buttons in the dialog box to clear the annotation text, and to copy the text to the Clipboard. You can also paste text from the Clipboard.

Pricing and Cost Estimates

All prices and estimates in the *3D Home Architect Deluxe* **Tips** are rough estimates. You will need to check stores in your local area for actual costs.

C Printing Blueprints

Printing Blueprints

Now What?

You've finished your home design, and would like to start taking steps toward the estimating and construction process. We can help. We have arranged for the services of a national home planning and computer drafting company to be available to you to professionally complete your drawings at affordable prices.

HomeStyles Modifications offers three levels of service to Brøderbund's *3D Home Architect Deluxe* users.

Basic Level – *"Plot Your Own 3D Home Architect Deluxe Floor Plan"*

HomeStyles Modifications will plot your *3D Home Architect Deluxe* plan design file on full-size blueprint paper to 1/4 or 1/8th inch scale. Then you can measure rooms, drop in scaled furniture and give the floor plans to a builder for a rough cost estimate. To order the basic level prints, simply email your file to: plan?@lifestylehomedesign.com along with your name, address, telephone and fax numbers. *HomeStyles* Modifications will contact you for credit card information by phone, or you can send a check or money order with a disk of your design along with your name, address, and telephone and fax numbers to:

HomeStyles Modifications
213 East 4th Street
St. Paul, MN 55101

Only $39.95 + $14.95 shipping and handling. Allow 5-7 working days for delivery.

Medium Level – *"Modify An Existing 3D Home Architect Deluxe Floor Plan"* – Call 1-888-720-8345 for an exact quote.

HomeStyles Modifications starts with a mail-order home plan that most closely resembles your dream home and adds your desired modifications. **3D Home Architect Deluxe** includes hundreds of pre-drawn home designs you can choose from that have complete blueprints available for purchase that have been drafted according to national building codes. They typically include foundation plan, all four elevations, roof diagram, building section, electrical plan and applicable details, and cabinet elevations. We can incorporate the changes you have designed in **3D Home Architect Deluxe** into the original architect's blueprints.

Call 1-888-720-8345 for an exact quote and where to send your DXF file or mail your disk. Average prices for medium-level services are $400-$600 for reproducible copies of an original drawing plus $600-$1200 for modifying the plan to your local standards with your desired changes so you can get an exact construction bid from your contractor or subcontractors.

High Level – *"Custom Drafting of Your Own 3D Home Architect Deluxe Floor Plan"*

HomeStyles Modifications will draft your plan according to national building codes including foundation plan, all four elevations, roof diagram, building section, electrical plan and applicable details, and cabinet elevations. *HomeStyles* Modifications can incorporate the changes you have designed in **3D Home Architect Deluxe** into the original architect's blueprints. *HomeStyles* Modifications can also work with you to help satisfy unique local requirements.

Call 1-888-720-8345 for an exact quote. Average prices for high-level services are $.75 to $1.25 per square foot to professionally computer draft your design concept. HomeStyles Modifications will add appropriate plan information to your floor plan concept so you can get an exact construction bid from your contractor or subcontractors. Your design concept saves you thousands of dollars in architectural design fees.

Call today for exact pricing and where to send your DXF file or mail your disk. (Prices subject to change.)

HomeStyles Modifications is an independent entity, not affiliated with Brøderbund or Learning Company Properties Inc.

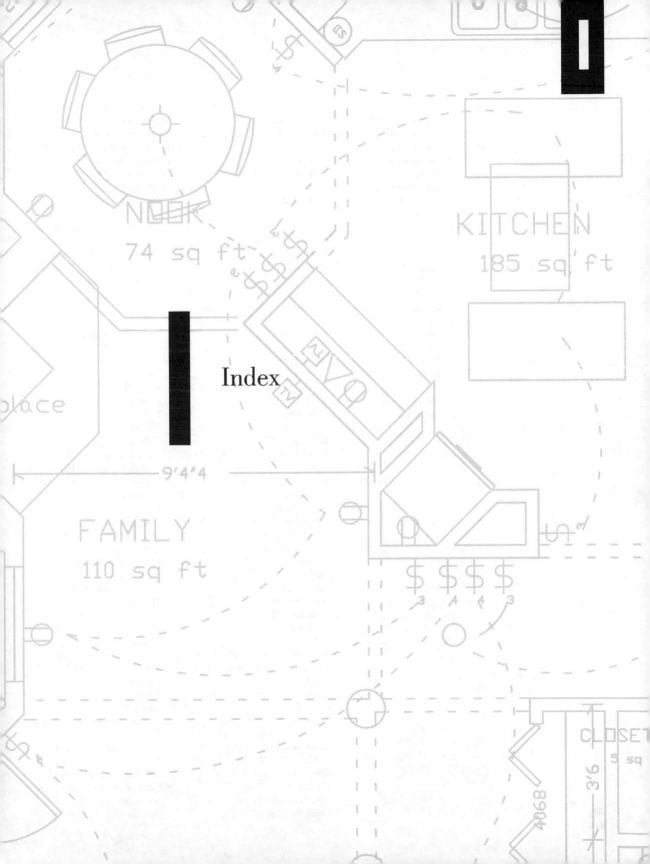

Index

Index

A

About command/tool, 244
Active Library box, 191
Add New button, 182
Adjust Color command/tool, 35, 104, 228–229, 232, 234
Adjust Color dialog box, 36, 104, 105, 234, 235, 236
All Rooms, 157–158
Alt key, 15, 18
Ambient Light, 58, 233
American HomeStyle magazine, 264
angled walls, 21
angles (view), 44
Annotate command/tool, 268
Appliances, 31, 79
Applied Materials command/tool, 42, 43, 57, 62, 195, 229, 245
Applied Materials View command/tool, 233
Applied Materials View window, 62, 213–214, 230, 245
Arial, 260
Arrange Icons, 241
arrows, 229
Assign Colors dialog box, 62, 209, 244, 245
attic, 240
Automatic Dimensions, 42, 43, 61, 73
Automatic Roof Designer
    displaying, 209
    functions of, 55
    gable roof built by, 115–116
    hip roof built by, 114–115
    shed roof built by, 117
    using Break Wall tool with, 129–131
    See also roofs
Autosave, 151

B

Back button, 191
Backdrop, 58, 234
backup files, 151
Balusters option, 87
Base Cabinet command/tool, 28, 73, 140, 186
Base Mould, 218
base moulding, 103, 218
Basic Level Design

Modification Service, 270
Basics command/tool, 244
Bathroom Fixtures, 191
bathrooms
    adding, 37–40
    fixtures for, 39
    naming, 38
    placing window in, 40, 69–70
    showers, 40
    walls for, 37–38
bathroom sinks, 39
Bathtubs, 191
Bay Window command/tool, 70, 139, 171, 176–177
bay window structures, 53
Beams command/tool, 165
Beam/Soffit, 42, 213
Beam (Wall Specification dialog box), 162
bedrooms
    four-wall enclosure defined as, 216
    naming, 25
    placing furniture in, 36–37
bifold door, 138, 169
Bifold Doors command/tool, 138, 166, 171
Bitmap (BMP) format, 153
bitmap images
    adding, 234
    Applied Materials view saved as, 57
    displaying, 233
    printing, 155, 156
bookshelves, 183
Bottom, 232
boundary lines
    adding, 215–216
    viewing, 42, 212
    See also lot
Bow, 7 Sect command/tool, 70
Bow Window command/tool, 70, 176
bow window structures, 53, 70–71
Box Window command/tool, 139, 171, 176, 177–178
Break Wall command/tool, 64, 127, 129–131, 137, 165, 189
Break Wall mode, 165
brightness of colors, 105
Brightness slider, 235
Build All Floors, 50, 222

Build button, 97, 99, 240
Build from Area, 222
Build from Room, 222
building code regulations, 206
building codes, 255
building inspectors, 249, 255
building site, 250–251
    See also floor plans
Build menu
    Base Cabinet command/tool, 186
    Bay Window command/tool, 171, 176–177
    Beams command/tool, 64, 165
    Bifold Doors command/tool, 171
    Box Window command/tool, 171, 176, 177–178
    Break Wall command/tool, 165
    Build/Move Lot command/tool, 42, 212, 215–216
    Cabinet command/tool, 179–185
    circular staircases, 202
    default settings in, 174
    Dimension Lines, 56
    Dimension Lines command/tool, 209–210
    Door command/tool, 166–169
    down staircases, 200–201
    Electrical command/tool, 203–206
    Fireplace command/tool, 84, 187–190
    Fixtures command/tool, 190–193
    Foundation Piers command/tool, 202–203
    Full Height Cabinet command/tool, 186
    Furniture command/tool, 193–194
    Garage Doors command/tool, 171
    Hatch Walls command/tool, 165
    Invisible command/tool, 164
    Outdoor Images command/tool, 195
    Outdoor Objects

IMPORTANT: READ CAREFULLY BEFORE USING THIS PRODUCT

LICENSE AGREEMENT AND LIMITED WARRANTY

BY INSTALLING OR USING THE SOFTWARE OR OTHER ELECTRONIC CONTENT INCLUDED WITH THIS AGREEMENT YOU ACCEPT THE TERMS OF THIS LICENSE WITH THE LEARNING COMPANY, INC., AND ITS AFFILIATES ("TLC"). IF YOU DO NOT AGREE TO THE TERMS OF THIS AGREEMENT AND YOU ARE ALSO THE ORIGINAL LICENSEE OF THIS PRODUCT ("ORIGINAL LICENSEE"), PROMPTLY RETURN THE PRODUCT TOGETHER WITH ALL ACCOMPANYING ITEMS TO YOUR DEALER FOR A FULL REFUND. THIS IS THE ENTIRE AGREEMENT BETWEEN THE PARTIES RELATING TO THIS PRODUCT AND SUPERSEDES ANY PURCHASE ORDER, COMMUNICATION, ADVERTISING OR REPRESENTATION CONCERNING THE PRODUCT. NO CHANGE OR MODIFICATION OF THIS LICENSE WILL BE VALID UNLESS IT IS IN WRITING AND IS SIGNED BY TLC.

LIMITED USE LICENSE. TLC and its suppliers grant you the right to use one copy of the accompanying product (the "Program") for your personal use only. This license, and the restrictions in this agreement, cover both the computer programs ("Software") and the other electronic content ("Content") of the accompanying product. All rights not expressly granted are reserved by TLC or its suppliers. This License does not constitute a sale and does not authorize a sale of the Program or anything created thereby. You must treat the Program and associated materials and any elements thereof like any other copyrighted material (e.g., a book or musical recording). This Agreement is governed by the internal substantive laws of the State of California (and not by the 1980 United Nations Convention on Contracts for the International Sale of Goods, as amended). In the event you fail to comply with any of the terms or conditions of this license, your rights to use the Program will end, you shall stop using the Program, remove the Program from your computer, and permanently erase all copies of the Program. You may be held legally responsible for any copyright infringement that is caused or encouraged by your failure to abide by the terms of this license.

YOU MAY NOT:

Use the Program or permit use of the Program on more than one computer, computer terminal or workstation at the same time.

Make copies of the materials accompanying the Program or make copies of the Program or any part thereof.

Except as permitted by the Program, copy the Program onto a hard drive or other device and you must run the Program from the CD-ROM (although the Program itself may copy a portion of the Program onto your hard drive during installation in order to run more efficiently).

Use the Program or permit use of the Program in a network or other multi-user arrangement or on an electronic bulletin board system or other remote access arrangement, or store it in a retrieval system or translate it into any other language.

Rent, lease, license or otherwise transfer this Program without the express written consent of TLC, except that you may transfer the complete Program copy and accompanying materials on a permanent basis, provided that no copies are retained and the recipient agrees to the terms of this Agreement.

Reverse engineer, decompile, disassemble or create derivative works of the Software. YOU MAY NOT MODIFY, TRANSLATE, DISASSEMBLE OR DECOMPILE THE SOFTWARE OR

ANY COPY, IN WHOLE OR IN PART.

Publicly perform or publicly display this Program.

Use any of the content for any commercial purposes or any purpose other than for incorporation into projects produced with the Software for home entertainment, personal and educational purposes except as outlined herein.

LIMITED WARRANTY. TLC warrants to the Original Licensee only, that the Program shall be substantially free from defects in materials and workmanship for ninety (90) days from the date of purchase. If within 90 days of purchase the media proves to be defective in any way, you may return the media to The Learning Company, Attn: Returns, 190 Parkway West, Duncan, SC 29334. Please include a copy of your sales receipt, packaging slip or invoice, along with a brief note of explanation as to why you are returning the Program.

EXCLUSIVE REMEDY. The Original Licensee's exclusive remedy for the breach of this License shall be, at TLC's option, either (a) the repair or replacement of the Program that does not meet TLCfs Limited Warranty and which is returned to TLC with a copy of your receipt; or (b) a refund of the price, if any, which you paid for the Program and associated materials. This Limited Warranty is void if the failure of the Program has resulted from accident, abuse, misapplication or use of the Program with incompatible hardware.

NO OTHER WARRANTIES. TLC, ITS AFFILIATES, AND ITS SUPPLIERS, IF ANY, DISCLAIM ALL WARRANTIES WITH RESPECT TO THE PROGRAM AND ACCOMPANYING MATERIALS, EITHER EXPRESS OR IMPLIED, INCLUDING BUT NOT LIMITED TO IMPLIED WARRANTIES OF MERCHANTABILITY, NON-INFRINGEMENT OF THIRD PARTY RIGHTS AND FITNESS FOR A PARTICULAR PURPOSE. TLC DOES NOT WARRANT THAT THE OPERATION OF THE PROGRAM WILL BE WITHOUT DEFECT OR ERROR OR WILL SATISFY THE REQUIREMENTS OF YOUR COMPUTER SYSTEM. THIS LIMITED WARRANTY GIVES YOU SPECIFIC LEGAL RIGHTS. DEPENDING UPON WHERE YOU LIVE, YOU MAY HAVE OTHER RIGHTS WHICH VARY FROM STATE/COUNTRY TO STATE/COUNTRY. TLC WARRANTS ONLY THAT THE PROGRAM WILL PERFORM AS DESCRIBED IN THE USER DOCUMENTATION. NO OTHER ADVERTISING, DESCRIPTION OR REPRESENTATION, WHETHER MADE BY A TLC DEALER, DISTRIBUTOR, AGENT OR EMPLOYEE, SHALL BE BINDING UPON TLC OR SHALL CHANGE THE TERMS OF THIS WARRANTY.

LIMITATIONS ON DAMAGES. This Program may contain significant or insignificant program errors, including errors which may cause an operational interruption of your computer system. The Program is provided "AS IS" and you assume responsibility for determining the suitability of the Program on your system and for results obtained. IN NO EVENT SHALL TLC, ITS AFFILIATES, OR ITS SUPPLIERS, IF ANY, BE LIABLE FOR ANY CONSEQUENTIAL OR INCIDENTAL DAMAGES WHATSOEVER ARISING OUT OF THE USE OF OR INABILITY TO USE THE PROGRAM OR PROGRAM PACKAGE, EVEN IF THEY HAVE BEEN ADVISED OF THE POSSIBILITY OF SUCH DAMAGES. THEY SHALL NOT BE RESPONSIBLE OR LIABLE FOR LOST PROFITS OR REVENUES, OR FOR DAMAGES OR COSTS INCURRED AS A RESULT OF LOSS OF TIME, DATA OR USE OF THE SOFTWARE, OR FROM ANY OTHER CAUSE INCLUDING, WITHOUT LIMITATION, PRODUCTS LIABILITY, CONTRACT OR TORT DAMAGES. THEIR LIABILITY SHALL NOT EXCEED THE ACTUAL PRICE PAID FOR THE LICENSE TO USE THE PROGRAM. BECAUSE SOME STATES/COUNTRIES DO NOT ALLOW THE EXCLUSION OR

LIMITATION OF LIABILITY FOR CONSEQUENTIAL OR INCIDENTAL DAMAGES, THE ABOVE LIMITATION MAY NOT APPLY TO YOU.

U.S. GOVERNMENT RESTRICTED RIGHTS. The Program and documentation are provided with restricted rights. Use, duplication or disclosure by the Government is subject to restrictions as set forth in subparagraph (c)(1)(ii) of The Rights in Technical Data and Computer Software clause at DFARS 252.227-7013 or subparagraphs (c)(1) and (2) of the Commercial Computer Software6Restricted Rights at 48 CFR 52.227-19, as applicable. The Contractor/Manufacturer is The Learning Company, Inc., One Athenaeum Street, Cambridge, Massachusetts 02142.

EXPORT RESTRICTIONS. You may not export or reexport the Software or any underlying information or technology except in full compliance with all United States and other applicable laws and regulations.

FURTHER ACKNOWLEDGEMENTS. You understand and acknowledge that (i) in order to utilize some features of the Program, you may need to purchase additional images, templates or other content; and (ii) TLC may, at its discretion or as required by its agreements with third parties, cease to support the Program. Support which TLC may cease to provide may include server access, web site support and the provision of enabling software. In the unlikely event this should happen, you agree that all monies paid shall be non-refundable.

MISCELLANEOUS PROVISIONS. If this Program was acquired outside the United States, then local law may apply. If you acquired this Software in Canada, you agree to the following: The parties to this License have expressly required that the License be drawn up in the English language/Les parties aux presentes ont expressement exige que la presente convention soient redigees en langue anglaise.

This License and your right to use the Program in any manner will terminate automatically if you violate or fail to comply with any part of this Agreement. Information in this Agreement is subject to change without notice and does not represent a commitment on the part of TLC.

SAVE THIS LICENSE FOR FUTURE REFERENCE